AF505083

INTERPRETING ABRAHAM

INTERPRETING ABRAHAM

JOURNEYS TO MORIAH

BRADLEY BEACH AND MATTHEW T. POWELL, EDITORS

Fortress Press
Minneapolis

INTERPRETING ABRAHAM

Journeys to Moriah

Copyright © 2014 Fortress Press. All rights reserved. Except for brief quotations in critical articles or reviews, no part of this book may be reproduced in any manner without prior written permission from the publisher. Visit http://www.augsburgfortress.org/copyrights/ or write to Permissions, Augsburg Fortress, Box 1209, Minneapolis, MN 55440.

Scripture quotations are from the New Revised Standard Version Bible, copyright © 1989 by the Division of Christian Education of the National Council of the Churches of Christ in the USA. Used by permission. All rights reserved.

Cover design: Erica Rieck

Library of Congress Cataloging-in-Publication Data is available

Print ISBN: 978-0-8006-9958-1

eBook ISBN: 978-1-4514-5237-2

The paper used in this publication meets the minimum requirements of American National Standard for Information Sciences — Permanence of Paper for Printed Library Materials, ANSI Z329.48-1984.

Manufactured in the U.S.A.

This book was produced using PressBooks.com, and PDF rendering was done by PrinceXML.

For
Richard G. Beach & Edward J. Powell

CONTENTS

Contributors ix

Preface xi

Part I. Traditional Readings

1. JUDAISM 3
   Jewish Uses of the Akedah—Genesis 22:1-19
   Rabbi John H. Spitzer

2. CHRISTIANITY 27
   Traditional Christian Interpretation of Genesis 22
   Carey Walsh

3. ISLAM 57
   Engaging with Abraham and His Knife: Interpretation of Abraham's
   Sacrifice in the Muslim Tradition
   Isra Yazicioglu

Part II. Modern Readings

4. KANT 87
   The Attack on Abraham
   Ronald Green

5. HEGEL 101
   Abductive Inference, Autonomy, and the Faith of Abraham
   Preston Stovall

6. KIERKEGAARD 131
   Resignation and the "Humble Courage of Faith" in Kierkegaard's Fear
   and Trembling
   Andrew Tebbutt

Part III. Post-Traditional Readings

7. KAFKA   149
A Tale of Two Abrahams
Matthew T. Powell

8. LEVINAS   169
Unbinding the Other: Levinas, the Akedah, and Going beyond the Subject
Laurence Bove

9. DERRIDA   187
Derrida and the Test of Secrecy
Chris Danta

Part IV. Today

10. Our Journeys to Moriah   213
Bradley Beach

Bibliography   221
Index of Names   229
Index of Biblical References   231
Index of Quranic References   233

Contributors

Bradley Beach received his PhD from Syracuse University and is Associate Professor of Philosophy at Walsh University. His philosophical interests are centered upon metaphysics, philosophy of religion and philosophical theology. He has published in philosophy of religion, metaphysics, and ethics.

Laurence F. Bove is professor of philosophy and provost at Walsh University in North Canton, Ohio. He received his BA and PhD in philosophy from St. John's University, New York. His presentations and publications examine issues concerning ethics, the philosophy of nonviolence, bioethics, social and political philosophy, and peace studies. He has written extensively on the nature and ethics of revenge. He co-edited *From the Eye of the Storm: Regional Conflicts and the Philosophy of Peace* (Rodopi, 1995), *Philosophical Perspectives on Power and Domination* (Rodopi, 1997), and *Introduction to Face to Face with the Real World: Contemporary Applications of Levinas*, a dedicated volume of *Philosophy in the Contemporary World*, 7, no. 1 (Spring 2000). Dr. Bove is a past president of the Concerned Philosophers for Peace.

Chris Danta is senior lecturer in English in the School of the Arts and Media at the University of New South Wales, Sydney. He is the author of *Literature Suspends Death: Sacrifice and Storytelling in Kierkegaard, Kafka and Blanchot* (Continuum, 2011) and the co-editor of *Strong Opinions: J. M. Coetzee and the Authority of Contemporary Fiction* (Continuum, 2011). He has also published essays in *New Literary History, Angelaki, Textual Practice, Modernism/modernity, SubStance* and *Literature & Theology*.

Ronald M. Green is the Eunice and Julian Cohen Professor for the Study of Ethics and Human Values in the Department of Religion at Dartmouth College. From 1992 to 2011 he served as Director of Dartmouth's Ethics Institute. In 1998, he was elected president of the Society of Christian Ethics. Professor Green is the author of nine books and over 160 articles on philosophical and applied ethics, including business ethics and bioethics. Two of his books, *Kierkegaard and Kant: The Hidden Debt* (State University of New York Press, 1992), and *Kant and Kierkegaard on Time and Eternity* (Mercer University Press, 2011), have played a major role in uncovering the depth and extent of Kierkegaard's relationship to Kant's philosophy. In 2005, Professor Green was named a Guggenheim Fellow.

Matthew T. Powell received his PhD from Marquette University studying the relationship between tradition and contemporary Western society through the lens of literature and philosophy. He has taught at Walsh University and has published extensively on the life and works of Franz Kafka.

Rabbi John H. Spitzer currently serves as associate professor of Jewish studies in the Theology Division of Walsh University (North Canton, Ohio). He holds a BA degree from Washington University (St. Louis, MO); a BHL, an MAHL, and Rabbinic Ordination from the Hebrew Union College-Jewish Institute of Religion (Cincinnati, OH); and a DMin from the Pittsburgh Theological Seminary. Rabbi Spitzer retired following thirty-five years of pulpit service and currently is the Director of the Walsh University Jewish/Catholic Studies Institute and Walsh University Lifelong Learning Academy.

Preston Stovall is a PhD candidate in philosophy at the University of Pittsburgh. He works on modal metaphysics and the philosophy of language, informed by interests in German idealism and classical American pragmatism.

Andrew Tebbutt is a doctoral student in the Department for the Study of Religion at the University of Toronto.

Carey Walsh received her (ThD from Harvard and is associate professor of Old Testament at Villanova University. She is the author of *Chasing Mystery: A Catholic Biblical Theology* (Liturgical, 2013), *Exquisite Desire: Religion, Erotics, and the Song of Songs* (Fortress Press, 2000), and *The Fruit of the Vine: Viticulture in Ancient Israel* (Eisenbrauns, 2000).

Isra Yazicioglu is an assistant professor of Islamic studies at St Joseph's University, Philadelphia, PA. Her research focus is Qur'anic hermeneutics, with special attention to the 20th century exegete Said Nursi, and the connection between sacred text, intellect, and spirituality. She authored the book *Understanding the Qur'anic Miracle Stories in the Modern Age* (Penn State University Press, 2013). Yazicioglu holds an MA in Islamic Studies and Christian-Muslim Relations from Hartford Seminary and PhD in Religious Studies from University of Virginia.

PREFACE

In preparing to write the introduction to this text, I walked next door to the office of my colleague and friend—a rabbi and doctor of theology. I asked him what was the first thing he thought about when I mentioned the Akedah. His response was both surprising and wonderfully revealing. He said, "I think of Abraham testing God."

Before we both knew it, nearly an hour had passed as we discussed various interpretations and applications of the narrative. And if I did not have a class to teach we might have talked another hour. In the course of our discussion we touched on matters religious, psychological, political, and pedagogical. We viewed the text, in turn, through sociological, historical, and hermeneutic lenses. And I learned something about my colleague that made me appreciate him more as a friend and a scholar.

That is, in the end, the true beauty of this gripping story of a father and son confronted by a divine command; that it not only compels conversation, but the conversations it compels reveal the deepest aspects of who we are. Many stories oblige discussion, but how many force us to reveal something essential about who we are in the process?

My colleague and I, as one would imagine from two theologians, discussed various midrashic meditations on the text. Did the knife actually pierce the skin of Isaac a little before Abraham was compelled to stop? How far? What exactly did Abraham tell Sarah before he took her son on their infamous journey? Was he lying if he told her it was for religious training? Exactly how much influence did Christianity exert on medieval Jewish exegesis? According to my colleague, at least enough for one midrash to reference the wood carried by Isaac in terms of the "cross we all must bear."

We also talked about the great joy each of us still finds in reading the text with students. How every lacuna in the text opens a world of interpretive possibilities. How each of the multitude of questions left open by the narrative presents a possibility to engage the students in thinking about these characters as people facing dilemmas and making choices. What did Isaac do when his father attempted to tie him up on the altar they constructed? What, if anything, did they say to each other on the way home? How did this event change their relationship? How could it not?

And, of course, we talked of Kierkegaard and *Fear and Trembling*. How did this rather short theological treatise, written in a language read by so few, come to have such a definitive impact on how we understand and discuss this singular chapter in Genesis? As my colleague pointed out, it would be an interesting experiment to see if any two scholars could discuss the Akedah narrative for more than thirty minutes without referencing Kierkegaard.

I would argue that the odds are not good. No matter the influence of Kierkegaard and his text, however, the reality is that in the end his voice (and his interpretation) is just one amidst a myriad of perspectives and arguments regarding a text ever pregnant with meaning. In our world today, Kierkegaard may exert a powerful influence over how we read Genesis 22 (as this very book will surely attest) but we are mistaken if we give that influence too much power to determine the shape and scope of our discussion about the text. This point is critical if we are to truly understand the breadth of influence that the Akedah narrative has exerted on all three Abrahamic religions and the entire Western intellectual tradition. This brief, nineteen-verse tale of a man told by God to sacrifice his "only" son has over the course of time generated discussions in every discipline of the humanities, and more than a few within the social sciences. It is a story compelling to those who are devoutly religious as well as those who hold no religious point of view whatsoever. And it is a story so simple in terms of conflict that it requires every reader to have an opinion on what it says about God, and about humans. That is, of course, the ultimate source of the influence of *Fear and Trembling* on our world today. In this text Kierkegaard offered a critical barometer in the history of the Western world for measuring the relationship between human and God. And, as a result, all subsequent measurements must be compared to his.

***

To be clear, though, the purpose of this particular text is not to present the full array of academic approaches to the Akedah story. Such an effort would require a volume (or volumes) much more extensive than this one. Instead, what we hope to present here is a history of critical reception. We wish to explore how our reading of the text has been affected by time. As our world has changed, how has our view of the story of Abraham and Isaac on Mt. Moriah? And, maybe just as importantly, how has *the way* we read the text changed? To that end, this book is presented in four parts. The first section explores the traditional interpretations of the Akedah story produced by the three Abrahamic religions: Judaism, Christianity, and Islam. Here the emphasis will be to explain the way the story was understood from within a faith perspective. In so doing, it should become clear how the text became foundational for the three predominant religious traditions of the West.

The second section of the book then attempts to gauge how readings of the Akedah story changed in what we now term the modern era. In other words, how did the Enlightenment project initiated in the wake of the Protestant Reformation affect our view of the story? This shift in the West from a primarily theocentric to an ever-growing anthrocentric point of view produced a fundamental challenge to the faith perspectives that defined the Abrahamic traditions, and to the very possibility of a revealed theology. Thus what we find in this part of the book are approaches to the text that evidence, in rather distinct ways, the expanding influence of the self in relation to the communal in terms of acquiring existential meaning and pursuing the quest for "truth." To this end, the impact of the Akedah story on three of the most prominent Enlightenment thinkers, Kant, Hegel, and Kierkegaard, is examined here.

The third section of the book emerges from a distinct presupposition, namely that within the West there is an emergent post-traditional perspective that has become more and more influential in terms of defining how we view those foundational narratives on which our religious traditions are grounded. Akin to the postmodern point of view, the post-traditional voice presents an attitude and viewpoint that stands outside of tradition, offering a critical perspective on the very nature and function of tradition within the world today. This part of the book will explore three of the most original voices of the twentieth century: Kafka, Levinas, and Derrida.

The final section of this book, subsequently, will attempt to draw some conclusions from the essays presented in the first three parts. The goal in this last part will not be to argue for some overriding unanimity, but to explore what the history of encounters with a specific text can tell us about who we are now in relation to who we were before. If there is anything to be learned from a project like the one we present here, it can only be achieved through comparison. The true art of this type of comparison, however, lies in discovering the tension between change and constancy. There is something of being human that has never changed. And there is the world today, ever new and remarkably different than anything that has come before. It is, therefore, the claim of this text that how we have read a narrative as seminal to the Western world as the Akedah story will not only tell us something of who we were and who we are, but also something about who we are becoming.

PART I

Traditional Readings

1

JUDAISM

Jewish Uses of the Akedah—Genesis 22:1-19

Rabbi John H. Spitzer

This article comprises a rabbinic analysis of one of the most significant and traumatic episodes in the life of *Avraham Avinu,* Abraham our Father, and certainly significant for his son, *Yitzchak* (Isaac). Known in Hebrew as the *Akedat Yitzchok,* the Binding of Isaac is found in the book of Genesis, chapter 22, verses 1 through 19. This is one of the most well-known and well-discussed texts of the Hebrew Bible. The point of view of this article includes both rabbinic interpretation and scholarly analysis, but the emphasis is on rabbinic interpretation. As such, the locus of the discussion is within the synagogue and the Jewish community. While this article doesn't claim to be exhaustive, it is my intention that the discourse peels away various layers of meaning to show how the text was used by Jews through the ages.

How the Rabbis Study the Text

The expression "peeling the layers" suggests the method of Torah study of the Jewish mystics. Imagining an onion, let the outer layer represent the Peshitta or the simple meaning of the text. It is the meaning we perceive from reading the text carefully, noting issues such as spelling and word choice. Peeling away this first layer uncovers the second, called *Remez* or the allusion. This is the awareness that there is something more in the text than initially meets the eye. It often surfaces when we compare two or more texts and it points us in a new and unique direction. The third layer is the *Drash* or the layer of explanation and interpretation. Because *Drash* is driven not only by the first two layers but also

3

by the times and needs of the Jewish people, the layer of *Drash* is the deepest, richest layer. What's more, it is always growing as each generation confronts the text in new and different ways depending upon its particular circumstance. Finally we arrive at the deepest layer, the layer known as *Sod*—the "Foundation" or the "Secret" inner source. This is the innermost part of the "truth" where we find the secrets of creation.[1]

How Do Jews Study the Text?

Dr. Norman Cohen taught these rules for Torah study.[2]

> 1. Read the text slowly, paying attention to each word, its spelling and its meaning.
> 2. Raise (and verbalize) every single question you have about the text. Be in dialogue with the text.
> Don't be afraid to raise the human questions—they are mirrors of ourselves.
> 3. Isolate one, specific moment in the text.
> 4. Look at the text and allow the characters who remain silent in the text to speak.
> 5. Use the larger context of the Bible to help understand the moment.

In this way, we become active readers who engage the text and the scholars who have previously engaged the text. We are able to "converse," as it were, with the great rabbis of the past and use their illumination of the textual meaning to be our starting place. To be an active reader is to engage a text in the light of one's own time and the body of interpretation and scholarship available at the given moment. In doing so, the reader is changed by the insights gleaned and nuances that are articulated. Indeed, the reader is transformed and re-shaped by the spiritual truths discovered. But beyond this, according to Barry Holtz, the interactive reader actually transforms and reshapes the text itself without adding or subtracting a single word. He suggests that active reading "calls forth response and dialogue on the part of the reader."[3] He takes

1. The rabbis believed that the Torah was the blueprint of creation. God consulted Torah prior to the creative act. Hence, the mystics believed that if one could indeed master the Torah in all its levels one could arrive at the very secrets of *Maase B'reishit*, the Work of Creation.

2. Dr. Norman Cohen, *Provost Emeritus and Professor of Midrash, Hebrew Union College Jewish Institute of Religion, New York (lecture notes recorded Oct. 19, 1991, Temple Israel, Canton, OH).*

3. Barry W. Holz, *Back To The Sources: Reading the Classic Jewish Texts* (New York: Summit Books, 1984), 17.

his cue from Wolfgang Iser, in Iser's influential essay, "The Reading Process: A Phenomenological Approach," which talks about the way that reader and work are intimately interconnected.[4] Iser suggests that what we read becomes abbreviated in our memory. The memory is recalled and set against a new background or circumstance that enables the reader to establish a new relationship with the remembered text. In doing so, the text reveals new connections with reality and new points of view relevant to the reader in his/her moment in time.

Engaging the Torah in this way allows one to be in dialogue with the text. This dialogic relationship, when coupled with the theology of divine revelation, suggests meanings far deeper than surface understandings. One who reads the text in this manner seeks the revelation for their moment and their issues.

Hence, when the rabbis study a text and peel away its layers in search for the *Sod*, they are not actually looking for the once-and-for-all truth or the final meaning. Rather, they search for the insight to understand the application of the text to their particular time and particular need. The text itself is like a faceted jewel and the active reader holds it up to the light, as it were, examining how the divine light shines off it and through it.

A Caveat

One whose interest in this article, or other Hebrew Bible texts for that matter, is piqued will want to delve deeper in their research. There is an ever-growing body of commentary on these texts in both the scholarly/secular world and the scholarly/religious world as well. In recent years, there has been a proliferation of "Messianic Jewish" and "Fulfilled Jewish" materials on Old Testament (Hebrew Bible) subjects. This caveat is not meant to discredit these sources, but rather to reinforce the premise of this article, which is to speak about the *Jewish* uses of the text. Various groups, Jewish, Christian, or otherwise bring their own lenses to textual study. If one is seeking a particular point of view, for example, a "Jewish" point of view, then the sense one brings to the text can be critical.

I use a common-sense approach to this issue, namely, that when one advances the belief that Jesus is the *Christos*, one fulfills the definition of being a *Christian*. Thus, for the purposes of this article, a "Fulfilled Jew" (meaning a Jew who finds Jesus as fulfilling the messianic promise of the first-century Jewish community) or a "Messianic Jew" (believing Jesus' messianic claims or the claims made about him) is functionally a Christian, even if they sometimes

---

4. In *New Directions in Literary History*, ed. Ralph Cohen (Baltimore: Johns Hopkins University Press, 1974), 125–47.

practice Jewish customs and ceremonies, such as making *kiddush*, blessing Torah, and wearing Jewish garb, and if they call their spiritual leaders "rabbi," and so forth. This becomes critical because Christians often see things in Torah that Jews don't or use texts in ways that Jews don't. For example, Christian interpretation often sees predictions of Jesus as Messiah in Hebrew texts that Jews do not see. Consider, for example, our text of the *Akedat Yitzchak*, the *binding* of Isaac. Note well, the word *AKaD* (root of Akedah) means "to bind." Yet many Christian interpreters will call this story "the sacrifice of Isaac." This is done, I believe, to point to and foreshadow what Christians believe to be the sacrificial nature of Jesus' death on the cross. For Jews, "binding" is a better word because it translates the Hebrew more clearly and Isaac, in fact, apparently walks away from Mt. Moriah, God having stayed his father's hand. Jesus, on the other hand, does not walk away from Calvary and is "sacrificed" on the cross (albeit, according to Christian theology, to be resurrected three days later and then walk away). The linking of these two stories, the first as a foreshadowing of the second as completion, may actually be called "Christian Midrash." Here we would have an instance of a Christian "use" of the Akedah. Later in this paper we will see midrashim in the Jewish world that will speak about an accomplished sacrifice of Isaac, perhaps as a response or reaction to the Christian passion.

THE MIDRASHIC APPROACH

The interpreting of biblical texts and biblical themes by the rabbis is often called "midrash" from the Hebrew root *DRSh* which conveys the idea of "to search." It is a process through which the rabbis, in their various times, sought to explicate the legal portions of Torah (*Midrash Halachah*) and the narrative, ethical and value-laden story texts (*Midrash Aggadah*).

Our rabbis taught that the revelation of Torah, the five books of Moses, was accomplished in two modalities. The written text, *Torah Shebichtav*, was dictated by God to Moses on Sinai. The second mode of revelation was an oral Torah, *Torah She'Baal Peh*. This "text" was passed on orally by Moses through a chain of tradition that included, ultimately, the books of Mishnah and Gemorah as well as the rabbis' midrashic commentaries.[5] They suggested that the written law was a direct and complete revelation to Moses who faithfully transmitted

---

5. When Mishnah, codified about 200 CE, and Gemorah, codified about 500 CE, are printed together they are known as Talmud. The Talmud is the classic compendium of the Jewish oral tradition. It has been commented upon through the ages to the present time. Most of the Talmud is concerned with halakah or legal matters. It does contain a significant amount of *Aggadah* or narrative material as well.

it to succeeding generations. This concept is known as the Masorah, or the faithful transmission of the tradition.[6] This fundamentalism[7] was described by Maimonides[8] in his commentary on the last Mishnah of the talmudic tractate *Sanhedrin*. Here, in his cooment on *Perek Helek*, (Tr. *Sanhedrin*, chapter 10, Mishnah 1) the RaMbaM articulates what came to be known as the Thirteen Principles of Faith. Principle 8 reads:

Principle VIII. That the Torah is from heaven [God]

And this is that you believe that all of this Torah that was given by Moses our teacher, peace be upon him, that it is all from the mouth of God. Meaning that it was received by him entirely from God. And it is not known how Moses received it except by Moses himself, peace be upon him, that it came to him. That he was like a stenographer that you read to him and he writes all that is told to him: all the events and dates, the stories, and all the commandments. There is no difference between "And the sons of Cham were Kush, and Mitzraim, and his wife was Mehatbe'el" and "Timnah was his concubine" and "I am Hashem your God" and "Hear Israel [*Hashem*[9] your God, *Hashem* is one]" for it was all given by God. And it is all *Hashem*'s perfect Torah; pure, holy, and true. And he who says that these verses or stories, Moses made them up, he is a denier of our sages and prophets worse than all other types of deniers [form of heretic] for he thinks that what is in the Torah is from man's flawed heart and the questions and statements and the dates and stories are of no value for they are from Moses Rabbeinu, peace be upon him. And this area is that he believes the Torah is not from heaven. And on this our sages of blessed memory said, "he who believes that the Torah

---

6. An example of the Masorah is found in tractate *Avot* of the Mishnah, perek one, which says, "Moses received the Torah from Sinai and gave it over to Joshua. Joshua gave it over to the Elders, the Elders to the Prophets, and the Prophets gave it over to the Men of the Great Assembly." One can see the rabbinic bias in this particular text as Moses' brother, Aaron the high priest, is excluded from this chain of traditional transmission.

7. Louis Jacobs, in his work *Principles of the Jewish Faith: An Analytical Study* (Basic Books: New York, 1964), draws attention to this fundamentalism in his introduction to the analysis of Maimonides's Thirteen Principles. Jacobs speaks of instances where new knowledge seems to contradict ancient formulations. He describes acceptance in the face of contradiction as "*sacrificium intellectus*."

8. Rabbi Moshe ben Maimon, known also a RaMbaM, 1135–1204.

9. "Hashem, "The Name," is one of a number of devices used as a substitute for the Tetragrammaton, *Yod He Vav He*. This most powerful name of God was pronounced but once a year by the high priest in the holy of holies on the Day of Atonement.

is from heaven except this verse that God did not say it but rather Moses himself did [he is a denier of all the Torah]." And this that God spoke this and that, each and every statement in the Torah, is from God and it is full of wisdom (each statement) and benefit to those who understand them. And its depth of knowledge is greater than all of the land and wider than all the seas and a person can only go in the path of David, the anointed of the God of Jacob who prayed and said "Open my eyes so that I may glance upon the wonders of Your Torah" (Psalms 119). And similarly the explanation of the Torah was also received from God and this is what we use today to know the appearance and structure of the sukka and the lulav and the shofar, tzitzis, tefillin and their usage. And all this God said to Moses and Moses told to us. And he is trustworthy in his role as the messenger and the verse that teaches of this fundamental is what is written (Numbers 16). "And Moses said, with this shall you know that Hashem sent me to do all these actions (wonders) for they are not from my heart."

Contemporary Orthodox Judaism, as represented by the Orthodox Union, simplifies the statement, to wit, "I believe with perfect faith that the entire Torah that we now have is that which was given [by God] to Moses."[10] In the spirit of contemporary fundamentalism ("God said it, I believe it, that ends it"), we might feel compelled to put our questions and concerns aside. If God spoke these words then we must live with the moral ambiguity of a father commanded by God to sacrifice the son, whom he loves, as a burnt offering.

Yet the rabbis, both ancient and modern, cannot allow this understanding of the text to stand. The very core of our being rebels at the very thought that God, who creates and loves and guides and teaches, would demand such a thing. Child sacrifice was a pagan practice, not a Jewish practice. The rabbinic treatment of the text we know as midrash calls upon us to address this question of morality and more, as well as the questions of meaning in every era of Jewish history. Rabbi Harold Schulweis speaks of our understanding of biblical text in relationship to the midrashic pursuit.

Rabbinic midrashim of dissent are numerous and religiously significant. These midrashim or rabbinic parables are elaborate metaphors and legends that fill the moral lacunae of biblical

10. "The RaMbaM's Thirteen Principles of Jewish Faith," Orthodox Union, http://www.ou.org/torah/rambam.htm.

narratives, unburdening the believer from a submissive reading of scriptures and a subservient stance toward the Sovereign Commander. In midrash, God hears moral arguments and cancels decrees. **In this way, the biblical text is not the last but the first word of God.** The Bible is not a closed book, but open to the multiple interpretations of its sages.[11]

Understanding Torah as God's *first* word allows us, in our time, to create not the last word, but the *next* word in an unfolding understanding of the revelation. Torah remains relevant through our reflection and growing understanding of the text.

THE LITERARY CONTEXT OF THE AKEDAH

One cannot help but see the parallelism between our text and the beginning of Abram's journey toward covenant.[12] The Torah portion called *Lech L'cha* (Gen. 12:1—17:27) depicts Abram's calling. God says:

> Get up from your land, from the place of your birth, from your father's house and go to the land that I will show you. And I will make you a great nation; I will bless those who bless you and make your name great, and you shall be a blessing.[13]

Abram rises to do this command without question. The text is simple and clear: "So Abram went as God had spoken to him."[14] The formula for separation from his ancestral culture and faith is likewise simple. He is commanded to separate from the local culture (land), from his community (place of birth) and from the family that nurtured him (father's house) and go to an unspecified place. Abram is a man of faith and a man of action, for he neither questions nor objects. Because he recognizes the voice of the one God, because he neither objects nor hesitates, Abram is called the first Jew and the one with whom God establishes the *brit*, the covenant. The covenant is reiterated and sealed several times[15] and

---

11. Harold M. Schulweis, *Consciences: The Duty to Obey and the Duty to Disobey* (Woodstock: Jewish Lights, 2008), 12. Emphasis mine.

12. Several characters in the Genesis narrative have their names changed at significant points in their lives. Three examples would be Abram who becomes Abraham (Gen. 17:5), Sarai becomes Sarah (Gen. 17:15), and Jacob who becomes Israel (Gen. 32:29).

13. Gen. 12:1-2. NB All Hebrew Bible references follow the Jewish Publication Society translation of the Hebrew Bible.

14. Ibid., v. 3.

in several ways as Abram journeys from Haran, where God called, to Beersheva, where yet another journey will begin.

We hear echoes of this first covenanting call as the Akedah begins in the next Torah portion, *Vayera* (Gen. 18:1—22:24). Beginning with Gen. 22:1 God calls out to Abraham in the imperative, "Abraham!" Like the first command ("get up and go!") this is followed by three descriptors, "take your son, your only son, the one whom you love." And finally, while the actions commanded are clear ("Go!", Genesis 12 and "Take", Genesis 22) the destinations are secret ("to the land that I will show you," Genesis 12, and "on one of the mountains that I will tell you," Genesis 22). Again, there is no hesitation and no questioning on Abraham's part. Indeed, Torah underscores Abraham's willingness to fulfill God's command: "And Abraham rose early in the morning," and busied himself with the preparations for the journey to the as-yet unspecified destination.[16]

The irony is not lost on the reader. The first call is a call to progeny and blessing and the second is a summons to sacrifice the fruits and proof of the first. The first is a summons to give up his past, while the second is a call to risk his future. In this irony we are tied up in ethical knots and struggle with the generations to understand what this story can mean. From the structure alone we know that it is a story of faith, of being tested, and of covenant.

It is an appalling story with its elements of God's command to a father, the father's acquiescence to this command with silence, and even sense of urgency to plunge the knife (he got up early . . .). We hear nothing from the son, or for that matter from the mother. But the midrash helps to fill in the silences in text, and to address what seems like obvious questions: Why indeed would God test Abraham? Should not the Omniscient One already know of Abraham's faith and character? Why does the text suggest that God *nissah et Avraham* (tested Abraham)? There are those who say that God didn't know the outcome of this test, that Abraham, a creation endowed with free will, might choose one path or another, and therefore God used the trial to acquire information about Abraham. The rabbis of the midrash, it would seem, were more inclined to suggest that God knew the outcome but "tested" in the sense of proving Abraham, a test so that Abraham would know the depths of his faith. In this sense, God does know how strong Abraham is, for if not, He would not have tested him. Genesis Rabbah[17] 55.2 transforms the idea of "testing" to learn

15. See ibid., 13:14-17; 15:1-7, 17-18; 17:1-27.

16. Ibid., 22:3.

17. Part of The Great Midrash (*Midrash Rabbah*), the collection of rabbinic interpretations of the Pentateuch and five scrolls of the Hebrew Bible, collected and published in Venice for the first time in 1545.

something into "proving" as in annealing. This is not an insignificant shift of nuance. It suggests that Abraham, rather than being the victim of a capricious God, is the hero or champion who is indeed capable of being tested.

> *The Lord trieth the righteous, etc.* (Ps. XI, 5). R[abbi]. Jonathan said: A potter does not examine defective vessels, because he cannot give them a single blow without breaking them. What then does he examine? Only sound vessels, for he will not break them even with many blows. Similarly, the Holy One, blessed be He, tests not the wicked but the righteous, as it says, "*The Lord trieth the righteous.*" [18]

Here, the Akedah, like the other Trials of Abraham[19] serves to announce his worthiness to the world, to declare him a righteous man and worthy of the covenant. This last test serves to anneal and strengthen him. In doing so, we find one answer to the question, "Why?" So that he (Abraham) would know; so that we (the world) would know, and so we (the Jewish people) would know—the strength of his faith; that he was worthy because of his righteousness; and, perhaps, why we in our turn suffer. There are others who suggest that the trial was not of Abraham, but of God. Abraham, knowing full well the promises God had made, namely the covenant, determined to fulfill the commandment to sacrifice his son. If God did not stop this act, then God was not faithful to God's promise. Hence, as the knife plunges toward the throat of his son, the *Malach* or messenger of God must cry out twice, "Abraham! Abraham!" to stop the deed. Such was Abraham's concentration and commitment.

Humanizing the Text

As noted, the biblical story leaves much unsaid. It is not a little disturbing to the reader that such a commandment to a father would go uncommented upon. To the rabbis, for whom the first commandment of Torah is "Be fruitful and multiply," and who understand the cosmic significance of Isaac as the fruit of God's covenantal promise, Abraham's silence is unbearable. They create the dialogue (which is missing in the Torah text) between Abraham and God at the moment of the command:

---

18. *Midrash Rabbah*, 55.2, ed. Rabbi Dr. H. Freedman and Maurice Simon, vol. 1, *Genesis* (London: Soncino 1939), 55.2 (p. 482).

19. The Rabbis of the Mishnah suggest that Abraham underwent Ten Trials, the last of which was the command to sacrifice his son.

> And He said: Take I pray thee, thy son, etc. (xxii, 2). Said He to
> him: "Take, I pray thee—I beg thee—Thy son." "Which son?" he
> asked. "Thine only son," replied He. "But each is the only one of his
> mother."—"Whom thou lovest."—"Is there a limit to the affections?"
> "Even Isaac," He said.[20]

Abraham has two sons, Isaac and Ishmael. In this midrashic dialogue we hear
a father's anguish. He understands the gravity of God's demand but cloaks his
anguish in a kind of name game until God makes it abundantly clear that
the lot falls to Isaac. The text goes on to tell us that once the commandment
was manifest, Abraham and his son and the servant lads journeyed toward "the
mountain that I will show you" for three days before "he lifted up his eyes and
saw the place afar off." From this the midrash infers that Abraham used the time
to mull over the commandment and its meaning. What would happen if he
refused to offer his son? What if he went through with it? What would Sarah
say? And only after he had thoroughly thought through the consequences of the
act did he look up and see the appointed place. These midrashim serve to give
Abraham a human face and heart, just like the human presence of the students
and sages who read the text in their own time.

We glimpse a similar human moment in stories about Sarah. While she
is not mentioned in the Akedah text, the rabbis cannot leave her out of the
story. They tell the story in the midrash that Abraham tells his wife that he and
the lad are going to pray, to offer sacrifice. Sarah awakens the next morning
and walking through the house finds the sacrificial knife and the firepot gone,
consistent with a father-son pilgrimage. But then she looks out to the yard and
sees the goat which had been designated as the sacrifice still tied up there. We
can feel her growing anxiety, concern and fear.

AGAINST CHILD SACRIFICE

A common understanding of the Akedah is as the text that denounces child
sacrifice in Judaism. Surely we know that there were many ancient cultures in
which the sacrifice of human beings was demanded. This was not only true in
the ancient Near East, but in South and Central America and Africa, and so
forth. In reading the Hebrew Bible, we encounter instances of traditions that
child sacrifice was practiced amongst Israel.[21] Perhaps, in the mind's eye of the

---

20. *Genesis Rabbah* 55.7.

21. See, for example Judg. 11, the story of Jephthah's oath and subsequent offering of his daughter. See
also 2 Chron. 28:3, dealing with the Valley of Gehennom where, during the time of King Ahaz, children
were purportedly sacrificed (passed through the fire) to the fire god Moloch.

author of the Akedah what was shocking or noteworthy about this story was not that God would require the sacrifice of the son, but that God would, in fact, stop it. This understanding is bolstered by the numerous places in Torah and the Prophets where we find prohibitions against following this pagan practice.

THE PARADIGM OF THE *OLAH*—THE BURNT OFFERING

The Hebrew text commands Abraham to take his son *v'ha'alehu sham l'olah*, to offer him up as an *olah*. *Olah* means more than just a sacrifice or offering. In the context of the temple in Jerusalem, the *Olah* was the burnt offering offered by the priests. It was to be an animal without blemish, ritually slaughtered by the priests and consumed by fire on the altar. All that was to remain was the ash from its sacrificial fires. The ashes had a special, spiritual quality about them. They effected ritual cleansing, about which we will speak later. But the idea that Isaac's slaughtering was a ritual slaughtering was manifest in the minds of the text's interpreters. It was even significant to Isaac.

The *Olah* offering was to be an animal without blemish and thus, even through its slaughter there could not be a *mum* (blemish). Fearful that he might flinch upon seeing the knife raised and thus cause his father to make a bad stroke, which would disqualify Isaac as a sacrifice, the rabbis have him say, "Father, I am a young man and am afraid that my body may tremble through fear of the knife and I will grieve thee, whereby the slaughter may be rendered unfit and this will not count as a real sacrifice; therefore bind me very firmly."[22] Hence, this story is called the *Akedat Yitzchak*, the binding of Isaac. This will become the paradigm for martyrdom in future generations.

We shall see in later midrashim and in the stories of oppressive times for the Jewish people that the slaughterer will inspect the knife for sharpness, and also to be certain there are no nicks in the blade so the death stroke will be smooth, quick and painless—even as the *shoichet*, the priestly slaughterer in the temple of old, or ritual butcher in the kosher meat market today, inspects his knife. In doing so, the sacrifice of the biblical son becomes the transforming symbol that will take the bloody slaughter of oppressed Jewish communities and turn them into sacrificial gifts to God.

Z'CHUT AVOT—THE SPIRITUAL MERIT OF THE FATHERS AND MOTHERS

As in so many religious traditions, contemporaries view their ancestors as spiritually superior to the current generation. So it is in Judaism. Even as the

---

22. *Genesis Rabbah*, 56.8.

Torah stories are filled with the foibles of Abraham, Isaac and Jacob, and the humanity of Moses, or the challenges presented by the kings of Israel and Judah in their generations, yet do we look back longingly on the previous generations and their piety, courage, spirituality, and closeness to God. In our very personal relationship with God, we pray that God will "cut us some slack" because of the goodness of our ancestors. Any casual reader of the Hebrew Bible will understand that this intercession of the merit of our ancestors was often invoked. At the incident of the golden calf when God's anger burns hot against the idolatrous behavior of the Jewish people, God declares to Moses, "Let my anger flare up against them and I shall annihilate them."[23] Moses intercedes for the people, urging God to remember His relationship with the ancestors. "Remember for the sake of Abraham, Isaac and Jacob, Your servants, to whom You swore by Yourself, and You told them, 'I shall increase your offspring like the stars of heaven'"[24] In other words, "God, since you knew our ancestors and the family, be gracious to us because of your relationship with them.

This idea, of the merit of our ancestors, is called *zachut.* Solomon Schechter[25] describes three iterations of *zachut: zachut avot* (the merit of the Fathers,[26] meaning our ancestors), the *zachut* of a pious contemporary, and the *zachut* of a pious posterity. For our purposes, we will focus on the first, *zachut avot.*

In a sense, the numerous times Torah speaks of "The God of Abraham, Isaac and Jacob" this value of *zachut* is invoked. It is more than a title for God, but rather a reminder to God that there is a historic relationship between God and our ancestors. When Jews are at prayer and invoke "Baruch Ata Adonai, eloheinu veilohei avorteinu, elohei Avraham, elohei Yitzchak, veilohei Yaakov,"[27] "Praised are You, Adonai, our God and God of our Fathers, God of Abraham, God of Isaac and God of Jacob," they are not only reminding

23. Exodus 32:10.

24. Ibid., v. 13.

25. Solomon Schechter, *Aspects of Rabbinic Theology: Major Concepts of the Talmud* (New York: Schoken Books, 1961), ch. 7.

26. Schechter points out that there is also *zachut imahot* or Merit of the Mothers. *Zachut avot* literally means merit of the fathers, but is used in the sense of our ancestors or the previous generations, especially the earliest generations of Abraham, Isaac and Jacob, Sarah, Rebecca, and Rachel and Leah.

27. The first benediction of the "Eighteen Benedictions," or the "Amidah," the central portion of Jewish daily worship services, begins with this benediction invoking the *avot* or the Fathers. In Reform Judaism, and now in Conservative and other contemporary interpretations of Judaism, the prayer formula includes the *imahot* or the Mothers of Israel as well.

themselves of this historic connection, but seeking to bring the deity close because of the merit of that relationship throughout history.

Zachut is also manifest by reminding God not only of God's relationship to the ancestors, but of God's promises to them. Returning to the Exodus 32 passage, God not only had an intimate relationship with Abraham, Isaac, and Jacob, but God had cut a *brit*, made a covenantal promise to them: "You swore by Yourself. And you told them. . . ." If the fathers merited a covenant and God promised, then the descendants of the fathers should continue to benefit from that promise. Because God is faithful and constant in God's promises, and because God is neither capricious nor changeable, this invocation of God's promise is almost rhetorical.[28]

But this story of the binding of Isaac is more extraordinary still. The rabbis, through the midrashim, emphasize the faithful and rational willingness of Abraham to fulfill this *mitzvah* and Isaac's willing and knowing submission. An interpretation of the phrase, "and they came to the place," (Gen. 22:9) says, "both carrying stones [for the altar], both carrying the fire, both carrying the wood. For all that, Abraham acted like one making wedding preparations for his son; and Isaac like one making a wedding bower for himself."[29]

The shared joy at the preparations for the sacrifice is somewhat puzzling, but is illuminated, I believe, by the wedding reference. The word used for "wedding" is *kiddushin*, or sanctification. A bride and groom sanctify their relationship by preparing the *chupah*, or marriage bower in Braude's translation. The image of *kiddushin* is also used by the rabbis to describe the moment at Mt. Sinai when God and the Jewish people created this covenantal relationship with God willingly offering Torah and the Jewish people willingly accepting it. So, this command to sacrifice Isaac is portrayed as a sanctifying act between Abraham and Isaac and God. A reiteration of the *brit*.

The *zachut* here is more than relational, or a reminding God of God's own promises, but a powerful emphasis on the merit of Abraham and Isaac's willing and active participation in this *mitzvah*. I suggest that this distinction between God's actions and promises and Abraham and Isaac's action is more than just nuance.

---

28. NB Gen. 18:23ff, in which Abraham intercedes with God on behalf of the righteous of Sodom and Gomorrah. Abraham argues, "shall not the Judge of all the world be Just?" Because we believe God is faithful and just, this statement on behalf of Abraham is a rhetorical question. We know the answer to be "yes" as soon as the question is asked.

29. *Sefer Ha-Aggadah, The Book of Legends from the Talmud and Midrash,* ed. Hayim Nahman Bialik and Yehoshua Hana Ravnitzky, trans. William Braude (New York: Schoken Books, 1992), 41.

Both Abraham and Isaac are pictured as making rational decisions to move forward with the deed regardless of the cost. The text tells us that Abraham "woke early" to perform the *mitzvah*. He journyed forth from Beersheba with Isaac and his two servant lads. The text tells us that he didn't see the place God intended until the third day. The rabbis, knowing that the journey between Beersheba and Jerusalem where Mt. Moriah is located was only forty-six miles, and a donkey could make the journey in a day, wondered at the three-day journey. They suggest, in the midrash, "'Then, on the third day, Abraham lifted his eyes and saw' (Gen. 22:4). Why on the third day? Why not on the first or the second? That the nations of the world might not say: God deranged Abraham so that he cut his son's throat."[30] The midrash further has Abraham sorting through the questions about this command . . . what would Sarah say? The rabbis want the Torah student to know that this wasn't an irrational, knee-jerk response on Abraham's part, but a thought-through rational decision to obey God's commandment.

As for Isaac, this was more than a journey with his father. He came to understand fully that he was to be the sacrifice. The midrash has the Satan attempting to dissuade father and son from going through with the deed.[31] In both cases the sacrifice and the potential sacrifice make knowledgeable statements that they are dedicated to follow through. Further showing Isaac's understanding of the situation, the midrash tells us that the binding was in fact his idea.

> When Abraham was about to begin the sacrifice, Isaac said, "Father, bind my hands and feet, for the urge to live is so willful that when I see the knife coming at me, I may flinch involuntarily [causing the knife to cut improperly] and thus disqualify myself as an offering. So I beg you, bind me in such a way that no blemish will befall me." So Abraham "bound his son well." (Gen. 22:9)[32]

It is, I believe, because of their reasoned and willing submission to what at least on the surface appears to be God's absurd commandment that Abraham and Isaac have a special *zachut* that is invoked by succeeding generations. Not

---

30. Ibid.

31. As in the book of Job, the Satan is not "the devil" but the advocate who tries and tests the system at hand. The midrash has the Satan try to dissuade Abraham from the act by pointing out that Isaac is the child promised to him and Sarah. Further, the Satan tries to dissuade Isaac by suggesting that his father must have gone mad in his old age.

32. *The Book of Legends*, 41.

solely because God knows God's creations, or because God makes promises to them, but because in spite of human nature, which loves life, and with full appreciation of the existential cost of following God's command, father and son moved forward.

Pulling together several sources, Schechter summarizes *zachut avot* thus:

> One Rabbi gets so exalted at the thought of the *Zachuth* of the Fathers that he exclaims to the effect: Blessed are the children whose fathers have a *Zachuth*, because they profit by their *Zachuth*; blessed are Israel who can rely on the *Zachuth* of Abraham and Isaac and Jacob, it is their *Zachuth* which saved them. It saved them on the occasion of the exodus from Egypt, when they worshipped the golden calf, and in the times of Elijah, and so in every generation. Indeed, Israel is compared to a vine, because as the vine is itself alive, but is supported by dead wood, so Israel living and lasting upon the deceased Fathers. It is by reason of this support, that the righteous deeds of the Fathers are remembered before God. "Who was so active before thee (God) as Abraham, the lover of God? Who was so active before thee as Isaac, who allowed himself to be bound upon the altar? Who was so active before thee as Jacob, who was so thankful to God?" **Therefore, whenever Israel comes unto distress they call into remembrance the deeds of the Fathers.**[33]

SEEING OURSELVES AS ISAAC: A RATIONALE FOR OUR SUFFERING

While we certainly wish to call upon the *zachut avot* when we confront our own imperfections and sins (see below), the Akedah also serves as a metaphor for our own meaning and merit, especially at times of distress and martyrdom. Consider the story recorded in 2 Maccabees 7 of the seven brothers and their mother during the Maccabean revolt against the forces of the Seleucid king, Antiochus IV Epiphanes, in the second century BCE. The story tells of the attempt of the king's soldiers to get the mother (known in tradition as Hannah) and her seven sons to commit apostasy by eating swine's flesh. Each son, in turn, bravely refuses and is brutally tortured until he dies. Finally the mother also succumbs. It is assumed that this text dates from about 124 BCE. The actions of the mother and her sons became one of the models for those who

---

33. *Aspects of Rabbinic Theology*, 174–75, aggregating references from *Agadath Bereshith* ch. 10; *Exodus Rabbah* 44.1; *Leviticus Rabbah* 36.2; *Canticle* [Song of Songs] *Rabbah* 1.4; *Sifre*, 73b. *The Book of Legends*, 41. Emphasis mine.

perish *Kiddush Hashem* as martyrs.[34] It is not difficult, therefore, to see the link between martyrdom and the binding of Isaac. Like Isaac, these seven brothers and their mother knowingly and bravely step forward for death. Theirs is a story surrounded by other stories of martyrdom in the books of the Maccabees.

These stories of willing sacrifice of one's life for the faith actually drew forth a cautionary response. 1 Maccabees 2:29-41 relates a pious group of Jews who fled the cities and villages during the early rebellion against the Syrian Greeks. They hid themselves away in the "wilds" in order to preserve their religious way of life. Antiochus's soldiers discovered them and brought forces against them to press the attack on the Sabbath.[35] The Jews chose death rather than take up arms on the Sabbath. Because of the willingness of Jews to die *Kiddush Hashem*, 1 Maccabees 2:41 reports that "that day they decided that, if anyone came to fight against them on the Sabbath, they would fight back, rather than all die as their brothers in the caves had done."

Mattathias, the priestly father of the Maccabee brothers, addressed the courage and faith needed to prosecute the war against the Hellenistic forces in what appears to be a deathbed oration in which he invokes Abraham's courage in keeping God's command.

> The time came for Mattathias to die, and he said to his sons, "Arrogance now stands secure and gives judgment against us; it is a time of calamity and raging fury. But now, my sons, be zealous for the law, and give your lives for the covenant of your fathers. Remember the deeds they did in their generations, and great glory and eternal fame shall be yours. Did not Abraham prove steadfast under trial, and so gain great credit as a righteous man?"[36]

The memory of Abraham's last trial becomes a cause for bravery and steadfast faith during the time of the Maccabean revolt. As the political situation deteriorated in Judea in the first and early second centuries of the Common Era, leading up to and through the Jewish Wars (66–73 CE) when Roman oppression brought new massacre and martyrdom to tens of thousands of Jews, and the Hadrianic persecutions known as the *Shemad*, one can only imagine how the image of Maccabean martyrdom with its biblical interpretation in the

---

34. For the Sanctification of The Name, that is, those who give their lives for their faith in God.

35. Josephus relates a similar story of Jews being suffocated while observing the Sabbath in a cave. See in the *Antiquities* 12.6.2

36. 1 Macc. 2:49-52.

light of the Akedah must have resonated with the Jews of that time. Shalom Spiegel, in *The Last Trial*, interprets the midrash.

> Into her mouth (the mouth of Hannah) the haggadah of the Talmudic Rabbis put words which expressed the mood of innumerable fathers and mothers during the Shemad period, the period of the Hadrianic devastations—parents who both mourned and rejoiced, mourning on the one hand because it had been decreed that their sons must be slain, rejoicing on the other hand because through their sons Heaven's glory was sanctified. "Their mother wept and said to them: Children, do not be distressed, for to this end were you created—to sanctify in the world the Name of the Holy One, blessed be He. Go and tell Father Abraham: Let not your heart swell with pride! You built one altar, but I have built seven altars and on them have offered up my seven sons. What is more: Yours was a trial; mine was an accomplished fact."[37]

A new theme immerges with regard to the Akedah. Whereas one thread of interpretation speaks of the perfections of Abraham's and Isaac's faith creating an account of *zachuit* for future generations, this new approach uses the Akedah to give meaning to the suffering brought about by terrible persecution. Indeed, in this comparison, the sacrifices of those who give up their lives *Kiddush Hashem* exceed the merit of our Father Abraham. His was a test while ours was an accomplished fact. As Spiegel says, "Is one who planned an act but does not act it out like the one who actually did act it out?"[38] This theme will be played out over and over again in the passing years as the Christian church comes into being and comes to power.

The period of the Crusades is legend for the martyrdom of the Jewish people throughout Europe. As Christian armies trooped across Europe to wrest the holy sites from the Muslims in 1096, 1146, 1187, and 1203, they often came across Jewish communities. *The New Jewish Encyclopedia* (p.101) speaks of an incident in York, England in 1190. As the Crusaders were preparing for their journey to Jerusalem, the Encyclopedia reports, "The ignorant mobs were incited by the leaders of the Crusades to pillage and massacre whole Jewish communities. The cry was: 'Before attempting to revenge ourselves upon the

---

37. Shalom Spiegel, *The Last Trial: On the Legends and Lore of the Command to Abraham to Offer Isaac As a Sacrifice; The Akedah* (New York: Pantheon, 1967), 14–15.

38. Ibid.

Moslem unbelievers, let us first revenge ourselves upon the "killers of Christ" living in our midst!"[39] One hundred fifty Jews were murdered.

This kind of savagery was not uncommon. Massacres occurred in Mainz, Worms, and Wevelinghofen, and numerous other locations. These events came to be remembered in *piyyutim*, liturgical poetry especially associated with the High Holy Day Services. The poems represented a commemoration of the gruesome memories and elevated them to the level of the Akedah. Elements ascribed to the Akedah find their way into these liturgical poems. The decision to die *Kiddush Hashem*, the ritual nature of the preparations such as inspecting the knife, the willingness of the victims to receive the cut are all present.

> Men, women and children, bridegrooms and brides, old men and old women, for the sanctification of the One Name, killed themselves—offered their throats to be cut—their heads to be severed, in ditches of water surrounding the town. Now there was a certain saintly man there, an elder, well on in years, and his name was Rabbenu Samuel bar Yehiel. He had an only son, a splendid looking young man, who with his father fled into the water and there offered his throat for slaughter by his father. Whereupon the father recited the appropriate blessing for slaughter of cattle and fowl, and the son responded with "Amen." And all of those who were standing around them responded in a loud voice, "Hear O Israel, the Lord our God, the Lord is One." O citizens of the world, take a good look! How extraordinary was the stamina of the son who *unbound* let himself be slaughtered, and how extraordinary was the stamina of the father who could resist compassion for an *only son*, so splendid and handsome a young man.[40]

Again and again we read in liturgical poems or in the chronicles of the times similar stories of Jews being slaughtered by others and viewing their sacrifices in the light of Abraham and Isaac. Most poignant are the stories of parents and friends slaughtering members of their families and loved ones and then turning the knife on themselves.[41] Speigel suggests that "the pattern of the original

---

39. David Bridger, *The New Jewish Encyclopedia*, ed. Samuel Wolk (New York: Behrman House Publishers, 1962), 101.

40. Ibid., 22 (emphasis original).

41. This has always been a controversial act. The defenders on Masada in 72 CE ended their lives prior to the Roman forces breaching the walls and carrying them off to slavery or worse. Josephus records (or invents) the oratory of Eliezer ben Yair, who exhorts the nearly one thousand defenders to take their

Akedah never ceased to hover before their mind's eye, as though no experience surpassed that one in sanctity. The victims themselves constantly set before their own eyes the example of the Patriarchs' behavior on Mount Moriah, and yearned to act their own parts in the image and likeness of the earlier dramatis personae."[42]

During this time of great persecution and martyrdom, the biblical story of Abraham and Isaac had the power to elevate the sacrifices Jewish people made in the face of Christian religious zeal. Whether a community locked in a building and burned to death, or individuals dispatched at the stake, or the "sacrifice" and suicide of communities who refused the invitation to grace, these became the subject of liturgical poetry comparing their decisions and deaths to that of Abraham and Isaac. In doing so, the dead were not just victims, but faithful saints even as the patriarchs. The blood and mud and pain and sorrow were elevated to the level of death for the highest cause and with the highest reward. But how could such a comparison be made when Abraham's hand was stayed and Isaac continued to live?

The Power of Resurrection, Blood, and Ashes

The central prayer of Jewish worship is called by a number of names. Most simply, that rubric of the service is called *T'fillah*, The Prayer. Another name is *Shemoneh Esre* which means "eighteen," enumerating the original number of benedictions making up *T'fillah*.[43] The first benediction is called *Avot*, or The Fathers, and is associated with Father Abraham (concluding with "Blessed are You, Adonai, shield of Abraham"). The second benediction, *Gevurot*, Power or Might, came to be associated with Isaac. This benediction suggests that God is powerful enough that God can *m'chaye ha'meitim*, revivify the dead. The midrash on the *Shemoneh Esre* associates *t'chiah hameitim* (resurrection of the dead) with Isaac. But again, if Isaac was not slaughtered, how could we make this connection?

own lives rather than submit. While many often speak of the *suicide* of the defenders, this is problematic to the rabbis and to Jewish tradition. Suicide, i.e., the willful destruction of the image of God in oneself, is considered a grave sin. So, the narrative is careful to explain that most people were killed by another, in this case, the father of each family, and only the father committed suicide.

42. *The Last Trial*, 24.

43. Eighteen, even though a nineteenth was added, and on Sabbath and festivals the intermediate blessings are reduced so the total is seven.

Speigel directs us to the midrash *Pirke R. Eliezer*:[44] "'And Isaac came to know *Resurrection of the dead as taught by the Torah*,'which is a gloss based on the reading of the Mishnah *Sanhedrin*, beginning of ch. Helek (10:1)." Indeed, in a number of places the knife is not stopped in midair on the way to the moment of slaughter but touches the neck of Isaac, at which point Isaac's soul flies forth and away.

> Now the moment the knife touched Isaac's throat his soul took flight. . . . Forthwith the Holy One said to Abraham: 'Lay not thy hand upon the lad.' Whereupon Abraham unbound the lad and his soul returned to him; and he stood up on his feet and recited the Resurrection-of-the-dead-benediction.[45]

Spiegel strongly suggests that this close identity of the binding of Isaac with resurrection was to make abundantly clear that the belief in *t'chiat meitim* was literal in the Jewish mind.

Following the destruction of the Temple in 70 CE, at a time when the Roman persecutions of the Jews and the nascent development of the Christian church parallel each other, to identify Isaac's binding on the altar with the supposed location of the sacrificial altar of the destroyed temple makes for interesting transformations. It underscores the idea of Isaac's moment being a moment of ritual sacrifice. As previously noted, Abraham inspects the knife, follows the sacrificial procedure and says the blessing for *shechita* (ritual sacrifice). Later generations who were brought to the point of slaughtering their children *Kiddush Hashem* and then following them by taking their own lives similarly would follow the formulas and practices for ritual sacrifice. The language of the *Mekilta de Rabbi Shimon bar Yohai*, with its sacrificial reference to "a quarter of a log" of blood,[46] will resonate with Christians as well as Jews.

> Rabbi Joshua says: "God spoke to Moses and said to him ["I am the LORD"] [Exod. 6:2]. The Holy One (blessed by He) said to Moses, **"I can be trusted to pay out the reward of Isaac son of Abraham, who gave a quarter of [a *log* of] blood upon the altar** and to whom I said:
>
> [Let the nations not say,] "Where is their God?" Before our eyes let it be known among the nations that **You avenge the spilled**

44. Ch. 31, as noted in *The Last Trial*, 34n.

45. *The Last Trial*, 30.

46. A log = two-thirds of a pint. A quarter log is the amount necessary for a ritually valid *shechita*.

blood of Your servants. Let the groans of the prisoners reach You; reprieve those condemned to death as befits Your great strength [Ps 79:10-11; emphasis original].

I am trying to bring them out of Egypt, and you say to me, "[Please, O Lord], make someone else Your agent"? [Exod. 4:13] (*Mekilta de Rabbi Shimon ben Yochai*, Wa'era)

The biblical passage describes how, as Abraham was in the act of slaughtering his son (some commentators say he raised the knife, others that he had begun the down stroke, and others that the knife had indeed entered the lad) an angel from God stopped Abraham. And when Abraham looked up he saw a ram caught in the thicket. The ram becomes the substitute sacrifice in place of his son.[47] The ram, then, as a replacement sacrifice, was burnt on the altar. A number of midrashim speak to the use of the ashes of that sacrifice. Spiegel cites *Midrash Tanhuma*: "Abraham requested of the Holy One, blessed be He, that so long as Israel make mention of Isaac's *Akedah* before Him, it continue to serve as an atonement for them, as though (Isaac) had been burned up on top of the altar. . . . Do Thou swear to me that Isaac's ashes will be heaped before Thee as a memorial for all time, as *though* I had sacrificed him."[48]

This remembers a time each year when the ashes on the temple's sacrificial altar were collected and heaped upon the Holy Ark; but here, the ashes themselves become endowed with *zachut*. They symbolize and remind God of the merit of our ancestors and entreat the Holy One for blessing.

The *Akedah* and Rosh Hashana

Rosh Hashanah,[49] the Jewish New Year, is part of a complex of holidays that address our human relationship with God, the identification, confession, and repentance of sin, and our hoped-for forgiveness.[50] Rosh Hashanah itself has several names. It is called *Yom Hazikaron*, the Day of Remembrance, and also

---

47. Gen. 22:13: *vay'alehu l'olah takhat b'no*, "and he offered it up as a burnt offering **in place of his son.**"

48. *The Last Trial*, 42n18 (emphasis original).

49. See Lev. 16:24: "In the seventh month, on the first of the month, there shall be a sabbath for you, a remembrance with shofar blasts, a holy convocation."

50. The High Holy Days, sometimes called the *Yomim Noraim* or Days of Awe, begin with preparation through personal introspection in the Hebrew month of Elul, and are marked by the Holy Day of Rosh Hashanah, the Jewish New Year, at the beginning of the month of Tishri and conclude with Yom Kippur, the Day of Atonement, ten days later.

Yom Teruah, the day of the blast of the shofar or ram's horn. In the Diaspora, outside of the land of Israel, it became the custom to observe two days of certain festivals due to issues of calendation and the difficulties of communicating the witnessing of the New Moon to the Diaspora. The Torah portion prescribed for the second day of Rosh Hashanah is the Akedah. The portion for the first day was designated as Genesis 21, which tells the story of God remembering Sarah when, even in her old age, she conceived and gave birth to Isaac. These two selections were complemented in the service with the reading of the *Haftarah*, the completion of the Torah reading, with selections on the first day of the birth of Samson and on the second day of the story of Jonah.

Dr. Lawrence Hoffman suggests that the unifying theme of these portions has to do with God remembering the Jewish people for blessing.[51] God took note of Sarah and remembered God's promise to her; God remembers the faithfulness of Abraham and Isaac and in that remembrance brings the blessing of life to their children. Each year, on the cusp of a new future when God judges the world and all who dwell upon it, Jews entreat God through the words of the *Machzor* (High Holy Day prayer book) to "Remember us unto life, O King who delights in life." Prayers such as this along with the Torah portion provide small "nudges" to God to consider the *zachut* of our righteous ancestors.

Substitution of the ram for the sacrifice also connects with the holiday because of the association between the *Akedah* and the sounding of the shofar. The ram's horn (or antelope horn) is ritually sounded during the Rosh Hashanah service and also at the conclusion of Yom Kippur. On Rosh Hashanah, the shofar is sounded in a series of calls in three sets. The second set is called *Zichronot*, or Remembrance, and speaks of the *Akedah*. In the Reform liturgy the sounding is preceded by, "We remember Abraham and Isaac walking together."[52] The sound is meant to remind God (and all of us) of that long ago act of faith. As the New Year begins and we are judged by the Judge of the world, we remind ourselves of the need for faith in the One who made a covenant with our ancestors, who stayed Father Abraham's hand and who prepared the ram as a substitute sacrifice.

51. Rabbi Lawrence A. Hoffman, PhD, the first Barbara and Stephen Friedman Professor of Liturgy, Worship and Ritual at the Hebrew Union College–Jewish Institute of Religion, New York. Lecture notes.

52. Chaim Stern, ed., *Gates of Repentance: the New Union Prayerbook for the Days of Awe* (New York: Central Conference of American Rabbis, 1978), 212

WHAT ARE THE TIES THAT BIND?

There is a great amount of literature that investigates and interprets the Akedah. Even in this brief study we have come a long distance from a story that justifies animal sacrifice as a substitute for child sacrifice. We have seen the test of Abraham transformed into a kind of test of God's remembrance and forgiveness, influenced by the *zachut* represented by the pile of ashes on the altar. The spiritual merit and faith of Abraham and Isaac yet speak to us homiletically; we could well ask what it is that continues to bind our children? In our contemporary society, do not the fathers and the mothers place expectations on their children that transform their lives? They are bound by our faith, making some into religious zealots who sacrifice their lives for our handed-down vision of God. Have we not bound our children by our patriotism, which often changes them into soldiers and exacts from them the ultimate sacrifice? We memorialize them and remember their sacrifices in hopes that we will be better people. And even if they return to us wounded of body, spirit, or mind, so often they are broken because of the experience. Like Abraham, we should remember that our decisions, our faith, and our worldview can often bind our children and shape their beings.

Reading the Akedah today tests our ability to accept its faith challenge or to rebel against what seems to be a morally untenable commandment. If God tested Abraham in order to find out what Abraham's faith was capable of making him do, given this commandment, then as many midrashim suggest, Abraham's zealous willingness to follow through must indeed make God tremble, if you could say such a thing![53]

Reading the Akedah today helps us appreciate that religious knowledge is/ can be dangerous. A scene not shown in the Torah text, but spoken about in the midrash, occurs the night before the beginning of the fateful journey toward Moriah. Abraham requests that Sarah prepare a feast to rejoice that in their old age they had a son. During the meal, "Abraham said to Sarah, 'You know when I was only three years old, I became aware of my Maker, but this lad, growing up has not yet been taught [about his Creator]. Now there is a place far away where youngsters are taught [about Him]. Let me take him there.' Sarah: 'Take him in peace.'"[54][/footnote] Who knew that "going off to religious school" could be so dangerous and life changing? Yet, indeed, religious faith can compel us to give our lives over to service, to action, even to death.

53. The rabbis often found themselves saying things that, in the face of faith, might seem either unrealistic or challenging. These statements are followed by the phrase *k'viyachol*, meaning, "if you could say such a thing!"

54. *The Book of Legends*, 40[footnote]null

The Akedah is a powerful story that resonates in each and every generation. We need only read it slowly and deliberately, pay attention, and apply the lessons and challenges of our own day to its words. In doing so, it will yield new worlds of meaning as we travel to that as-yet unidentified mountain . . . raising our eyes and seeing it afar off.

2

CHRISTIANITY

Traditional Christian Interpretation of Genesis 22

Carey Walsh

From its beginnings in the New Testament, the Christian interpretation of Genesis 22 saw connections between the near sacrifice of Isaac and the crucifixion of Christ. Christian interpreters focused on the element of sacrifice in the tale while their Jewish counterparts tended to concentrate on the relationships between God, Abraham, and Isaac. The other elements of the story also typical in Jewish interpretation, for example, the conversation between father and son, the location of the sacrifice, and the knowingness of Isaac, by comparison receive scant attention in the Christian exegetical tradition.

The term most commonly used to depict the story of Genesis 22, Akedah—the *binding* of Isaac—is typical of Jewish, but not Christian interpreters, who focus primarily on the spiritual meanings of the divine command to sacrifice.[1] Therefore, I will refer to the story of Genesis 22 throughout this essay as "Abraham's offering." There is a potent irony here. For Christian interpreters the horror in this tale, of a father offering his son, is diffused by its later actually happening in the Gospels. Origen, for instance, notes a comparison between Abraham and the God of Jesus Christ. Both are willing to offer their sons in a "magnificent generosity" whereby Abraham offers a mortal son *not* put to death, and God delivers the immortal son *to* death.[2] In one story the sacrifice of the

---

1. Claus Westermann, *Genesis 12–36: A Commentary*, trans. John J. Scullion (Minneapolis: Augsburg, 1985), 354.

2. Origen notes a probable connection with Rom. 8:32, suggesting that Paul has this story of Isaac in mind: "He who did not spare his own Son but handed him over for us all, how will he not also give us everything else along with him?" *Homilies on Genesis* 8, 8, in Origen, *Homilies on Genesis and Exodus*,

son is averted, though the horror at what nearly happened lingers. In the second story in the Gospel there is no reprieve. The sacrifice of the son occurs, and its horror is recalibrated as the gift of grace in atonement. Christ is sacrificed, but this action effects a divine forgiveness for all. The horror in the second story, it would seem, was worth it for the soteriological gain it wrought.[3] One live son, Isaac, is saved by the substitution of a ram. The other, dead son, Jesus, becomes saved and *saving* through substitutionary atonement. As Luther remarked, interpretation of this difficult story must rely, not on reason, but on the word, "namely, that he who is dead lives, and he who lives, dies."[4]

The early Christians sought to understand Jesus by reading their Scriptures, that is, the books of what later became the Old Testament. This led to a general shift in attention from the Torah, the first five books of the Bible, which is central for Jewish interpreters, to the Prophets.[5] Christian Bibles positioned the prophetic corpus in the last part of the Old Testament before the New in order to point the way to Christ, while the sequence of the material in Jewish Bibles remains Torah, Prophets, and Writings. Also, the Christian shift in perspective meant that the Torah tended to be read *as* prophetic, that is, as prefiguring Jesus. Early Christians, it should be recalled, viewed Israel's history as their own history.[6] It is also important to note that at the time of Christianity's spread in a Greco-Roman world, texts were viewed as oracular, that is, as containing hidden divine messages.[7] The first communities of the Way did not understand why their rabbi had been executed and so they turned to their

trans. Ronald E. Heine, Fathers of the Church, vol. 71 (Washington, D. C. : Catholic University Press, 1982); Mark Sheridan, ed., *Genesis 12–50*, vol. 2 of *Ancient Christian Commentary on Scripture: Old Testament* (Downers Grove, IL: IVP Academic, 2002), 108.

3. The gospels themselves, especially Mark, wrestle with the violence of the crucifixion. Modern theology revisits the violence grounding atonement notions. See Stephen Finlan, *Problems with Atonement: The Origins of, and Controversy about, the Atonement Doctrine* (Collegeville, MN: Liturgical, 2005); Gil Bailie, *Violence Unveiled: Humanity at the Crossroads* (New York: Crossroads, 1997); Regina M. Schwartz, *The Curse of Cain: The Violent Legacy of Monotheism* (Chicago: University of Chicago Press, 1997); and especially, Jürgen Moltmann, *The Crucified God: The Cross of Christ As the Foundation and Criticism of Christian Theology* (Minneapolis: Fortress Press 1993).

4. *Luther's Works*, American Edition, edited by Jaroslav Pelikan and Helmut T. Lehman (Philadelphia: Fortress Press, and St. Louis: Concordia, 1957–86), 4:113.

5. P. R. Ackroyd and C.F. Evans, eds., *The Cambridge History of the Bible: From the Beginnings to Jerome* (Cambridge: Cambridge University Press, 1970), 413.

6. George Lindbeck, "The Story-Shaped Church: Critical Exegesis and Theological Interpretation," in *The Theological Interpretation of Scripture: Classic and Contemporary Readings*, ed. Stephen E. Fowl (Oxford: Blackwell, 1997), 42.

7. Ackroyd and Evans, *Cambridge History of the Bible*, 454.

Scriptures for illumination of God's meaning. They were convinced that Jesus' death and resurrection happened "according to Scriptures" and so it was natural that they looked into those Scriptures with new eyes.[8] Genesis 22, along with the stories of the Passover lamb (Exodus 12),[9] the scapegoat (Leviticus 16),[10] and the suffering servant songs (Isa. 42:1-4; 49:1-6; 50:4-9; and 52:13—53:12) particularly aided in their understanding of Christ's sacrificial death.[11]

Overall in the history of Christian interpretation of Genesis 22, the connection between Isaac and Christ is positive and illuminating of God's mission. Abraham is seen as an exemplar of faith.[12] And throughout Christian tradition, interpreters follow Origen's lead on the legitimacy of interpreting Scripture by means of Scripture, that is, drawing connections between texts in the Bible.[13] Origen exercised a tremendous influence on the subsequent late patristic and medieval exegetical tradition in general, and specifically with this story of Abraham's offering in at least three essential facets: (1) his insistence that biblical interpretation involved intertextual associations between the Old Testament and the New, (2) an emphasis on understanding the literal as well as the spiritual sense of biblical texts, and (3) a conviction that the multivalence of Scripture was the result, not of indecision on the part of the interpreter, but of the divine source of the texts. The multiplicity of meanings resulted from the grandness of divine inspiration and the limitations of the human mind to ever grasp this grandness fully.

Origen was of the Alexandrian school, which employed insights from Greek philosophy and rhetoric to understanding Scripture. Hence allegory was a means to interpret what a passage meant both on the literal or "physical" level and on the "ethical" or spiritual level.[14] In discussing his approach, Origen used an analogy with the human person: just as the person is comprised of body, soul, and spirit, so too does Scripture have a literal, moral, and spiritual aspect.[15] Scriptural passages often had more than one meaning, but these never

8. G. W. H. Lampe, ed., *The Cambridge History of the Bible: The West from the Fathers to theReformation* (Cambridge: Cambridge University Press, 1969), 156.

9. Cf. 1 Cor. 5:7; John 1:29, 36; Rev. 6:1; 14:4; 17:14.

10. Finlan, *Problems with Atonement*, 21; *Epistle of Barnabas* 7.7; Gal 3:13; 2 Cor. 5:21; Rom. 3:25; 6:6; 7:4; 8:3.

11. Shalom Spiegel, *The Last Trial*, trans. Judah Goldin (New York: Random house, 1967), 83–84.

12. R. W. L. Moberly's comprehensive study demonstrates the largely positive interpretation of the test in Christian interpretive history: *The Bible, Theology, and Faith: A Study of Abraham and Jesus* (Cambridge: Cambridge University Press, 2000).

13. Sheridan, ed., *Genesis 12–50*, 111.

14. Robert M. Grant with David Tracy, *A Short History of the Interpretation of the Bible*, 2nd ed., (Philadelphia: Fortress, 1984).

contradicted one another. The act of interpretation was aided by the same gift of divine grace that had authored Scripture in the first place.

Allegorical interpretation enabled Origen to tap into the homiletic potential of even difficult passages, such as Genesis 22, without ignoring their literal sense. The principal aim of scriptural exegesis, for Origen, was in discovery of its "intellectual truths," that is, the spiritual ones, over the historical sense, but he nevertheless did not ignore that history, as his critics often claimed.[16] A Platonist influence can be seen in Origen's view that the historical details served as the mirror through which divine, intellectual truths were reflected. These truths, since they are of divine origin, are timeless and available through interpretation of any passage from the canonical whole. Origen's allegorical method upheld both the rationality of Christian faith to people familiar with Greek philosophical ideas and the usefulness of Scripture for the spiritual life. In this respect, Origen's interpretative outlook exemplifies a chief characteristic of patristic exegesis, namely its orientation toward theology, and its insistence on the unity of theology with life.[17] Patristic exegetes were plenty rigorous and critical in their analysis of scriptural texts. But since they shared the faith they studied, they were not reductive in ascertaining meanings. They assumed polysemy—many meanings—in Scripture. They assumed beauty, richness, and revelation were present in the text. The original context, what the author meant, was "only one of its possible meanings and may not, in certain circumstances, even be its primary or most important meaning."[18] To read as a believer, Henri de Lubac noted, essentially collapses the distance between past and present, in a way that it does not for the historian. The story becomes the believer's own story.[19]

Origen's influence, as we noted above, extended into medieval exegetical practice, with a further elaboration of the allegorical method. The late patristic and medieval periods established the interpretative notion that Scripture had at least four senses of meaning, those located in the text's (1) letter, (2) allegory, (3) moral lesson, and (4) anagogy, its final goal or eschatological meaning.[20]

15. Ackroyd and Evans, *Cambridge History of the Bible*, 467.

16. Principally interpreters of the Antiochene school, Jerome, and Augustine, who all emphasized the historical and literary details of a passage to a greater extent than did the Alexandrians. However, Origen's understanding of allegory differed from that of Philo, in that for Origen both the sign and the thing signified were historical. Beryl Smalley, *The Study of the Bible in the Middle Ages* (Notre Dame: University of Notre Dame Press, 1989).

17. James L. Kugel and Rowan A. Greer, *Early Biblical Interpretation* (Philadelphia: Westminster, 1986).

18. David C. Steinmetz, "The Superiority of Pre-Critical Exegesis," *Theology Today* 37 (1980): 28.

19. Henri de Lubac, "Spiritual Understanding," in *Theological Interpretation*, ed. Fowl, 16.

In addition, Origen's impact was felt particularly through the *Glossa Ordinaria*, in wide use in the Middle Ages. This was a compendium of the biblical texts with standard glosses, that is, expositions, notes, and theological insights added for the purposes of biblical instruction in the schools. It served as a means of making the patristic tradition available and intelligible and was used both in lecture by the instructor and for copying by students. The *Glossa Ordinaria* included homilies from Origen (as well as other church fathers) and so his allegorical exegetical method was widely diffused. [21] With the Renaissance and Reformation of the 16th century, the allegorical method waned. The Renaissance ignited a renewed interest in the historical context of ancient texts, including the Bible, and the Reformation stressed a subjective, immediate understanding of Christ through reading Scripture directly and without the aid of either allegorical methods or the patristic tradition of the church.[22] For the Reformers, the text was the sole source of revelation and not, as it was for the Catholic Church, Scripture *and* tradition.

From the Enlightenment on, biblical interpreters focused not on connections between texts and the two Testaments but on discrete stories, and in this case of Abraham's offering, on the troubling aspects in the divine command itself. Immanuel Kant, for example, could not reconcile a command to kill one's son with a universal moral duty within us. The contradiction cannot go away, and so he professed uncertainty about it being God's voice that had issued the command.[23] From Julius Wellhausen (1844–1914) on, with the rise of historical criticism, interpreters have been concerned primarily with the origin of the story. There is widespread scholarly agreement that it is an etiology, that is, an explanation of a cultural fact, detailing the abolition of human sacrifice (Isaac) by substituting an animal (the ram caught in a thicket).[24] In this historical-critical perspective, then, the story helps to name a probable cultic site, Mt. Moriah, important at the time of the author(s).[25] Let us turn now

20. Henri de Lubac argues that the medieval exegesis of four senses of scriptural meaning still follows Origen's vision of a literal and spiritual sense, with the latter three senses constituting spiritual understandings. *Medieval Exegesis: The Four Senses of Scripture,* vol. 2, trans. E. M. Macierowski (Grand Rapids, MI: Eerdmans, 2000), 25, 56, 76–89, 212–13.

21. As Beryl Smalley notes, "To write a history of Origenist influence on the west would be tantamount to writing a history of western exegesis," *The Study of the Bible,* 14.

22. Grant and Tracy, *A Short History,* 93–94.

23. Westermann, *Genesis 12–36,* 354.

24. For a comparative study of the Akedah with child sacrifice in ancient cultures, see *The Sacrifice of Isaac: The Aqedah (Genesis 22) and its Interpretations,* ed. Ed Noort and Eibert Tigchelaar (Leiden and Boston: Brill, 2002).

to Christian traditional interpretation of Abraham's offering, which begins as early as the New Testament.

Scripture on Abraham's Offering

> By faith Abraham, when put to the test, offered up Isaac, and he who had received the promises was ready to offer his only son, of whom it was said, "Through Isaac descendants shall bear your name." He reasoned that God was able to raise even from the dead, and he received Isaac back as a symbol. Hebrews 11:17-19

There are two interpretations of the tale of Abraham's offering in the New Testament: first, in this passage, Heb. 11:17-19; and second, in James 2:21. It is never mentioned by Jesus or any of the Gospels. The Hebrews passage is part of a list of acts of faith by the patriarchs and other significant figures in the Old Testament, for example, Abel, Noah, Moses, and Gideon. And, of all the acts in which Abraham demonstrated his faith, it is his willingness to sacrifice his son that is recalled in Hebrews.

For the author of Hebrews, Abraham's willingness links sacrifice to faith, for himself, Jesus, and, as a type, for all subsequent believers. But this link is severed in modernity, whose premium on individualism enhances self-protectiveness.[26] Sacrifice in the modern milieu is more generally viewed as a choice that Abraham and Jesus were entitled to make, but is no longer assumed to be constitutive of faith. Our own individualism, then, is off the hook and we can remain appalled by Abraham's choice. Traditional Christian interpretation, as exemplified in the Hebrews passage, far from obscuring the text's meaning, allows us to see the fundamental link between sacrifice and faith.

The primary significance of the story for the author of Hebrews lies, then, in Abraham's unwavering demonstration of faith in his God.[27] Hebrews 11, it

25. Hermann Gunkel, *Genesis*, trans. Mark E. Biddle (Macon, GA: Mercer University Press, 1997), 233–40; Jon D. Levenson, *The Death and Resurrection of the Beloved Son: The Transformation of Child Sacrifice in Judaism and Christianity* (New Haven: Yale University Press, 1993), 112–14.

26. For a masterful analysis of modernity's impact on biblical interpretation, see Hans W. Frei, *The Eclipse of Biblical Narrative: A Study in Eighteenth and Nineteenth Century Hermeneutics* (New Haven: Yale University Press, 1974).

27. Due to its unique style and vocabulary in contrast to those demonstrated in the Pauline letters, the authorship of Hebrews has long been debated, even from patristic times. For instance, Tertullian suggested Barnabas; Origen, Luke. The consensus of modern biblical scholarship is that Hebrews was written not by Paul, but rather another, anonymous author. Luke Timothy Johnson, *The Writings of the New Testament: An Interpretation* (Minneapolis: Fortress Press, 1999), 458–61.

shall be recalled, makes the difficult yet true claim that "faith is the realization of what is hoped for and evidence of things not seen" (Heb. 11:1), and Abraham's willingness to sacrifice his own son testifies, paradigmatically, to such faith. The contradiction between God's promise to Abraham of many descendants through Isaac and God's command to sacrifice the same son must have been acute for the patriarch. Abraham, for the author of Hebrews, negotiates that contradiction by listening to something unseen, unknown, namely, an intuition that somehow the painful contradiction is illusion. The notion of resurrection is precisely that "evidence unseen" and so for Hebrews, Abraham is theologically light years ahead of his time. He has faith in a belief that is revealed only with the resurrection of Christ. Luther agrees with the author of Hebrews that Abraham's belief in resurrection is what enables him pass the test.[28] Nowhere in the Old Testament is belief in resurrection overtly evident, with the exception of Dan. 12:2, a relatively late text, written sometime in the 2nd century BCE: "Many of those who sleep in the dust of the earth shall awake; Some to everlasting life, others to reproach and everlasting disgrace." [29]

So, it is Abraham's preternatural faith that emboldens him to obey God's command. The invisible—"evidence unseen"—takes precedence over the seen, namely, his own son. Abraham's faith in this unknown, later doctrine is then affirmed when he received Isaac back "as a symbol" (Heb 11:19). The Greek here, *parabolē*, "symbol," from which the English "parable" is derived, is helpful for it signifies something unseen. Isaac, as *parabolē*, is more than a spared son. He now symbolizes the unseen truth of resurrection.[30] The spared son symbolizes that something new is afoot in the divine sphere, which is Christ. Abraham does not merely pass God's test, and get his son Isaac back; he gets a glimpse of New Testament truth, namely, that someday even the death imperiling his son will have no sting (1 Cor. 15:55). In fact, as Jean Danielou has asserted, *two* aspects of the mystery of Christ are typified in this story: the resurrection, as we noted above, but also Christ's passion, in the suffering that Isaac endures.[31]

Things then do not return to normal after Abraham's test. They are brand new. The threat of Isaac's death is not suppressed or ignored in Hebrews 11. It

28. *Luther's Works*, 4:96.

29. Ezekiel's tale of dry bones (Ezek. 37:1-13) is a figurative metaphor for the restoration of Israel after its tragic exile. Elisha revives a dead boy (1 Kgs 4:18-37), much as Jesus revived Lazarus, but these stories denote revivification, not resurrection. The difference is that Israel, the boy, and Lazarus, though revived, will eventually die (John 11:1-44).

30. Rom. 6:5; 8:17.

31. Jean Danielou SJ, *From Shadows to Reality: Studies in the Biblical Typology of the Fathers*, trans. Wulstan Hibberd (CreateSpace, 2011), 123.

is simply surpassed with a greater truth, that of resurrection. Abraham and Isaac are not wounded by their harrowing ordeal. For the author of Hebrews, they come away unscathed and rejuvenated, with Isaac the enduring "symbol" that death is not the end (v. 19). In fact, Luther stresses that they both come away giddy with victory, a victory over death; Isaac's physical death yes, but also the dread with which death grips mortals. As a result of their obedience, Abraham and Isaac witness, Luther maintains, a divine truth, that death is mere sport for God.[32] As a result, they walk away existentially freer than their contemporaries.

The saving of Isaac prefigures the resurrected Christ. The connection of Isaac with Christ will shape all subsequent Christian interpretations of Abraham's offering, as we shall see. In fact, the King James translation makes the connection even more explicit with the phrase "his only begotten son" (v. 17), while the New American Bible translation has "only son." Here the King James is closer to the Greek original, "*monogenē*," "only born," of Hebrews 11, while the New American is closer to the Hebrew *yakhid* of Gen 22:2: "only one."[33]

Jesus himself does not mention the story of Abraham's offering explicitly though he speaks of Abraham on numerous occasions. When he teaches about everlasting life as always having been God's plan, he asserts that the God of the fathers, of Abraham, Isaac, and Jacob, is a God of the living. Jesus is telling the stunned crowd that Abraham and Isaac (and Jacob) are still alive. He may or may not be alluding to the story of Abraham's offering, but he does relate the idea of resurrection with Isaac explicitly (Matt. 22:32; Luke 20:37). Luther follows this logic and is assured that all the patriarchs, Abraham, Isaac, and Jacob, who placed their hope in God believed in the resurrection of the dead.[34]

Abraham's demonstration of faith is echoed in the Pauline letters, even though the Genesis 22 story is not explicitly recalled. For Paul, Abraham is clearly the father of faith because he believed and obeyed God (Gen. 15:6) long before the covenant of circumcision was enacted (Gen. 17:10). The sequence is crucial for Paul's theology and mission to the Gentiles. Abraham becomes the example of faith in God *before* the law (e.g., circumcision), and so validates the inclusion of faith-filled Gentiles to God's saving mission alongside the faith-filled *and* law-abiding Jews. Gentile Christians are part of God's promise through Isaac.[35] Abraham is the linchpin for universal salvation in Christ and for Paul it rests on the patriarch's faith.

---

32. *Luther's Works*, 4:117.

33. The Septuagint, the Greek translation of the Old Testament, has "loved son, whom you love" twice using the verb *agape*, "(selfless) love."

34. *Luther's Works*, 7:116.

35. Rom. 9:7-8; Gal. 3:16, 18; Gal. 4:22-24, 28.

The second New Testament passage that makes explicit use of the story of Abraham's offering occurs in the book of James. The relation between *faith*—believing that God was in Christ—and *works*—obeying God's commandments—is an ongoing dispute in the New Testament. For Paul, faith is paramount. For James, works also matter. James uses the example of Abraham, this time specifically with the offering of Isaac, in nearly the opposite sense from Paul. Abraham is celebrated not only for his faith, but for the unity of his faith and works in the ordeal: "Was not Abraham our father justified by works, when he offered his son Isaac upon the altar? You see that faith was active along with his works, and faith was completed by the works" (James 2:21–22). James credits Abraham's active obedience to the divine command to sacrifice his son as the patriarch's (estimable) work.

John Calvin takes a different tack in understanding this passage in James.[36] He states that this work of Abraham in Genesis 22 *did not* win Abraham righteousness with God because God had earlier credited him with it in Gen. 15:6. Calvin argues that "it is absurd for the effect to precede the cause," and Abraham was justified long before even Ishmael, the older brother, was conceived. Therefore, Calvin points out, the verse in James expresses the *declaration*, not the *imputation* of righteousness, as that had already occurred long before.[37] Calvin returns to Genesis 22 to discuss the divine promise made after the ordeal, in verses 16–18. There it appears that Abraham is rewarded with a promise of descendants and blessing, and so on, but this, Calvin correctly notes, is simply a repetition of the promise Abraham has already received (Gen. 13:16; 15:5; 17:7). God is indeed generous here as "he will repay to works what He had freely given before the works."[38]

The interpretive strategy of both Paul and the author of Hebrews is typological. This method examines Old Testament figures and events as prefiguring or foreshadowing figures and events in the New.[39] Typology, from the Greek *typos*, meaning "stamp," notes an impression in a text, a meaning not apparent before New Testament times. "A type," Danielou notes, "is an

---

36. The Protestant Reformers tended to align themselves with Paul on the faith side of the faith and works dispute, in reaction to what they saw as the works-based sacramental system of the Catholic Church.

37. John Calvin, *Institutes of the Christian Religion*, trans. Henry Beveridge (Grand Rapids, MI: Eerdmans, 1953), 370.

38. Calvin, *Institutes*, 375–76.

39. Nicholas Lash, *Theology on the Way to Emmaus* (Eugene, OR: Wipf & Stock, 2005); Francis M. Young, *Biblical Exegesis and the Formation of Christian Culture* (Cambridge: Cambridge University Press, 1997), 152–57; Ackroyd and Evans, *The Cambridge History of the Bible*, 413.

event which offers likeness to something in the future, but yet does not really fulfill this something."[40] It is instead suggestive, allusive, even perhaps *enticing* of a fuller truth not yet revealed. Christians believe revelation occurs in the Old and New Testaments and in their juxtaposition. Gospel events recapitulate the saving acts of God in the Old Testament.[41] The Second Vatican Council (1962–1965) confirms this view in its Dogmatic Constitution on Divine Revelation, drawing on a quotation by Augustine: "God, the inspirer and author of both Testaments, wisely arranged that the New Testament be hidden in the Old and the Old be made manifest in the New."[42]

Typology differs from allegory in important ways. An allegory has an abstract concept attached to a concrete image in a text. The abstraction is then somewhat privileged over the concrete image or can be detached from its historical sense.[43] Allegory assumes a hidden meaning, then, that can exist independently of the literal sense. Typology also assumes a hidden meaning, but one that comes to light in consort with the New Testament.[44] In typology, both concrete and hidden meanings remain important. In fact, typology insists on a *revelatory* connection between two events. In this instance, Genesis 22 does not contain Christ's crucifixion in some sort of Bible code that cruelly leaves its intended original audience in the dark. Rather, the text is polyvalent, full of meanings always, and additional theological resonances become clear after the crucifixion.

In allegorical interpretation, the abstract idea, in this case, say, of faith or obedience, is prominent over the literal details of an Abraham, Isaac, Mt.

---

40. Danielou, *From Shadow to Reality*, 125.

41. Andrew Louth, *Discerning the Mystery: An Essay on the Nature of Theology* (Oxford: Clarendon, 1983) 96–131; Robert Louis Wilken, *The Spirit of Early Christian Thought: Seeking the Face of God* (New Haven: Yale University Press, 2003), 71–77; Lampe, *The Cambridge History of the Bible*, 157.

42. "Dogmatic Constitution on Divine Revelation," in *The Conciliar and Postconciliar Document*, vol. 1 of *Vatican Council II*, Austin Flannery OP, ed., (Northport, NY: Costello, 1975), 750–65.

43. Recent scholarship offers a useful discussion of the complex hermeneutic and philosophic issues involved in these two terms, which are beyond the scope of the present discussion. A third term, figural, has now come into use to address the "intelligibility discovered in the relation between two events comprising a single divine performance in history." John David Dawson, *Christian Figural Reading and the Fashioning of Identity* (Berkeley: University of California Press, 2002), 86. See also the helpful discussions in Fowl, *Theological Interpretation*, and Peter W. Martens, "Revisiting the Allegory/Typology Distinction: The Case of Origen," *Journal of Early Christian Studies* 16 (2008): 283–317; Frances M. Young, *Biblical Exegesis and the Formation of Christian Culture* (Cambridge: Cambridge University Press, 1997).

44. See Christopher R. Seitz, *Figured Out: Typology and Providence in Christian Scripture* (Louisville: Westminster/John Knox, 2001).

Moriah, and an impending sacrifice. Modern biblical criticism tends to confuse these two strategies of interpretation and reject them both as "'reading into" (eisegeting) a biblical text meanings that were likely not there for the original authors.[45] Modern study aims to "draw out" (exegete) meanings that the authors likely intended.[46] Recall that for modern people, the Bible is to be read and studied. For the early Christians, it was oracular and also written somehow with the guidance of the Holy Spirit.[47] Jesus himself used typology when he told the story of his death and resurrection by drawing on the story of Jonah in the belly of the big fish for three days (Matt. 12:38-42; Luke 11:29-32). His is typological interpretation because it reveals a connection between events; the details of the Jonah story matter alongside what they portend of Jesus' death. Typological interpretation was long viewed as legitimate in Christian tradition because it had apostolic beginnings with Christ and Paul.[48] It was as well long considered spiritually efficacious because reading was closely linked to the process of illumination and conversion, what Ellen Davis terms an "openness to repentance."[49] Let us turn now to how Christians have interpreted the specific details in the story of Abraham's offering.

45. Allegorical, not typological, interpretation would tend to diminish texts of any serious historical meaning. Ackroyd and Evans, *Cambridge History of the Bible*, 379. For an excellent discussion of early interpretive methods, see Steinmetz, "The Superiority of Pre-Critical Exegesis," 27–38.

46. Stephen Fowl, "Introduction" *in The Theological Interpretation of Scripture*, ed. Fowl, xvii; Ellen F. Davis, "Teaching the Bible Confessionally in the Church," in *The Art of Reading Scripture*, ed. Ellen F. Davis and Richard B. Hays (Grand Rapids, MI: Eerdmans, 2003), 13. In recent decades, however, a growing contingent of biblical scholars has turned its attention to pre-modern exegesis. Brevard Childs was an early and highly influential proponent of a canonical approach that looked to the history of interpretation along with historical critical analysis. For more recent studies see: Stephen E. Fowl, *Engaging Scripture: A Model for Theological Interpretation* (Eugene, OR: Wipf & Stock, 2008); Wilken, *The Spirit of Early Christian Thought*; Gary A. Anderson, *The Genesis of Perfection: Adam and Eve in Jewish and Christian Imagination* (Louisville: Westminster/ John Knox, 2002); Davis, "Teaching the Bible Confessionally"; Louth, *Discerning the Mystery*; *The Ancient Christian Commentary on Scripture*, published by InterVarsity Academic, and *Brazos Theological Commentary on the Bible*, by Baker Academic press, are new commentary series that incorporate patristic and medieval exegetical insights on texts.

47. De Lubac, "Spiritual Understanding," 12; Ackroyd and Evans, *Cambridge History of the Bible*, 461, 474.

48. Ackroyd and Evans, *Cambridge History of the Bible*, 466.

49. Davis, "Teaching the Bible Confessionally," 16; de Lubac nicely focuses the distinction by stating that the reader is interested in his or her own conversion and not merely the psychology of Old Testament characters, 14.

"God tested Abraham" (v. 1)

The first thing to note is that the story differs from other Abraham narratives by stating its theme at the front: God tested Abraham.[50] For Origen, this is the only reason for the divine command and Abraham passes the test, because as Hebrews 11:17 shows, he did not hesitate: "Abraham . . . was ready to offer his only son."[51] Luther adds psychological insight to his exegesis of verse 1 by noting that the command drastically affects Abraham for the rest of the chapter. After God's command, he notes, Abraham can "see nothing else. Everything fades out in him."[52]

The central theological question of the passage becomes why God would need a test of Abraham at this point. And here the interpreters readily protect God's omniscience. The test is never because God does not know what Abraham will do, but for other reasons. St. Thomas Aquinas, as was his wont, dissects the issue into various parts. There are, he reasons, two kinds of tests, those that lead to some good, and those from the devil that deceive and trick people. Aquinas rules out the possibility that this could somehow be a test from the devil. Further, Aquinas reasons, the good can be for Abraham's sake or for the sake of others. Aquinas deliberates that the test in Genesis 22 is obviously for the good, and for the sake of others, not Abraham. The patriarch's example of faith, which triumphs over the testing of "fleshly concerns," that is, that he would love his son, helps Christians in their own "fleshly" struggles. "For if concupiscence triumphs," Aquinas warns, "the person does not love God in a perfect manner, nor does he love in a perfect manner when the concerns of the world either frighten him or exert an undue influence upon him."[53]

Luther understands the testing of Abraham to be a signal opportunity for readers to see that "good fruits come from a good tree," namely, Abraham.[54] He highlights the aspect of contradiction in the test. Isaac is the son of all of

---

50. Westermann, *Genesis 12–36*, 354–55. Westermann argues that the story conforms to a threefold test narrative structure: (1) lay the task on the protagonist, (2) the protagonist carries out the task, (3) the protagonist discovers whether or not he has passed the test. Jon Levenson insists that verse 1 is not a theme, adding that it is typically only Christian interpreters who see one theme in the story. *The Death and Resurrection of the Beloved Son*, 125–26.

51. Sheridan, ed., *Genesis 12-50*, 102; Origen notes that Abraham's quickness is characteristic, as he had left his homeland when God first called him, Gen 12, *Homilies on Genesis* 8, 4.

52. *Luther's Works*, 4:109.

53. St. Thomas Aquinas, "Commentary on St. Paul's Epistle to the Thessalonians," in *The Collected Works of St. Thomas Aquinas*, (electronic edition (InteLex Corporation, 1993), 24.

54. Martin Luther, "Sermon on the Eleventh Sunday after Trinity: A Picture and an Example of a True Saint and a Real Hypocrite," in *Sermons of Martin Luther*, electronic edition (Intelex Corporation, 1995), 4:341.

God's promises to Abraham and he is the one whom Abraham must sacrifice. God throws Abraham into a kind of theological catch-22 that must have vexed him sorely. The verb for "test" (Hebrew: *nasah*) means both "test" and "tempt," and so Abraham would likely have been weighing what to do.[55] To Abraham, God was a best friend, and not an enemy or tyrant. Hence this test from God, Luther argues, must have brought on an internal struggle within Abraham and doubts about whether or not he had displeased God at some point. In fact, Luther adds, Abraham's ordeal was harsher than Mary's when she lost her son, Jesus, in Jerusalem (Luke 2:41-50), because at least she would know that he was alive.[56] It is Luther, then, with his psychological acuity, who comes closest to voicing the discomfort modern readers often have with the nature of God's test, and by implication, the nature of God. Abraham is known as the father of faith for the three monotheistic faiths—Judaism, Christianity, and Islam—that share his story. And his harshest credential for being the father of faith was his willingness to forgo his own biological fatherhood by killing his son. Some important lessons undoubtedly are being stressed in the story about loyalty, devotion, and priorities, but the horror can easily obstruct them.

Abraham's climactic demonstration of his faith has become, particularly for modern eyes, almost the exact opposite of these lessons; a crystal clear example of what *not to do* in the name of faith. Abraham seems fanatical and modern Americans certainly shy away from any displays of overcommitment. Regina Schwartz and others have come to critique the byproduct of such radical monotheism, namely, its "violent legacy."[57] There is no simple, wholesale answer to the problem of violence in the name of religion, but the biblical texts themselves, this story included, contain multiple meanings that together safeguard against their misuse. Reading for these multiple meanings does not diffuse the terror in what Abraham was prepared to do, but it does yield an inner critique or deconstruction of the *subsequent* need for fanaticism. Attending to these meanings does not soften Abraham for us. Isaac is in an abusive home. And, the legacy of child abuse will shape his character as passive, unable to control his children, and the most opaque of the patriarchs. He will be duped,

---

55. *Luther's Works*, 4:91.

56. Ibid., 94.

57. Schwartz, *The Curse of Cain*. See also David Blumenthal, *Facing the Abusive God: A Theology of Protest* (Louisville, KY: Westminster/John Knox, 1993); and David Penchansky, *What Rough Beast? Images of God in the Hebrew Bible* (Louisville, KY: Westminster/John Knox, 1999). This is the prime sticking point, as well, for the so-called New Atheists—Richard Dawkins, the late Christopher Hitchens, Sam Harris, and Daniel Dennett—who posit that the violence of the biblical faiths too easily outweighs whatever gains they could have wrought.

acted upon, by his own son, Jacob, on his deathbed. The narrative cycle of Isaac as victim continues his passivity throughout his life. And since Sarah dies in the first verse of the next chapter, 23:1, the rabbis believe Abraham's actions essentially killed her. The effects of the terror of his near sacrifice, then, are preserved in the Isaac narrative cycle and they implicitly critique the originating violence at Abraham's hands. In addition, historical criticism has shown that its original cultural context had included child sacrifice, so that this story was really meant to signal its cessation with a different, loving kind of deity. It was, in other words, a story of violence averted. Still, amidst these subtleties of interpretation, there lingers a harrowing dimension of God. Christopher Seitz's insight is particularly apt with respect to the story of Isaac's near sacrifice: 'The problem with historical criticism was that it had failed to do constructive theological work involving the identity of God in the most basic sense."[58]

"Go to the land of Moriah" (v. 2)

Jewish interpreters discuss the location of the divine test, Mt. Moriah, in considerable detail. This is understandable since Mt. Moriah is traditionally considered to be the location where Solomon's temple was later built (2 Chron. 3:1). St. Jerome concurs with Jewish interpreters here, based on his personal experiences traveling from Hebron to Jerusalem.[59] Verse 14 states that it occurred at "the mount of the Lord," which biblical tradition locates in Jerusalem (2 Chronicles 3; Psalm 76; Isaiah 2; Zechariah 6).

Jewish interpreters tend to derive the place name, Moriah, from the noun "fear" or "awe," *yira'*, because this term suggests a stance for worship. Jerome uses instead the similar *ra'ah* , "see," and understands "Moriah" as a causative, "cause to see," meaning "enlightening," place. From there, he argues, God's oracle[60] came forth, first in law and then with the Holy Spirit.[61] Both verbs are later used in the story. In verse 12: "You fear God"; and in verse 14, when Moriah is named as the place where God "will be seen," "as it is said to this day," suggesting a site of continuing worship. In this view, for Judaism, the story of

---

58. Seitz, *Figured Out*, 4.

59. He adds that Abraham must have been living in Gerar, rather than the Oaks of Mamre at the time, to account for a three day journey. Luther too ponders the journey's length and posits that the distance from Mt. Moriah to the servants left behind to be about a quarter of a mile. *Luther's Works*, 4:109.

60. The Hebrew term for the holy of holies, *debir*, shares the same root with the word for "word," *dabar*.

61. Jerome, *Saint Jerome's Hebrew Questions on Genesis*, trans. C. T. R. Howard (Oxford: Clarendon 1995), 55.

Abraham's offering in Genesis 22 provides the theological foundation for the temple.[62]

Most Christian interpreters also presume that Mt. Moriah is in Jerusalem. Caesarius of Arles states outright that the place of Isaac's sacrifice is where Jesus is later crucified.[63] Hence, even the story's very geography is typologically forecasting the future execution of Christ. Luther, however does not think Mt. Moriah is in Jerusalem because the entire region around the city is mountainous and it would not, then, have been possible for Abraham to see it from afar (v. 4).

After the ordeal, Abraham names the site "'The Lord will see' as it is said to this day, 'On the Mount of the Lord it shall be seen'" (v. 14). Luther confirms that *grammatically* the latter phrase is passive, "The Lord shall be seen." But he adds that *theologically*, the active sense, "The Lord will see" is also correct since God "saw to it" that a ram would be there.[64] Origen's exegesis, by contrast, focuses not on the tense of the verb, but rather on the spiritual opportunities afforded by the detail of vision. Origen notices that since God is not anthropomorphically equipped with eyes to see, the mention of his vision must have a nonliteral, spiritual meaning. He states:

> A clear way of spiritual understanding is opened for those who know how to hear these words. For everything which has been done reaches to the vision, for it is said that "the Lord saw." But the vision which "the Lord saw" is in the spirit so that you too might see these things in the spirit which are written, and just as there is nothing corporeal in God so also you might perceive nothing corporeal in all these things, but you too might beget a son Isaac in the spirit, when you begin to have the "fruit of the spirit, joy, peace."[65]

Jerome picks up on the phrase in verse 14, "as it is said to this day." He comments further that the "Lord sees" is a saying for the Jews of his time when they are in distress. They use the phrase in troubled times for consolation in the belief that God will see or care, just as he did in the story of Abraham's offering. "To this day," when the ram's horn is sounded at the Jewish celebration of the New Year, it commemorates the substituted ram in this story and is thought to invoke God's mercy.[66]

---

62. Levenson, *The Death and Resurrection of the Beloved Son*, 115.

63. Sheridan, ed., *Genesis 12–50*, 111.

64. *Luther's Works*, 7:138–39.

65. Origen, *Homilies on Genesis* 8, 10.

The Sacrifice of the Son

It was noted above that Christian interpreters view the near sacrifice of Isaac as prefiguring Christ's crucifixion.[67] Barnabas is explicit that the sacrifice of Isaac is a foreshadowing of Christ's passion.[68] Augustine writes of Isaac, "the prefiguration was not achieved without

bloodshed, in the one case by the slaying of a ram..., See Gn 22:13. in this way the resurrection was symbolized, but the reality of it was reserved for our true Lord."[69] He emphasizes here, not what *Abraham* is doing, but what *God* is, namely, preparing the way for resurrection. The primary spiritual lesson, even though a test, is precisely not, then, to earn God's favor, but to discover within oneself faith. Even the poignant detail of verse 6 that "Abraham took the wood of the burnt offering and laid it on Isaac" reminds interpreters like Origen of Christ having carried his own cross on the *via dolorosa*. Origen further uses this narrative detail about Isaac carrying his own wood to suggest that Isaac is both victim *and* priest in performing the ritual sacrifice as Christ did.[70] For Clement of Alexandria, Isaac is a type for Christ in numerous aspects: carrying his own wood, being the son, and being the intended victim.[71]

Augustine examines what lesson the sacrifice of a son could hold. His exposition shows his typological interpretation in action. Thus he defines the hard lesson:

> In a word, not to value above God what God gives us. We are still dealing only with the literal meaning of what was done, before we come to the inner secret of the thing signified, that is to what lies hidden in this mystery or sacrament of Abraham being ordered to kill his only son. See note 8 above. And when he wants to take it away from you, don't let him go down in your estimation, because God is to be loved free? Sermon 2[72]

66. Spiegel, *The Last Trial*, 92.

67. Caesarius of Arles, Sermon 84, in *Sermons*, trans. Mary Magdeleine Mueller, OSF, Fathers of the Church, vol. 47 (Washington, D-.C: Catholic University Press, 1982), 16; Augustine, "Exposition of Psalm 51," in *Expositions of the Psalms, 51–72*, trans. Maria Boulding, The Works of Saint Augustine vol. 3/17 (Hyde Park: New City Press, 2001), 341.

68. *Epistle of Barnabas* 7:3, in *Genesis 12–50*, ed. Sheridan, 90.

69. Augustine, "Exposition of Psalm 51," "Verses 1-2: The Hidden Meaning of the Title," *Expositions of the Psalms, 51–72*, 17.

70. Origen, *Homilies on Genesis* 8, 6.

71. Sheridan, ed., *Genesis 12–50*, 104–05; cf. Tertullian, *Adversus Marcionem*, 3.18; Augustine, *Civ.* 16, 32.

Augustine notices a sacrament within the frightening story. Augustine distinguishes between the literal meaning of a biblical text and its signified "inner secret," the symbol. But he insists that both meanings retain their importance in Christian interpretation. Isaac never becomes merely an allegory for our instruction. Augustine maintains that Isaac "really was born to Abraham, and that he also represented something else. The same is true about his obeying God when ordered to sacrifice his son."[73]

History and symbol are always held in tandem in Augustine's exegesis and this is why he is a useful guide of what the typological method can unearth. For him, it is not the words of the biblical text that assume primary importance, but rather the doctrine they are expressing.[74] This emboldens him to interpret a lesson that is there for all. For Augustine, more so than for other patristic interpreters such as Origen, the history in biblical stories remains significant because it is the domain of divine-human interaction. His is a fully realized incarnational view of history. God entered history in the person of Jesus and so the details will always matter. Divine history, for Augustine, is evident in the Bible in a twofold way. It is a record of *res gesta* —action in God's past, and another element, *res gestura*—of what God will do.[75] Abraham, as it were, is undergoing his own passion, one that prepares Christian readers for Jesus.

A THREE-DAY JOURNEY

A significant difference between Jewish and Christian interpreters occurs with verses 3–4. At issue is how the phrase "on the third day" should be understood: "he arose and went to the place of which God had told him. On the third day Abraham lifted up his eyes and saw the place afar off."

Grammatically in Hebrew, there are no periods to end sentences, and so the phrase "on the third day" could go with either sentence in verses 3–4.[76] The interpretative question becomes, did Abraham leave on his journey after three days of preparation, saddling the donkey, gathering his servants, cutting wood, etc.? Or, did he complete the journey on the third day? Did he set out or arrive "on the third day"? Christian interpreters stress that Abraham arrived on the third day as a typology of the resurrection and even the trinity.[77] In verse

72. Augustine, "Sermon 2: Abraham, Tested by God" in *Sermons (1–19) on the Old Testament*, trans. Edmund Hill, The Works of Saint Augustine, vol. 3/1 (Hyde Park: New City Press, 1990), 178.

73. Ibid.

74. Ackroyd and Evans, *Cambridge History of the Bible*, 574.

75. Ackroyd and Evans, *Cambridge History of the Bible*, 553.

76. Instead, stress markers are added much later. Also, the separation of content into verses is quite late, occurring sometime in the late Middle Ages.

3 "Abraham rose early in the morning" after having heard God's command in verse 2. Luther applauds the patriarch's eagerness to obey.[78] This detail in verse 3 shows that Abraham did not delay and supports the interpretation that he *arrived* rather than *set off* "on the third day."

Origen considers the general duration of the journey to be spiritually significant. Such a long amount of time allows Abraham rigorous contemplation of his life, Isaac's life, and the impending sacrifice, and this too is all part of God's testing. Origen and Luther both stress that a journey of three days, the whole time knowing the nature of the command, becomes a test of emotional endurance for Abraham. Luther and Calvin argue that Abraham suffered three days of fatherly torment and the "darts of Satan," which are misgiving, doubt, and second-guessing.[79] Luther champions Abraham as a model of fortitude too since it is a wonder he did not die of grief at any point during the three long days.[80] Calvin is clear that the death of a child under any circumstance would be terrible. A fatal sickness or murder by another is one thing, he notes, but Abraham journeys with the awful foreknowledge that his son will die by his own hand.[81] Abraham, Origen surmises, would struggle between "affection and faith, love of God and love of the flesh."[82] In addition, the hike includes an ascent, up a mountain. Since Abraham's offering occurs above the surrounding highlands, Origen argues, the movement upward symbolically shows the patriarch exalted by faith. Abraham, he states, becomes a model for all Christian pilgrims as he "abandoned earthly things and ascended to things above."[83] He then preaches about this spiritual sense:

> "Offer your son'" not in the depths of the earth nor "in the vale of tears," but in the high and lofty mountains. Show that faith in God is stronger than the affections of the flesh. For Abraham loved Isaac his son, the text says, but he placed the love of God before love of the flesh."[84]

---

77. *St. Jerome's Hebrew Questions*, 178–79. For Caesarius of Arles, the three days to the sacrifice also brings to mind the trinity; Sheridan, ed., *Genesis 12–50*, 103.

78. *Luther's Works*, 4:99.

79. Ibid., 4:110.

80. Ibid., 109.

81. Calvin, *Institutes*, 392.

82. Sheridan, ed., *Genesis 12–50*, 103.

83. Origen, *Homilies on Genesis* 8, 3.

84. Origen, *Homilies on Genesis* 8, 7.

NARRATIVE ACTION

The next issue dealt with by Christian interpreters is not limited to specific verses but involves all of the actions in the scene. Abraham is the subject of many verbs and engages in mundane tasks such as saddling his donkey that presumably servants would do. The details of his active participation, then, also testify to the patriarch's obedience. He "rose" early, "saddled" his donkey, "took" two servants, "cut" the wood, and "hiked" up to Mt. Moriah (v. 3); "took" the wood, "laid" it on Isaac, "carried" the fire and knife (vv. 6–7); "built" an altar, "arranged" the wood, "bound" his son, "placed" him on the wood (v 9); and "reached" out and "grabbed" the knife (v. 10). It is quite clear from this litany of verbs that Abraham is active and willing, rather than begrudging in his obedience. He is not simply going through with God's command. He is performing it meticulously. With all of the patriarch's activity described, Cyril of Alexandria imagines how difficult the job of a painter would have been in depicting this story since he would have to produce so many paintings.[85] The careful description of all of Abraham's actions enhances the taut, dramatic tension in the story.

Luther asserts that all of these verbs truly testify to Abraham's "extraordinary obedience" because Abraham has 318 servants (Gen. 14:14) who would otherwise likely perform these tasks.[86] Origen additionally credits Isaac with willing obedience because he walks side by side with Abraham, rather than behind him: "the two of them went together" (v. 6). Luther, though, disagrees and claims instead that even though Isaac is old enough to carry a donkey's load worth of wood, that is, he is a grown man, Isaac does *not know* he is to be killed upon it.[87] This detail of walking together, a united front, is important for Origen, for it reveals Isaac as a victim to Abraham's role as a priest, and also allows him to "contribute equally with the priesthood itself." Luther does credit Isaac later for his unknowing willingness in that he allows his father to bind him as a butcher would. Isaac at that point, Luther notes, is letting his father perform the priestly duty of the rite of burnt offering. Luther states: "The son is obedient, like a sheep for the slaughter, and he does not open his mouth. With the exception of Christ we have no similar example of obedience."[88]

At the same time, the interpreters notice that all this activity is narrated without a word about Abraham's internal world. For Luther, the very details

---

85. Sheridan, ed., *Genesis 12–50*, 107.

86. *Luther's Works*, 4:109. Later, he cannot help himself wondering if there is any faith without works since there is so much "saintly obedience" in Abraham's actions, 113.

87. Ibid., 111.

88. Ibid., 114–15.

of Abraham's preparation suggest emotions too great to be described. Luther imagines the father's torment in something otherwise as pedestrian as saddling his donkey. Throughout his reflections on the story, Luther remains acutely sensitive to the psychological drama beneath the detailed description of Abraham's actions. Luther wonders: "Should he not have deliberated further in a matter so sad and astonishing?" And further, should he not have asked for his wife Sarah's counsel? Luther asserts that all the emotion lies as it were *behind* the details, namely, that Abraham is "so absorbed, he barely knows what he's doing." [89]

The scene with all of Abraham's deliberative action and the length of the journey is tense, fraught with unspoken emotion. The narrative is indeed gripping for what it does not say, namely, the emotional hell this father and son must have been going through. When Isaac asks, "behold, the fire and the wood; but where is the lamb for a burnt offering?" (v. 7), Jewish interpreters wonder if the son knows what the father is up to.[90] They debate if Isaac is naïve, sad, obedient, or frightened. Luther argues that Isaac is obedient, even "solicitous about the glory of God" in asking about the sacrifice, but unknowing about its intended victim.[91] Indeed, the narrative tension in this story of Abraham's offering remains so high that it has long been considered a masterpiece of the Old Testament, to be sure, and also in the annals of world literature itself. E. Auerbach's seminal study, *Mimesis*, favorably contrasts the aesthetic conventions of this biblical tale with Homer's depiction of Odysseus's homecoming in the *Odyssey*.[92] Auerbach argues that the narrative's subjective austerity is what makes the tale so gripping; that Abraham's internal struggle is omitted, with only the external tasks, for example, walking together, saddling his donkey, and carrying the wood, , provided in its stead.

The Servants and Donkey Remain Behind (v 5)

No detail is left unexamined by Christian interpreters in this important tale. In verse 5, Abraham tells his servants to remain behind with the donkey while "I

89. Ibid., 108.

90. For a thorough and excellent analysis of how the narrative structures work to heighten the emotional tension, see Meier Sternberg, *The Poetics of Biblical Narrative: Ideological Literature and the Drama of Reading* (Bloomington: Meir Sternberg (Author) ›Visit Amazon's Meir Sternberg PageFind all the books, read about the author, and more.See search results for this authorAre you an author? Learn about Author CentralIndiana University Press, 1987).

91. *Luther's Works*, 4:111.

92. E. Auerbach, "Odysseus' Scar," in *Mimesis*, trans. Willard R. Trask (Princeton: Princeton University Press, 1974), 3–23.

and the lad go yonder and worship, and come again to you." Luther provides spiritual insight from this verse. He advises that we should do as Abraham did: "When we wish to ascend to God, we should come with Isaac alone, that is, with Christ through faith; the servants and ass, that is, our works, we should leave below." [93] Caesarius of Arles asks why the text has the servants stay "with the donkey" and concludes that the animal is a symbolic of their weak faith. At times, typology could work overtime and try to render hidden meaning from every detail. Caesarius, in this instance at least, might have been better off taking a page from Freud's playbook and acknowledging that sometimes a donkey is just a donkey.

Caesarius of Arles, alas, has a darker supersessionist reading of the significance of the servants remaining behind with the donkey.[94] The servants, he asserts, represent the Jewish people, and the donkey represents the synagogue.[95] For Caesarius, it is as if the servants—the Jews—are guilty by association with the beast of burden. They are, for Caesarius, as stubborn as the donkey they are left with, and Abraham somehow knows that they cannot handle the truth that he is obeying. It is evident from such hostile typological exegesis that Caesarius's faith for Christ has slipped into an anti-Semitic triumphalism that has proven far more stubborn in Christian history than any donkey.

The interpreters are vexed by the potential deception of Abraham with the servants. Does Abraham lie to his servants by saying that he and his son are off to worship *and return?* For he knows that obeying God's command will mean that he returns alone. Origen is convinced that Abraham is not lying to the servants because, following Hebrews 11:19, he believes in the resurrection.[96] Hence somehow, even if Isaac is slaughtered, Abraham will not return to the servants alone. Luther adds that this is why the two must go alone for the rest of the way: only they know the truth of resurrection.[97] Caesarius also believes that the patriarch is not lying, but he draws instead on Abraham's own history

93. Luther, "The Sermon for the Fourth Sunday after Trinity," in *Sermons of Martin Luther*, 4:100.

94. With the inclusion of the New Testament as scripture, some Christian fathers argued that the Old Testament was no longer necessary, that it had been superseded by the revelations in the New Testament. Marcion is the most well-known proponent of this view. The view was rejected as heresy by the church, but a sort of crypto-Marcionism persists in Christian attitudes toward, and unfamiliarity with, the Old Testament. The Second Vatican Council, in its Dogmatic Constitution on Divine Revelation (*Dei Verbum*) sought to repair the anti-Semitism and supersessionism by advocating that both Testaments be read for God's saving actions.

95. Sheridan, ed., *Genesis 12–50*, 104.

96. Ibid.

97. Luther, *Luther's Works*, 4:119.

rather than the verses in Hebrews to make the point. Abraham, he reminds us, believes in a God who gave him a son from a sterile woman, so he goes into the journey knowing that "nothing is too wondrous for the Lord" (Gen 18:14).[98]

Augustine too believes that Abraham has not lied to the servants when he tells them to remain behind. His reasoning parallels that of Caesarius in that he draws on Abraham's own personal history rather than the New Testament passage. He reasons against any deception on the patriarch's part:

> On the contrary, in his heart there was always the same unshaken and absolutely unfailing faith. Abraham reckoned, you see, that the God who had granted that one who did not exist should be born to aged parents would also be able to restore him from death. The text quoted in note 1. The reference in the Revisions is to II,22,2.
> What God had already done was much greater—when Abraham saw himself given a son after all hope had faded—was indeed, if you consider the human limitations, impossible. So he gave his mind wholly to faith. He did not believe that anything was impossible to the creator. Having begotten a son by trusting God, he later on trusted God when he gave this order.[99]

These Christian exegeses of Abraham's guilelessness add a vital theological realism to Christian interpretation of Abraham's offering. If Abraham obeys God's command to sacrifice his son because he somehow intuits a resurrection that is not revealed until Christ, then he is no doubt admirably precocious. But the nature of his faith is then proleptic—that is, built on the future event in Christ's resurrection, as it was for the author of Hebrews. This notion has the effect of diminishing the actual lived faith of Abraham's personal history. It is akin to the Christian today who believes because of an afterlife in heaven. Abraham is the father of faith because this has been proven over and over again *within* his life. He emigrated without knowing his destination, performed a new rite of circumcision on himself and all the men of his household (Gen. 17:23-27), and had a son when he was one hundred years old and Sarah, who had been barren her entire life, was in her nineties (Gen. 17:17; 21:5). After some initial incredulity, Abraham had faith in this God who had given him Isaac against all odds.[100] That birth had certainly gone against reason and physiology, so why would his faith not transcend them again? This patriarch had learned

---

98. Caesarius, Sermon 84, 18; Sheridan, ed., *Genesis 12–50*, 104.

99. Augustine, "Sermon 2: Abraham, Tested by God," 176.

100. They end up naming the boy "Isaac" from the Hebrew for laughter.

through experience that nothing was too wonderful for God. The present and future are intertwined: *res gesta, res gestura*. God can do what God has done. This is what biblical faith asks us to trust.

Once the servants are left behind, father and son walk together for the rest of the journey. Their conversation consists of a terse two verses, verses 7–8.

> So they went both of them together (6b). And Isaac said to his father Abraham, "My Father!" and he said, "Here I am, my son." He said, "Behold, the fire and the wood; but where is the lamb for a burnt offering?" Abraham said, "God will provide himself the lamb for a burnt offering my son." So they went both of them together. verses 6b–8

I have included the ending of the previous verse, 6b, because the same phrase occurs at the end of verse 8 and so frames the conversation in the scene. The syntactic frame emphasizes that Abraham and Isaac are united. In addition, the conversation begins as the story itself had with one character calling and the other responding with "here I am!" In the Bible, this phrase connotes ready attentiveness, not mere location. Isaac (and God) easily knows where Abraham is. Isaac shares with his father that he sees all the preparations are intact for a sacrifice except the main element, the victim. Abraham answers only "God will provide the lamb for a burnt offering my son" (v. 8). For Origen, his answer refers to Christ, and he uses this passage to illustrate in essence how typology works: "Abraham's response, sufficiently accurate and cautious, moves me. I know not what he saw in his spirit, for he speaks not about the present, but about the future. . . . He responded to his son's inquiry about present things with future things."[101]

The lamb in Abraham's response is a type that includes the multiple meanings of: (a) Christ, (b) Isaac, and (c) Abraham's trust in his Lord. Abraham is not lying to his son, Isaac; rather, he is trusting in God utterly. Luther also insists that Abraham is not lying to his son, because it is true that God will (later) provide it in the form of a ram caught in a thicket.[102] Abraham's answer also demonstrates a fatherly mercy in not telling Isaac his fate. At the same time, Luther is convinced that the lost transcript of their conversation would have included "no doubt" the doctrine of the resurrection of the dead, which they both knew.[103] The rabbis, however, notice the ominous juxtaposition of "burnt

---

101. Origen, *Homilies on Genesis* 8, 6; Sheridan, ed., *Genesis 12–50*, 105.

102. Luther, *Luther's Works*, 4:112.

103. Ibid., 113. Such theological talk, though, might have aroused Isaac's suspicions.

offering" with "my son" in verse 8.[104] For them as well, Abraham is also not lying; instead he answers his son with brutal, if uncaught, honesty.

THE SUBSTITUTED RAM

The story of Abraham's offering has a dual typology of Christ: Isaac, the willing son, and the ram substituted at the last moment. Innocence is thus doubly emphasized. And so Origen maintains that the ram is a type of Christ in flesh, while Isaac is a type of Christ in spirit: "Christ suffered, therefore, but in the flesh, of which this ram is a type. . . . But the Word continued 'in incorruption,' which is Christ according to the spirit, of which Isaac is the image. For this reason he himself is both victim and priest."[105] And, as Tertullian stressed, the fact that Isaac's sacrifice is *not* carried out, shows that it was meant as a type for Christ's later sacrifice.[106] The passion, he adds, is so great a mystery that it ought to be prefigured. The ram is the substitution offered by an angel of the Lord (v. 13). Many Christian interpreters note the allusion to atonement. The ram caught in a thicket (wood) is like Christ on the cross.[107] For Ambrose, the ram is the Word "full of tranquility and restraint and patience."[108] Athanasius adds a theological reason for the substitution as well. He states that there is a delay, a reprieve in the story because the death of Isaac could not buy freedom for the world; only the savior could do so.[109] The ram caught in a thicket prefigures Christ for Augustine as well. And it is for him a nice example of how all the pages of the Old Testament "keep vigil" for the events of Christ's coming.[110] Here, the ram caught in a thicket heralds that "other Ram," Jesus and his cross. "We can even say that the ram was a symbol of Christ, for to be held fast by the horns is like a crucifixion. So all this obscurely prefigures Christ."[111] Chrysostom

104. *Genesis Rabbah*, trans. H. Freedman, (London: Soncino, 1939), 1:494.

105. Origen, *Homilies on Genesis* 8, 9; Sheridan, ed., *Genesis 12–50*, 109.

106. Tertullian, *Marc.* 3, 18.

107. Augustine, *Civ.* 16.32; The ram is held fast by the thicket, as Christ wore a crown of thorns; Ephrem the Syrian, "Commentary on Genesis" in *Selected Prose Works*, trans. Edward G. Mathews Jr. and Joseph P. Amar, Fathers of the Church, vol. 91 (Washington, DC: 1994), 169; Caesarius of Arles, in Sheridan, ed., *Genesis 12–50*, 104.

108. Ambrose, *Letters*, trans. Mary Melchior Beyenka, OP, Fathers of the Church, vol. 26 (New York: Catholic University Press, 1954), 115–16.

109. Sheridan, ed., *Genesis 12–50*, 110.

110. *Augustine in His Own Words*, ed. William Harmless (Washington, DC: Catholic University of America Press, 2010), 227.

111. Augustine, "Exposition of Psalm 51," 342.

calls the thicket a type of cross, so that Abraham witnesses the truth of Christ in shadow, long before.[112]

Luther draws a parallel with Christ's two natures here. Isaac stands as Christ's divine nature, which does not die, while in the ram "here Christ, the Son of God, is prefigured, who like a mortal man died on the cross. Yet the divine nature did not die, the human nature being sacrificed in its place."[113] Modern biblical scholars, by way of contrast, consider the substitution to reflect a cultural transition in ancient Israel from human to animal sacrifice.[114] The etiological view does not fully explain why there is no condemnation in the narrative itself about the divine command.[115]

"Now I Know" (v 12)

After twelve verses fraught with dramatic tension, the angel of the Lord intervenes and the ordeal ends (v. 12). In the Bible, angels are simply messengers from God who otherwise look entirely ordinary, except for their sudden appearance. From the Hebrew *mal'akh*, meaning "messenger" or "angel," they appear at crucial times in biblical narratives and serve as what Karl Barth termed "the ambassadors of God."[116] They are not the winged, chubby babies of Renaissance art. Barth reminds us that divine presence in the Bible is never harmless and sentimental, but is formidable, and usually life changing.[117]

The angel of the Lord says to Abraham, "Now I know" that you fear God (v. 12). Christian interpreters are bothered by the adverb "now" since it might well suggest that the Lord and his angel did not previously know something. They want at all times to preserve God's omniscience. Origen says that the adverb is added in verse 12 for our sake, as a way to highlight that Abraham has clearly passed the test. He adds too that "now" there is also a certainty in Abraham's inner heart; he knows for sure that he is fully obedient to his God, regardless of the command.[118] "Now" is written to guide spiritual hearers of the tale with their own discernment and to confirm the peace of unconditional faith

112. Sheridan, ed., *Genesis 12–50*, 110.

113. "Sermons on Gospel Texts for Advent, Christmas, and Epiphany," *Sermons of Martin Luther*, 1:284.

114. Jon D. Levenson, *Death and Resurrection of the Beloved Son*, 112–14; Gunkel,*Genesis*, 233–40.

115. Konrad Schmid, "Abraham's Sacrifice: Gerhard von Rad's Interpretation of Genesis 22," *Interpretation* 62 (2008): 269; Levenson, *Death and Resurrection of the Beloved Son*, 113.

116. Karl Barth, *Church Dogmatics*, vol. 3, pt 3, ed. Geoffrey W. Bromiley and Thomas F. Torrance (Edinburgh: T& T Clark, 1936), 477.

117. Ibid., 489.

118. Origen, *Homilies on Genesis* 8, 8; Sheridan, ed., *Genesis 12–50*, 107–08.

within Abraham. Hence, Origen makes the spiritual interpretation explicit, with the exclamation "now" as directive: "So, therefore, we appear at least to engage in business for the Lord, but the profits of the business go to us. And we appear to offer victims to the Lord, but the things we offer are given back to us. For God needs nothing, but he wishes us to be rich, he desires our progress through each individual thing."[119] Augustine follows suit: "You must know then, dearly beloved, that God's testing is not aimed at his getting to know something he was ignorant of before, but at bringing to light what was hidden in a person. . . . People are not as well known to themselves as they are to their creator."[120]

Aquinas is also quick to affirm God's omniscience in the tale. He interprets the phrase "now I know" in verse 12 with the use of an analogy with Christ's own knowledge:

> The meaning is not that He who knows all things from eternity began to know at that moment, but that He made known Abraham's devotedness by that declaration. In a similar way the Son is said to be ignorant of the day of judgment, because He did not impart that knowledge to the disciples, but replied to them, Acts 1:7: "It is not for you to know the times or moments which the Father hath put in His own power."[121]

God (and Christ) knows all things, but we his disciples come to understanding in divine mysteries. Here, then, God makes "known Abraham's devotedness" so that we too can "now" grow in our own devotedness to the Lord. Aquinas sees a patient, nuanced pedagogy always at work in God's revelation in Holy Scriptures.

Luther's tack is somewhat different as he seeks to defend Abraham rather than God in his discussion of the adverb "now" in verse 12. Abraham, he says, "was previously good and obedient." What transpires in his offering of Isaac is that the inner state of Abraham is manifest outwardly, that is, it is revealed. The difference is important for Luther because Abraham is an exemplar of faith: "He does not say: Now you have become Godfearing; but by this work it is revealed and made *known* that you fear God." "Now" for Luther is a grammatical marker signaling a revelation, a manifestation of something—Abraham's faith—that was *always there*. He continues on a philosophical bent, "Hence these are two

---

119. Origen, *Homilies on Genesis* 8, 10.
120. Augustine, "Sermon 2: Abraham Tested by God," 177.
121. Aquinas, "Compendium on Theology," in *The Collected Works of St. Thomas Aquinas*, 300.

distinct things, to *be* or *become* something, and that something *be made known* or *revealed*. There are many things that are known to God alone, but when it is revealed it also becomes known to man."[122]

THE FEAR OF GOD

The angel of the Lord intervened to stay Abraham's hand from killing his son (v. 12). We learn at that point that Abraham has passed the test, as Abraham clearly "fears God." This phrase, a biblical trope, deserves some comment. The "fear of God" denotes a posture of reverence and awe toward the holy, more than it does outright fright. It describes an attitude of humility in God's presence and so is often used in scenes of worship or supplication. When the book of Proverbs begins "The fear of the Lord is the beginning of wisdom," (Prov. 1:7), the author summons the humble posture typical of worship for the study of life's ways.[123] Abraham has amply demonstrated that he reveres the Lord since he has the knife lifted to slay his son.

The concluding verses, 15–19, as we noted above, are a repetition of the promise made to Abraham earlier (Gen. 12:2-3; 15:5-6; 17:4-8). Therefore, they cannot be a reward for Abraham's ready display of obedience in offering his son. Origen understands the repetition of the promise to be a confirmation of Abraham "of faith," that is, in his willingness to sacrifice his son, for what earlier had been a confirmation "of flesh," that is, with his undergoing the rite of circumcision (Gen. 17:4-8). Abraham, through his will and body, had amply demonstrated his trust in God and so received a doubled promise. Origen then notices an added detail in verse 15 that the promise is "from heaven," whereas earlier it had been "from earth."[124] By and large, however, Christian interpreters do not spend much time on these concluding verses and view their overall effect as confirmation of God's promises.

Augustine is the notable exception. Isaac is a type of Christ, and the repeated promise of many descendants is a prefiguring of Christ's many followers, that is, the church. The angel says to Abraham, "Because you have done this, and have not withheld your loved son, I will bless you and I will

122. Luther, "A Lesson in Mercy, the Mote and the Beam," 38; also, Luther, "Sermon on Eighth Sunday after Trinity," *Sermons of Martin Luther*, 4:278–279. Vol. 4 of *Sermons of Martin Luther*. Electronic edition. Charlottesville, VA: InteLex Corporation, 1995. All of these sermons are from *The Sermons of Martin Luther*, ed. John Nicholas Lenker, vol. 4 Grand Rapids, MI: Baker, 2000).

123. Westermann, *Genesis 12–36*. The notion of the "fear of God" in found primarily in three biblical traditions, Deuteronomy, Psalms, and Wisdom. The consensus in source theory is that the phrase is in the narrative is E, the Elohist.

124. Origen, *Homilies on Genesis*, 9, 1.

multiply your descendants as the stars of heaven . . . and by your descendants shall all the nations of the earth be blessed: (vv. 16–18).

With "son" as Christ also and "descendants" his church, Augustine offers an ecclesiological reading of the promise: "no sooner had the Head been foretold than the body must be too."[125] These verses do not merely repeat an earlier promise. They bear new revelations from God about the church. Augustine continues on verse 18: "The Spirit of God began—God himself began—to want to preach to Abraham about the Church, and to do so he discarded figurative language. He proclaimed Christ in a figurative way but foretold the Church quite openly."[126] That is, whereas Christ was *figuratively* present as Isaac in the story of Abraham's offering, the church is *directly indicated* in this reiterated promise of descendants. Augustine's exegesis accounts for the seeming repetition; it contains new revelation. The promise to Abraham has always involved a multitude of descendants through Isaac. But after his near sacrifice as a Christ figure, the multitude *is* the church that emerged after Christ's death and resurrection.

Conclusion

In conclusion, Christian interpreters have demonstrated a careful, theologically nuanced exegesis of the story of Abraham's offering. They have sought to draw out connections between God and Abraham as father, and Christ and Isaac as son. As a result, they enable us to reflect more deeply on the tensions between faith, obedience, and love in Christian life. It is clear from their steadied exegesis that Abraham's offering is not at all about *blind* faith or *blind* obedience. Abraham, and Jesus as well, take their long, gritty journey in a faith that is arduous. The biblical meaning of faith is trust. Abraham is deservedly the father of faith because he trusted God throughout the journey to Mt. Moriah. His was a faith that was never simplistic or robotic. With his beloved son on the line, it could not afford to be.

The Christian interpreters, because they are confessional, know something that perhaps we sometimes forget, namely, that faith *is* painstaking, contradictory, and really difficult to maintain. They understand Abraham to be an example for Christian faith not because he never wavers, but in watching closely *how* he does not. Their typological forays were never intended as literary whimsy, interpretation for its own sake or for the sake of cleverness. They

---

125. Augustine, *Expositions of the Psalms 1–32*, (III/15) Works of Saint Augustine (New York: New City, 2000), 342.

126. Ibid.

were motivated by a homiletic desire to make the God in this story known as the same God of Jesus Christ. They viewed Scripture, both Testaments, as a unity that revealed God's nature and contained spiritual instruction. The lessons Abraham learned, since they were timeless and divine, were lessons that Christian followers could learn right alongside him. His willingness to put nothing, *no one*, before God is the theological lodestar of the story.

It is true that Christian interpreters saw the good news in the story in part because they went looking for it through typology. But it is also true that they found the goodness in the details themselves. There was in the end no horrific killing because the God who led Abraham his entire life was leading him still through this, his worst ordeal. And that consistent, dependable, providential God is the same God leading Jesus and all of us through our ordeals. By reading about Abraham, we see the hint of what is to come with resurrection of Christ. But we also learn something more about God by watching Abraham, a father torn between two loves. We witness that "father" is much more than a domestic role of authority. It is in fact the central Christian mystery, "a highly condensed expression of love that suffers unimaginably and yet finds resources to love more still."[127]"Faith," as Barth says, "is holding, in spite of all that contradicts it, once for all, exclusively and entirely to God's promise and guidance."[128] The Christian interpreters probe beyond the idea that obedience is pleasing to God. It is certainly that, as the angel of God let Abraham know. Abraham's obedience, they notice, enables God to take him to a new level, past the point where death stings. Luther makes this distinction: "Natural death, which is the separation of the soul from the body, is simple death. But to feel death, that is, the terror and fear of death—this is indeed real death. Without fear death is not death; it is a sleep, as Christ says (John 11:26)."[129]

Abraham, by his obedience, glimpsed death from God's perspective and was thus freed from fear of it. Christians who truly understand the resurrection share precisely this freedom with Abraham. Daring to stare into this story of willingness to sacrifice can spiritually unhook us too from this fear. Augustine sees Abraham as an example for Christian faith not because he never wavers, but in watching closely *how* he does not. His passion, in Augustine's reading, readies us for reflection on Christ's own passion. Scripture itself is teaching us how to walk slowly and meditatively through the Stations of the Cross, rather than jump to Easter. God is in each step of the way. He was for Abraham, and Jesus, and for each one of us.

127. Davis, "Teaching the Bible Confessionally," 13.

128. Karl Barth, *Dogmatics in Outline*, trans. G. T. Thompson (New York: Harper, 1959), 15–21.

129. *Luther's Works*, 4:114.

3

ISLAM

Engaging with Abraham and His Knife: Interpretation of Abraham's Sacrifice in the Muslim Tradition

Isra Yazicioglu

As it is in Christianity and Judaism, the story of Abraham's attempt at sacrificing his son is a scriptural story in Islam. In this essay, we shall first look closely at the Qur'anic version of the story and then discuss some of the ways in which the text has been interpreted in the Muslim tradition. Before we delve into our venture, two notes, or perhaps disclaimers, will be in order.

The first assumption that guides this study is to look at the Qur'anic story as a story in its own right, rather than as a story originating in the Bible or Judeo-Christian sources. To be sure, it is a fact that the Qur'an emerges as a text after the Bible, and the story is very similar to the biblical one. It would be neither desirable nor possible to forbid a historian try to do her historical work to investigate the ways in which the Judeo-Christian sources may have informed Muhammad's milieu.[1] Nevertheless, ultimate explanations of origin will always involve an existential decision, and thus, rather than settling origin claims, this essay is interested in the Qur'an's "self-perception" and the reception of a Qur'anic story by Muslim interpreters.[2] Throughout the essay, I treat the

---

1. To be sure, there is no neutral history and a historian's existential commitments will also shape his historical theories. For a good and pertinent example, see W. A. Bijlefeld, "Controversies around the Qur'anic Ibrahim Narrative and Its 'Orientalist' Interpretations," *The Muslim World* 72 (1982): 81–94.

2. Indeed, different implicit existential conceptions of "genuine revelatory" moments will often accompany the search for "origins" of a scriptural passage. Some place the spark of innovation on Mount Sinai, or rabbinic innovation, some with Jesus Christ, others in ancient Near Eastern creativity, while some others assume that sheer luck, mad human subconsciousness, and historical accidents are the origin

Qur'an as a separate unit in itself, and while acknowledging similarities with other traditions, I resist a hierarchical model that deems the Qur'an as always "derivative" of biblical and postbiblical literature.[3]

My second disclaimer is that this essay does not aim to be exhaustive or representative of all of the main responses to this Qur'anic story. Instead, it is a selective presentation to give a taste of the meaningful ways in which the interpretive tradition received this provocative and invocative story. In what follows, I shall first look at the presentation of Abraham in the Qur'an and then introduce the Qur'anic story of Abraham's attempt at sacrificing his son.

Abraham in the Qur'an

The Qur'an is a compilation of passages that the Prophet Muhammad claimed to have received from God through the mediation of the angel Gabriel. The purported narrator throughout the text is God, who is understood to be addressing humanity through the Prophet Muhammad. These passages, which were revealed to the Prophet over a period of about twenty-three years (610–632 CE), form a discourse that is quite unexpected for an ear attuned to biblical style. For it does not follow a particular chronology: unlike the Bible, the Qur'an does not start with a creation story and move along a trajectory of salvation history. Nor does it offer a biography of Muhammad's life or a story of his ministry, though allusions to them are present. Moreover, with the exception of Joseph story, the Qur'an does not contain extended narratives, either. While it mentions many of the figures that are also mentioned in the Bible, such as Adam, Noah, Moses, and Jesus, their stories are never told in one place. Instead, each of these figures appear and re-appear throughout the text; snippet stories about each are presented elliptically, and placed in an exhortational context. The story of Moses, for instance, is told in more than fifty different places in the Qur'an, each providing an excerpt or an episode of Moses' life and ministry, and they serve to illustrate central Qur'anic themes, such as the oneness of God and life after death.

---

of all. Keeping William C. Smith's advice, I shall instead try to reflect a phenomenological approach, that which does not take upon itself the final decision on the question of origin, and instead gives the outsiders a taste of an insider's encounter with the text.

3. Indeed, "scholars have habitually traced interpretive lines that assume that the putative hybrid, the 'Judeo-Christian,' is superior to Islam, that the Bible and post-biblical literatures are prior to the always derivative Qur'an and that the story trade between Jews, Christians and Muslims only ever went in one direction, *to*, the East from a (qualifiedly Eastern) proto-West." Yvonne Sherwood, "Binding–Unbinding: Divided Responses of Judaism, Christianity, and Islam to the 'Sacrifice' of Abraham's Beloved Son," *Journal of American Academy of Religion* 72, no. 4 (2004): 829.

One of the major claims of the Qur'an is that the Creator of the universe has spoken to humanity throughout time and across different lands. Starting with Adam and ending with Muhammad, countless prophets and messengers of God have been sent to disclose the meaning of life and the divine purpose to humanity (e.g., Q. 4:164; 40:78). Prophets and messengers are presented as exemplary human beings, including Abraham. In the Qur'an, Abraham is not the first monotheist; instead he follows the path of previous messengers who proclaimed the oneness of God, such as Noah. Nevertheless, he is highlighted as a crucial example of a monotheist and people are time and again called to follow the "creed of Abraham" (*millati ibrahīm*) (Q. 2:135; 2:130; 3:95; 6:161, etc.). Abraham is presented as an exemplary human being who opens himself up to divine guidance and receives it, and responds fully with gratitude and surrender to God. And God takes Abraham as his "friend" (*khalīl*): "Who could be better in religion than those who direct themselves wholly to God, do good and follow the religion of Abraham, who was true in faith? God took Abraham as a friend"(Q. 4:125).[4] This title *khalīl* became an epithet for Abraham in the Muslim tradition, including Persian and Turkish literature.[5]

In the Qur'an, Abraham searches for God amidst his pagan society and questions the idol worship. He turns away from the worship of the passing by declaring "I do not love those that set" (Q. 6:76), a phrase that became a cornerstone in Islamic spirituality. Abraham is then guided by God to the path of "truth": the worship of the Eternal One. His public mission also starts early: as a youth, he engages his father (Q. 19:42-46) and people, trying to convince them out of their idolatry. The people in response throw him in fire, but he is saved from it by God (Q. 2:258; 6:80-81; 21:51-78; 26:70-89; 29:16-27; 37:83-98; 43:26-28). The Qur'an also alludes to Abraham's migration, with Lot, away from his people to a land that has been blessed, with no reference to the geographical site (Q. 21:71). His migration is more often termed as a "migration to God," emphasizing the spiritual motive behind the physical move (Q. 29:26; 37:99).

In the Qur'an, Abraham is also the recipient of a divine promise, and unlike the Hebrew Scriptures, and more like the New Testament, the emphasis here is on the spiritual legacy he is promised. God shall make Abraham a leader in faith

---

4. Unless otherwise noted, all the translations of the Qur'an are cited from M. A. S. Abdel Haleem, *The Qur'an: A New Translation* (Oxford: Oxford University Press, 2005).

5. Thus, for instance, in Turkish literature—similar to Arabic and Persian usage—Abraham is referred to as *Halilullah* (Friend of God), *Halilurrahman* (Friend of the Merciful), and *Halil-i Akdes* (Friend of the Exalted One). See also Annabel Keeler, *Sufi Hermeneutics: The Qur'an Commentary of Rashid al-Din Maybudi* (Oxford: Oxford University Press, 2006), 215–18.

(*imām*) for all people and this promise will extend to those of his progeny *only if* they follow Abraham's path of faith and submission (Q. 2:124). The Qur'an is unequivocal that physical descent from Abraham is of no value in itself. The descendants of Abraham have indeed been given Scripture and wisdom, "but some of them believed and some of them turned away" (Q. 4:54–55), and the former shall prosper and the latter will not.

Abraham's sons, Isaac and Ishmael, are mentioned much more briefly and often in the same breath as righteous messengers who called to the path of God (e.g. Q. 2:133, 136, 140; 3:84; 4:163; 14:39), and at other times separately (e.g. Q. 6:118; 12:38; 19:54). While the Qur'an recounts the good news of Isaac's birth to Abraham and Sarah twice, it does not refer explicitly to Hagar, nor to any tension between Sarah and Hagar. It is implied, however, that Abraham in time separates Ishmael and Hagar from Sarah, for he settles "some of [his] offspring" in a different place, in "a barren valley"(Q. 14:37), understood to be in "Becca" (Q. 3:96), an ancient reference to Mecca. It is on one of his visits to Mecca that Abraham builds with Ishmael a temple for worship of God, the precursor to today's Kaaba (Q. 2:127–128), which is the site of pilgrimage (*hajj*) in Islam. While the Kaaba was associated with Abraham in pre-Islamic Arab traditions, from a biblical perspective the association of Abraham and Ishmael with Mecca may come as a surprise.[6]

The Qur'anic Passage on Abraham's Attempt at Sacrifice

Abraham's attempted sacrifice of his son is narrated in Sura 37, right after the brief mention of how Abraham challenged idol worship among his people, and the angered interlocutors of Abraham decided to throw him into a blazing fire (Q. 37:83-98). The text alludes to Abraham being saved from the fire, his migration for God, and then moves right onto the sacrifice story:

> They wanted to harm him, but We [God] humiliated them. He [Abraham] said, "I will go to my Lord: He is sure to guide me. Lord,

6. A Muslim commentator, Muhammad Asad, suggests a reconciliation: "At first glance, the Biblical statement (Genesis xii, 14) that it was 'in the wilderness of Beersheba' (i.e., in the southernmost tip of Palestine) that Abraham left Hagar and Ishmael would seem to conflict with the Qur'anic account. This seeming contradiction, however, disappears as soon as we remember that to the ancient, town-dwelling Hebrews the term 'wilderness of Beersheba' comprised all the desert regions south of Palestine, including the Hijaz." According to Asad, "this is by no means improbable if one bears in mind that for a camel-riding bedouin (and Abraham was certainly one) a journey of twenty or even thirty days has never been anything out of the ordinary." Asad, *Message of the Qur'an*, (Gibraltar: Dar al-Andalus, 1984), 26n102 [in ref. to Q. 2:125.]

grant me a righteous son." So We gave him the good news that he would have a patient son. When the boy was old enough to work with his father, Abraham said: "My son, I have seen myself sacrificing you in a dream. What do you think?' He said, "Father, do as you are commanded and, God willing, you will find me steadfast." When they both submitted to God, and he had laid his son down on the side of his face, We called out to him, "Abraham, you have fulfilled the dream." This is how We reward those who do good—it was a test to prove. We ransomed his son with a momentous sacrifice, and We let him be praised by succeeding generations. "Peace be upon Abraham!" This is how We reward those who do good: truly he was one of Our faithful servants. (Q. 37:99–111)

Perhaps the first striking feature of this passage is that it does not name the son involved in the sacrifice. As shall be discussed later, the question whether it was Ishmael or Isaac was debated in the exegetical tradition. As far as the Qur'an is concerned, the story has the same "punch line" regardless of who the son was, for both Ishmael and Isaac are honored in the Qur'an, and neither one is presented as having a more privileged connection to God than the other.

Another important feature of the story, which is again different from the biblical narrative, is the conversation between Abraham and his son, and the son's explicit consent to the sacrifice. In fact, Abraham discloses to his son not only his intention but also his source of inspiration. In other words, he does not simply say to him, "God wants me to sacrifice you," but rather that he sees in a dream that he is sacrificing him. Thus, his question to his son "what do you think?" could be interpreted both as consulting about sacrifice: "Shall I go ahead with God's command?" as well as about the inference "is this dream a divine command?"

Next, the son and the father both surrender (*aslama*) to what they perceive to be the will of God. In that very moment of submission, Abraham is called and the very "fulfillment" (lit. "confirmation") of the dream is announced. Before continuing to narrate what happens next, the text clarifies that this was all a "clear test" (*balāun mubīn*) and that Abraham and the son are rewarded as doers of good.

The sacrifice of the son is replaced by a "momentous sacrifice," which is again noteworthy in its lack of detail. Muslim commentators often understood the ransom to be sacrifice of a ram, as noted in the Genesis narrative. Also, a strong connection was made between this "momentous" ransom provided by God and the Festival of Sacrifice that Muslims celebrate in pilgrimage season every year (Q. 22:26–37), in commemoration of Abraham's legacy. We shall treat the sacrifice ritual later as a performative interpretation of the story.

INTERPRETATION OF ABRAHAM'S SACRIFICE IN THE MUSLIM TRADITION

The Qur'anic story of Abraham's attempted sacrifice is significant for the Muslim tradition in that it involves one of the major examples of "submission" to God (*islām*), which lies at the heart of the religion endorsed in the Qur'an. (eg. Q. 2:132–33; 3:19, 67, 85; 22:78). The text is provocative and different interpreters engaged with it over the ages. I shall present my sampling of Muslim reception of the story as follows.

First, we shall look at how the story has been understood in the exegetical tradition (*tafsīr*), as it is displayed in some of the classical running commentaries on the Qur'an. Here, I would like to especially give a taste of a common tendency in classical exegesis, as well as in the popular stories about prophets (*qisās al anbiya* literature), which John Renard names as "historical prophetology." This is an "approach [that is] largely interested in the story line and in gathering the myriad anecdotal details that render a story, credible, engaging and true-to-life, with a generous enough sprinkling of the fantastic to make it marvelous."[7]

To be sure, classical exegesis goes beyond historical prophetology in seeking to understand the implications of the sacred text. Thus, in the second part, we look at the question of the counter-intuitiveness of the divine command as it is discussed by the famous theologian-exegete, Fakhr al-dīn al-Razi. We shall also note a famous mystic's disagreement with Razi's interpretation.

Third, we shall discuss examples of how Muslim interpreters took this story as edifying for them, taking the Qur'anic notion that the prophets' conduct is exemplary for believers (e.g. Q. 33:21; 60:4–6). They engaged with the question of how to apply the story to a believer's life. Clearly, there was a clear consensus throughout—which was made very explicit, for instance, by the Muslim scholar, Ibn Hazm—that no Muslim should ever even think of offering her child as a sacrifice to God. What was, then, the lesson of this story? We shall see two crucial ways in which the tradition received the story as teaching a profound lesson.

---

7. John Renard, *All the King's Falcons: Rumi on Prophets and Revelation* (New York: SUNY Press, 1998), 3.

HISTORICIZING AND DRAMATIZING: THE SACRIFICE STORY IN HISTORICAL PROPHETOLOGY

Many of Muhammad's earliest opponents dismissed the Qur'an as "fables of the ancients," that is, as stories assembled from older sources and falsely presented as God's words (see Q. 6:25; 8:31; 9:105; 16:24). In contrast, both the early and later commentators of the Qur'an regarded the similarity between the Qur'an and pre-Qur'anic sources as a badge of honor.[8] For they affirmed the Qur'anic claim that it was a fresh revelation from God "confirming what has been sent down before," and regarded the continuities across the texts as "vertical." That is, the same God, who had spoken earlier through Torah and the Gospels, was now speaking through Muhammad. Thus, the similarities between the Qur'an and previous traditions were interpreted as the consistency of the divine speaker, while the divergence of the Qur'an from the previous scriptures was interpreted as divine clarifications as to what has been lost or misunderstood over time by previous communities. (Needless to say, what constituted "divergence" from the Qur'an was open to interpretation.) Given these assumptions, it is not surprising that from early on Muslims were interested in how other communities related to the Qur'anic stories, willing to adopt information from the Bible and other sources, albeit with a grain of salt.

In addition to being receptive to seeing similarities between the Qur'an and sacred traditions of other communities, some Muslim exegetes also took advantage of the fact that the Qur'anic story telling—if it can be called as such—was very elliptical and succinct. Thus, they were often excited about "filling in" the details of a very succinct Qur'anic story from Judeo-Christian sources.

Popular storytelling about prophets, the *qisās al anbiya* tradition, was even more enthusiastic than classical Qur'anic exegetes in telling the lives of Qur'anic prophets in rich detail, placed within a universal history of struggle between good and evil.[9] These traditions incorporated biblical, rabbinic, and Christian motifs, as well as other oral sources, and probably also a good deal of imagination. In what follows, we shall first look at some of the famous stories related in Muslim circles around this Qur'anic passage.

THE SON: ISAAC OR ISHMAEL?

As noted earlier, the Qur'anic narrative does not clarify who the son is. Earlier exegetical sources tend to identify the "'to-be sacrificed son" (*al-dhabīh*) as Isaac, and later interpreters incline more toward Ishmael, especially after the tenth

8. Ibid., 1.
9. See ibid., 3–4.

century.[10] Today, most ordinary Muslims would think that the Qur'anic text actually mentions Ishmael as the son.

For those who identified Isaac as the intended sacrifice, the fact that the Torah/Old Testament identified the sacrificial son as Isaac was a crucial evidence. For those who identified it as Ishmael, the biblical reference was not as trustworthy at this point. For them, biblical reference to Isaac being Abraham's "only son" in the binding story was a problem, for clearly there was no time that Isaac was the only son, and these exegetes felt they should be more cautious toward the biblical version.

Different ways of construing when the story took place also led to different identifications of who the son was.[11] These kinds of arguments from chronology of events are not decisive since the Qur'an is not chronological in its style. A textual clue for identifying the unnamed son "gifted" to Abraham (Q. 37:101) as Isaac was that all the other references to the good news of a son mentioned in the Qur'an referred to Isaac. Based on the same references, others argued that the unnamed son must have been Ishmael for the couple is promised the good news of Isaac "and after him Jacob" (Q. 11:71). Thus, if Abraham was already given the good news of Isaac's progeny, how could then he be commanded to slaughter Isaac? This must have been a strong argument. What also tilted the balance toward Ishmael was his connection to the Kaaba and pilgrimage rituals, which also included animal sacrifice that came to be understood as a commemoration of Abraham's attempt at sacrificing his son.

As Firestone suggests, the identification of Ishmael as the son involved in the sacrifice may have become popular also as part of Jewish-Muslim polemic. Indeed, some of the Muslim commentators may have been reacting to the

10. Reueven Firestone, in his detailed study of narrations around the Qur'anic story of sacrifice, notes the tenth century to be the turning point for the opinions shifting from Isaac to Ishmael. See *Journeys in Holy Lands: The Evolution of the Abraham-Ishmael Legends in Islamic Exegesis* (Albany, NY: SUNY Press, 1990), 150–51. Even after the tenth century, the exegetical sources did not ever erase the silence of the text. Hence, for instance, in sixteenth century, al-Suyuti records different accounts that highlight either Isaac or Ishmael as the intended sacrifice. Interestingly, some Muslim interpreters, such as Rumi (d.1273) and Ibn 'Arabi (d. 1240), refer to *both* Ishmael and Isaac as the son involved in the event. Similarly, some contemporary commentaries still cite the evidences for both sides, and eventually leave the identity of the son undecided, noting the scholarly disagreement over the subject.

11. For instance, some said the event must have happened after Abraham migrated to Damascus (migration alluded to in v. 101), and therefore it must be Isaac. Some others disagreed, saying that since the text mentions the good news of Isaac right after the story of sacrifice (v. 112), the son involved must have been Ishmael. For a summary of this debate on the identification of the unnamed son by a classical commentator, see Fakr al-din al-Razi, *Tafsir al-Kabir* (Egypt: al-Matba'ah al-Bāhiyah al-Misrīya, n.d.), 26:153ff.

popular Jewish view of the exclusion of Ishmael from the covenant, from whom Muhammad is believed to have descended. Moreover, some Muslims even saw in the identification of Ishmael as the *dhabīḥ* ("the one to be sacrificed") a sign of God's preference of Arabs over Jews. The disagreement over the identification of the son also was used in Persian–Arab polemics, since the former traced their lineage to Isaac.[12]

Within the Qur'anic view, however, there is a clear resistance to such boasts over lineage, and the concept of being a Muslim is clearly not predicated on one's bloodline or a particular historical community. In fact, not only are Ishmael and Isaac both spoken of highly in the Qur'an, but both are also regarded as part of the "believing community" that the reader is invited to join (e.g., Q. 2:132–36).Moreover, as noted earlier, the Qur'an is very clear that divine blessing is not conditioned upon lineage. Perhaps the silence of the Qur'an regarding the identity of the son is a way of protecting the lesson of the story from being lost in inter-communal competition.

ABRAHAM'S DREAM

In the Qur'anic passage it is clear that both Abraham and his son take the dream as a divine command. Classical commentators such as al-Tabari (d. 923), Zamakhshari (d. 1144), and al-Tabarsi (d. 1154) narrate a story according to which, when Abraham was given the good news of a son (in this version, Isaac), he was so excited that he vowed to sacrifice it to God once he was born:

> Gabriel said to Sarah, "I am giving you the good news of a son named Isaac, and after Isaac, Jacob." She slapped her forehead in surprise. . . . Sarah said to Gabriel: "What is a sign of this?" He took a dry twig in his hand and bent it between his fingers. It quivered and turned green. Then Abraham said, "He will therefore be a sacrifice to God!"[13]

Then Abraham forgot his vow, and the dream that he saw years later was a divine reminder of this vow. In a view ascribed to Imam Abu Hanifa (d. 767), this story thus explains why a sacrifice was still necessary, even after it was announced that Abraham fulfilled the vision, for he had to also offer an expiation of his vow.[14] This additional story may have also lessened the

---

12. W. Montgomery Watt, "Isḥāḳ," *Encyclopaedia of Islam,* 2nd ed., ed. P. Bearman, Th. Bianquis, C.E. Bosworth, E. van Donzel,and W.P. Heinrichs, (Leiden: Brill, 2011).

13. Tabari on the authority of al-Suddi, cited in Firestone, *Journeys in Holy Lands,* 108–9.

uneasiness of the divine command by putting the responsibility on Abraham's shoulders: it was Abraham's own vow that made him liable for such a test.

THE "FLESHING" OUT OF THE EMOTIONS

It is noteworthy that many of these additional stories dwell on the emotions of the son and the father. In one account, the son tells his father, "father, bind me tight lest my blood spatter on you," or "father, bind me tightly lest I lead you astray."[15] In other accounts, the son and the father are both crying right before the sacrifice; they cry so much that the soil on which Ishmael/Isaac is lying gets soaked. In some versions, the son makes references to his mother, asking the father to pass his garment and convey his greetings to her.[16] The son also encourages Abraham to go ahead with the sacrifice even if he trembles and tries inadvertently to resist:

> Do not sacrifice me while looking at my face lest you feel compassion for me and fail to take my life. And if I regret [my decision] and shrink [from the deed] and struggle against you, [then fear not]. But tie my hands to my neck then place my face upon the ground.[17]

There is also the crucial temptation prelude noted in different traditional sources, according to which Abraham, Ishmael/Isaac and Hagar/Sarah are tempted by Satan one by one. Thus, for instance, Satan comes to the mother and informs her of what Abraham is intending to do with her son, and the mother first does not believe: "Certainly not! He is even more compassionate toward him than I!" She then asks why would he ever consider to do such a thing, and when Satan says because of God's command, she responds, "If God commanded that of him, then he should do it!" Under similar provocation, the son gives a similar response to Satan.[18] Satan also approaches Abraham in the form of an old man and says, "Heaven forbid! You will sacrifice an innocent boy?" When Abraham informs that it is God's command, the old man

14. Elmalili Hamdi M. Yazir, *Hak Dini Kur'an Dili*, ed. I. Karacam, E. Isik, N. Bolelli, A. Yucel (Yenibosna, Ist: Feza Yay, 1992) 6:444.

15. Suyuti, *Durr*, 5, 284, lines 5ff., cited in Norman Calder, "From Midrash to Scripture: The Sacrifice of Abraham in Early Islamic Tradition," in *Interpretation and Jurisprudence in Medieval Islam*, ed. Jawid Mojaddedi and Andrew Rippin (London: Ashgate, 2006), 382.

16. Firestone, *Journeys in Holy Lands*, 117–19.

17. Attributed to Mujahid (119/722) in Suyuti, *Durr*, 5, 280, lines 20ff, cited in Calder, "From Midrash to Scripture," 390.

18. Firestone, *Journeys in Holy Lands*, 111–12.

insists that it must have been a Satanic suggestion. When the old man sees that Abraham is set on the sacrifice, he pleads, "O Abraham, you are a leader whom people follow. If you sacrifice him, then [all the] people will sacrifice their children!"[19] The old man's arguments sound very reasonable, indeed.

Such stories not only help the reader visualize the event told in the Qur'an and dwell in that very challenging moment of sacrifice, but also ease the emotional and theological challenges in reading the story. By *acknowledging* all the fears and anxieties that can be invoked by such an unusual command, these stories also seem to *release* them.[20] It seems to me that these tales are in effect communicating to the reader, "yes, the command seems appalling (killing an innocent boy!), very painful to carry out (both the father and the son are crying!), or even bordering on setting a dangerous precedent (what if human sacrifice becomes a tradition!), but it was none of these. It was God's command, and there was a point to it *other* than all these scary ones."

WAS THE SACRIFICE A DIVINE COMMAND?

One might argue, however, that in the Qur'anic narrative it is not entirely clear that the sacrifice of the son was indeed a divine command. Classical exegetes often note that the dreams of prophets are not like ordinary dreams; they are truthful dreams, and a channel of God's revelation. As a widely read sixteenth-century "digest" commentary, Jalalayn *tafsir*, puts it, "the visions of prophets are [always] true and their actions are [inspired] by the command of God, exalted be He."[21] It was also noted that Abraham saw the dream three nights in a row, which convinced him that it was not a satanic suggestion but instead a truthful dream.

As these explanations strengthened the notion that it was indeed a divine command, they also subtly challenged it to some extent. For, as the famous medieval commentator Fakhr al-din al-Razi (d. 1209) put it, if it were entirely clear to Abraham that a prophet's dream equals a genuine revelation, why would Abraham think about it after the first night? Why would he consult with his son and proceed only after the son supports his interpretation? And yet if it

19. Ibid., 112.

20. As Sherwood notes, these stories also reveal that the traditional readers noticed what we *moderns* notice: the incredible demand put on the father and the son, and the counter-intuitiveness of the divine command. Thus, they challenge the assumption that only through the Enlightenment that the notions of humaneness and rationality are introduced to religion (Sherwood, "Binding–Unbinding," 855).

21. Jalal al-din al-Mahalli and Jalal al-din al-Suyuti, *Tafsir al-Jalalayn*, ed. 'Abd Allah Rabi Mahmud (Lebanon: Maktaba Lubnan, 1998) 594. The English translation is by Feras Hamza, from www.altafsir.org.

was a mere dream, then how is it possible that a prophet, who is an exemplary individual for all believers, tries to sacrifice his son based on a mere dream? Razi's solution is to suggest a combination: perhaps the dream he saw was also confirmed by an additional clear revelation.[22]

Razi also raises the question whether it is possible to talk about God as having commanded something, and then, before the command was carried out, having abrogated that command. For Razi, the answer is in the positive: it is quite possible that God first commands the sacrifice of the son, and then abrogates that command by stopping Abraham from doing it.[23] Razi presents the issue as pertaining to jurisprudence (*usūl al- fiqh*), the method of interpreting the divine commands, but it also reveals Razi's theological conviction that God may command something without actually wishing that thing to happen. After all, Razi was an Asharite theologian.

The relation of human actions to God's will and power was the topic of the earliest controversy in Muslim history and for the Asharite position—which became the mainstream opinion by eleventh century—the distinction between God's will and God's approval was a crucial one. The idea was that nothing, including human actions, happened without God's will, which was to be distinguished from the fact that God willed the consequences of bad human choices to happen without being "pleased" with them. As was crystallized in the work of a later classical theologian, al-Nasafi, (d. 1309), the conclusion was that

> God is the creator of all the actions of His creatures whether of
> Unbelief or of Belief, of obedience or disobedience. And they are all
> of them *by His Will* and Desire, by His judgment, by His ruling, and
> by His decreeing. His creatures have actions of *choice* for which they
> are rewarded or punished. *And the good in these is by the good pleasure
> of God, the vile in them is **not** by His good pleasure.*[24]

In other words, people make choices and God willingly creates the results of those choices. Hence, nothing happens without God's will and power, and yet humans also have responsibility for the bad results because they are the ones who make choices. (To offer a modern analogy, a publisher may publish an author's article without agreeing with all that is expressed therein. Without the

---

22. Razi, *Tafsir al-Kabīr*, 153.

23. Razi, *Tafsir al-Kabīr*, 155.

24. Sad al-Din Taftazani, *A Commentary on the Creed of Islam: Sad al-Din al-Taftazani on the Creed of Najm al-Din al-Nasafi*, intro. and trans. E. E. Elder (New York: Columbia University Press, 1950), 80 (italics and emphasis added).

publisher's consent and power, not a single word will be published, and yet that does not mean the publisher is "pleased" with every single word in the article.) Asharites argued that when God creates an unjust act of a human being upon the person's choice, God does not become unjust because he creates the injustice *for* that person *as* his/her injustice, not as God's injustice.[25] To be sure, God is responsible in the larger scheme of things, for having allowed humans choice. Yet, in the larger scheme, there is no real ugliness or injustice since God has given freedom of choice to human beings for an overall wise and good purpose.[26] This good purpose is to provide room for humans to develop their capacities, to bring out their good qualities such as their sense of justice, courage, and creativity, and thereby to manifest God's beautiful qualities, such as his wisdom, mercy, justice, and majesty, a point that was especially central to Sufi thought.

An implication of the Asharite position on the issue for the sacrifice story is that since God's will and approval are not the same thing, God may have commanded the sacrifice of the son without approving such human sacrifice. Razi argues that a command may have a purpose other than being carried out. He offers an analogy to illustrate his point: think of a servant and a master—the master can assign to the servant a very difficult task to be carried out in a few days. Even as he is commanding the task, the master's aim may be to simply train the servant in obedience, and once the servant displays the willingness to do it, the master can cancel the task.[27]

Razi also records dissent from this view. He reports that Mutazilites, who were the opponents of Asharites, along with many Shafiis and Hanafis, disagreed with the possibility of God commanding something and then abrogating it. Hence, they suggested that Abraham was actually never commanded to carry out such a sacrifice; there was no such command in the first place that was being abrogated in a later stage. According to this view, Abraham was only commanded with making preparations for sacrifice and showing submission to God's will, and being ready to follow the command to

25. Al-Ash'ari (d. 936), the founder of the Asharite School, argues that while in regard to human beings whoever wills or performs folly is foolish, this rule does not necessarily apply to God. In fact, according to al-Ash'ari it does not even apply to all humans, either. As an example, al-Ash'ari brings the case of Joseph in the Qur'an, who, in the face of insistent temptation for adultery, said that he preferred prison to that sin. Here, al-Ash'ari notes that although Joseph willed a folly to take place (i.e., to be innocently put in prison as he was threatened) he was not himself unjust for willing such injustice, because he willed as the injustice of another. Abu'l Hasan Ali Ibn Ismail al-Ash'ari, *al-Ibana 'an Usul ad-diyanah,* intro. and trans. Walter C. Klein (New Haven, CT: American Oriental Society), 104.

26. Taftazani, *A Commentary on the Creed of Islam,* 87.

27. Ibid., 157.

sacrifice *if* it was given. Razi retorts back by saying that if the sacrifice command was not ever given, then why was a ransom provided for the son?[28]

What is also at stake here is another major controversy of Islamic theology: whether God could command something that is detestable (*qabīh*) according to human criteria. The Mutazilite view, which eventually became marginalized in the majority (Sunni) discourse, argued that things and actions have a good or bad essence to them, which are transparent to human reason, and that God's commands are congruent with those essences. That is, God prohibits something because it *is* evil, and he commands something because it *is* good, and human reason can witness to that. Hence, Abraham being commanded with something that is otherwise a sin does not make sense for Mutazilites. After all, if the sacrifice of the son is not evil, then why does God stop Abraham from doing it, and if it is indeed evil, then was God ignorantly commanding something evil?[29] On the other hand, what became the Sunni orthodoxy insisted that good and bad were contextual and relative, and *strictly speaking* God's actions were not compelled by our human considerations of good and evil.[30] Thus, Razi says that to judge the divine command on the basis of what seems good or evil to human reason is invalid. To be sure, he is willing to grant the "ugliness" of child sacrifice cited by Mutazilites. He argues, however, that it does not necessarily make the command an evil command. For the goodness of the command is not always determined by what the command is but at times is determined by its context and purpose. Hence, God commanded the sacrifice of the son for a different purpose, not for it to be undertaken, but for the resolve of Abraham to manifest.[31]

Muhyiddin Ibn 'Arabi (d. 1240), the famous Muslim mystic, also had an interesting position on whether Abraham was ordered by God to sacrifice his son. Ibn 'Arabi has had an enormous influence on Muslim spirituality and thought, which earned him the title of the Greatest Master, *Shaykh al-Akbar*. According to him, each messenger figure embodies a crucial stage in the spiritual journey toward God. The prophets are models to all believers in that

---

28. Ibid., 155.

29. Ibid., 157.

30. I would like to stress the "strictly speaking" qualifier here, since the traditional Muslim controversy over whether God was bound by that which binds our sense of morality has been overstated to some extent in current Western scholarship, giving the misleading impression that the "arbitrary" nature of God's will has won over God's wisdom in Sunni theology. Yet Sunni theologians did not ever reject the notion of compatibility of God's commands with human nature (*fiṭra*), or God's wisdom in giving particular guidelines for human life, even as they affirmed the unboundedness of God's will.

31. Razi, 155.

their "voyages are bridges and passageways constructed so that we might cross over them toward our own essences and our own beings."[32]

According to Ibn 'Arabi, Abraham represents the station of "rapturous love" in the journey toward God.[33] The epithet friend [*khalīl*] of God was given to Abraham because he was "penetrated" [*khallala*] by a "rapturous love by which the lover is wholly permeated by the beloved."[34] Even in this high station, Abraham had more to learn. In regard to Abraham's dream regarding the sacrifice, Ibn 'Arabi notes that Abraham mistakenly took the dream at face value.[35] To be sure, most of the things that prophets observe in the realm of dream are necessarily true, for they come from the "World of Absolute Image-Exemplars" (*mithāl al-mutlaq*), which has a correspondence with reality that is outside the plane of Imagination.[36] Now, Abraham thought that the dream he saw about sacrificing his son was such a one, but actually it was the kind of a vision that did not directly correspond to reality, a vision that had to be interpreted to apply to reality. According to Ibn 'Arabi, interpretation means to connect the apparent form to something beyond the form, and this was what was called for in the case of Abraham's dream:[37]

> The state of sleep is the plane of Imagination and Abraham did not interpret [what he saw], for it was a ram that appeared in the form of Abraham's son in the dream, while Abraham believed what he saw [at face value]. So his Lord rescued his son from Abraham's misapprehension by the Great Sacrifice [of the ram] which was the

32. Ibn 'Arabi, *Kitāb al-isfār 'an natāij al-asfār* [Book of the Unveiling of the Effects of the Voyage], *Le Dévoilement des Effets du Voyage*, Arabic text ed., intro. and trans. D. Gril (Combas, 1994), §45, cited in Michel Chodkiewicz, "The Endless Voyage" http://www.ibnarabisociety.org/articles/endlessvoyage.html.

33. Ibn 'Arabi, *The Bezels of Wisdom*, intro. and trans. R. W. J. Austin (New York: Paulist Press, 1980), 91ff.

34. Austin, "Introductory Note," in ibid., 90.

35. It is interesting that elsewhere, in *Futūhāt*, Ibn 'Arabi regards this test as a test Abraham had to go through to focus his yearning squarely on God, and not anything else. (*Fut.*, 2, 10, cited in Chodkiewicz, "The Endless Voyage," who also notes that while Ibn 'Arabi includes this discussion under his chapter on Isaac, in his *Futūhāt* he refers to Ishmael as the son involved in the sacrifice.)

36. William C. Chittick, "Ibn 'Arabi's Own Summary of the *Fusūs*: 'The Imprint of the Bezels of the Wisdom,'" *Journal of the Muhyiddin Ibn 'Arabi* Society 1 (1982): 17, http://www.ibnarabisociety.org/articlespdf/naqshalfusus.pdf. (For Ibn 'Arabi, the term "Imagination" has a special connotation that is different from what we mean by "imagination" in everyday usage, hence its capitalization by the translator.)

37. Ibn 'Arabi, *Bezels*, 99.

true expression of his vision with God, of which Abraham was unaware.[38]

Ibn 'Arabi reads God's address to Abraham stopping him from sacrifice in Q. 37:104-105 [*ya Ibrahim qad saddaqta al-ru'yā*] in the sense of, "O Abraham, you *believed* your dream" instead of "O Abraham, you *fulfilled* your dream." Ibn 'Arabi's reading actually offers a more literal reading of the verb *saddaqta* mentioned in the verse. He further supports it by pointing out how God does *not* say to Abraham, "you were right in what you believed."[39] Hence, the "ransom" provided by God was ransom only from Abraham's perspective; in reality it was the real sacrifice intended by God. The case of Abraham the Friend of God becomes a teaching moment for all believers, showing that "in respect of any vision we may have of the Reality *in a form unacceptable to the reason . . .* we must interpret that form in accordance with a doctrinal concept of Reality, either from the standpoint of the recipient of the vision or the [cosmic] context [of the vision] or both."[40] It is interesting how Ibn 'Arabi both affirms the role of reason in interpretation and qualifies that affirmation. Reason is to be the arbiter of what is real, but it must at the same time conform to a proper vision of "Reality."

"It Was Clearly a Test": The Story as a Clear Lesson

Even though Razi, his opponents, and Ibn 'Arabi understood Abraham's dream differently, they all responded to the Qur'anic statement that what Abraham went through was a *clear* test. Indeed, the very plain sense of the Qur'anic story seems to have oriented Muslim readers toward attending to the lesson of the story. The emphasis on the lesson side of the story is brought out very well by Ibn Hazm, an eleventh-century Spanish Muslim scholar (d. 1064). Interestingly, Ibn Hazm's comment on Abraham's attempted sacrifice is found within his discussion of whether women could be prophets. In defense of women's prophethood, Ibn Hazm first defines prophethood as getting a direct and clear message from God, a message that is *qualitatively* different from an inspiration, thought, dream, or feeling that normal people can experience. To show that women did have such encounters, Ibn Hazm cites the Qur'anic references to Sarah, Mary, and the mother of Moses. In order to emphasize the seriousness and qualitative difference of such revelatory experience, he analyzes

38. Ibid.
39. Ibid.
40. Ibid., 109 (italics added).

the case of the latter. He notes that Moses' mother received not only a divine promise but also an instruction: she is instructed by God to put her baby in a chest and leave it in the river (Q. 20:39; 28:7). According to Ibn Hazm, if she was *not* a prophet who received a genuine revelation, and instead she threw her baby into the river because of a dream she saw or because of a feeling she had, she would be "committing an act of extreme insanity and a heinous crime." To emphasize the distinction between prophets and others, he says: "*if any of us* did such a thing, it would be an extreme transgression (*ghaya al-fisq*) or an extreme case of insanity," which would require being placed in "a mental institution (*bimaristan*)."[41] Similarly, Ibn Hazm notes that Abraham's attempt at sacrificing his son, if it is taken out of its prophetic context, would not make any sense whatsoever. If Abraham attempted to sacrifice his son because of "a mere dream," or "a doubt that came to him," *he* and "*anyone who is not a prophet,*" would be "an extreme transgressor or an extremely crazy person (*majnunan fi ghayati al-junūn.*)"[42] Thus, the situation of the prophets is exceptional and the exact same act under all other circumstances would be insanity.

That the Muslim tradition—similar to Christianity and Judaism—categorically prohibits human sacrifice is relevant to Ibn Hazm's insistence that in the absence of an exceptional situation of prophecy, the attempt of sacrifice would be simply insane or absolutely reprehensible. Thus, the Qur'anic story is to be read within the confines, or rather the *horizon*, of an established ethical framework: since sacrificing a human being as an offering to God is *out of question* in the "sacred law" (*shari'a*), the story has to be received as an instruction about something else. In the next section, we shall look at two examples of how the sacrifice story was read as "something else," that is, a lesson in spiritual formation. In the writings of the famous spiritual master Rumi, as well as the annual performance of pilgrimage rites, we see how a profound attitude of submission was understood to be the lesson of the Qur'anic story.

Sacrifice Story and Spiritual Formation

Jalal ad-Din Rumi (d.1273) was another towering figure in the Muslim tradition, whose works enjoyed popularity by Muslims and non-Muslims alike. Unlike his contemporary Ibn 'Arabi, who wrote in an abstract and dense style, Rumi wrote more in everyday language, incorporating different parables and stories from everyday life. According to Rumi, the Qur'an's essential message

---

41. Abu Muhammad 'Ali bin Ahmad Ibn Hazm, *al-Fasl fi al-milal wa al-ahwai fi al-nihal*, ed. M. I. Nasr and A. 'Umayra (Beirut: Dar al-Jil, 1982), 5:120 (italics added).

42. Ibid., 121 (italics added).

is to show how the world is a mirror revealing the Creator, who constantly arranges and maintains the whole universe every moment. Life is a journey to God, and God speaks to a human being within her context. Divine love calls each soul back to himself. Each soul knows and loves the source of all beauty, the Divine, and yet each person needs to go through a conscious process so as to discover that hidden yearning within himself. Thus, the references to cleansing of the soul and maturing through the "heat" of divine love are frequent motifs in Rumi's work.

Rumi's reference to the sacrifice story comes in the midst of his famous parable about a chickpea.[43] The chickpea, boiling on the stove, starts jumping around in the cooking pot, and screams to be taken out. It complains to the housewife who put it there, asking her why she is doing this to it; if she cared enough to buy it from the market, why is she now throwing it to fire? The housewife in response pushes the chickpea back into the pot with her spoon, saying, "Boil nicely and don't jump away from one who makes fire. I do not boil you because you are hateful to me: nay, it is that you may get taste and savor."

Alternatively, she tries to convince the chickpea to be generous. She exhorts it to think of the pain and difficulty of the guest and to be generous to the guest. Just as it received generosity in the spring, and was nourished in the fields, now is the chickpea's turn to be generous. One should be generous to the guest, so that the guest will leave happily and go back with a good report to the king who has sent that guest.[44]

The conversation between the chickpea boiling in the pot and the lady of the house goes on, as she tries to convince the chickpea to receive the cooking process as a kind opportunity rather than a curse, as a result of being loved rather than being despised. Their conversation is glossed by Rumi as a metaphor for the relationship between the Merciful Creator and the human being who goes through troubles and challenges. Rumi exhorts the reader to see all that befalls one as meaningful, being sent for a wise and merciful purpose, to transform the self for the better. It is normal that the soul first sees many events as bitter, and wants to escape, but in reality they are essential for its transformation for the better. Elsewhere, Rumi notes that the difficulties in life are painful to the person who is not conscious that God's mercy is unbounded and who resists

43. Rumi, *The Mathnawi of Jalalu'ddin Rumi*, trans. and comm. R. A. Nicholson (Cambridge: E.J. Gibb Memorial Trust, 1930), 4:4160ff. In place of a page number, the references to *Mathnawi* are cited with the book plus verse number within the text, as indicated in the Nicholson edition. All references to *Mathnawi* will be cited in this form, and unless otherwise noted the translation cited is from Nicholson.

44. Ibid.

change for the better. For Rumi, the Qur'anic prophets are great examples of being receptive to growth and transformation, and they display the wisdom of perceiving God's mercy even at the face of most difficult events.

> The wise man is as a guest-house, and he admits all the thoughts that occur to him, whether of joy or of sorrow, with the same welcome, knowing that, like *Abraham*, he may entertain angels unawares. Let grief as well as joy lodge in the heart, for grief is sent for our benefit as well as joy. Endure woe patiently, like *Joseph* and *Job*, and regard it as a blessing, saying with Solomon, "Stir me up, O Lord, to be thankful for Thy favor which Thou hast showed upon me! [Q.27:19]"[45]

For Rumi, the story of Abraham's attempt at sacrificing his son—whom he often refers to as Ishmael and occasionally as Isaac—is yet another good example of trusting the wisdom and mercy behind everything, and submitting to the One. Thus, in his parable of the chickpea, the housewife says: "O chickpea! I am *Khalīl* [Abraham], and you are my son, lay your head before the knife, for, I see in my dream that I am sacrificing you." (3:4174) Like Ishmael, one need not worry or be afraid before the knife of "calamity," which is a blessing in disguise sent by God. And what is to be slaughtered by such calamities is *not* the real head, but that which blocks one from God, while the "real head," cannot be ever severed, nor can it die. (3:4175-76)

For Rumi, therefore, the story of submission of Abraham and his son before that apparently painful divine command serves as a clear reminder that God is the one whose love and power can be trusted unconditionally. And, therefore, the story can be translated to everyday life as a willingness to see even the most unexpected event as being commissioned by the One who is both loving and majestic. The binding of Abraham's son is the manifestation of this crucial willingness to leave a forgetful and confused attitude toward life and oneself. The point is to be wakeful to the divine wisdom and mercy that runs the world, which in turn makes submission to God possible. Rumi emphasizes that God's eternal wish from the believer is *not* that his head be severed, rather that he *submit* to God, and thus, he exhorts: "[O Muslim!] do seek to [genuinely] submit to Him!" (3:4175).

---

45. This translation is from E.H. Whinfield's abridged translation of 5: 3676-3 in *Masnavi i Ma'navi: The Spiritual Couplets* (London: Trübner, 1887), reprinted as *Teachings of Rumi* (New York: E.P. Dutton, 1975), 267–68. Cf. Nicholson's.

For Rumi, a meditation on *who* God is (Merciful? Powerful? Wise?) is essential for surrender to God. Thus another very interesting commentary by Rumi on the binding of Ishmael/Isaac comes after a complex parable in the *Mathnawi*. The parable has its turns and twists, but it is basically about a great king who falls in love with a handmaiden, buys her, and brings her to his palace, only to see her fall sick. The king consults all kinds of physicians, but to no avail. Finally, he cries out to God, and God in response sends a special physician to his aid. The heavenly physician diagnoses that the woman is in love with a goldsmith in Samarkand. The man is brought from there and she is united with him. She heals and after six months of her union, there comes an apparently ruthless procedure to turn her love from the man to the king. The physician gives a medicine to the man, which causes him to lose beauty and strength gradually, till the maiden starts disliking him. The man eventually dies, and then the maiden is united to the king (1.35–220).

The story is again metaphorical, the sick lady representing the human soul, and the king the Divine (1. 220–245). God is in love with the human being, but the human being is in love with the passing passions of life, and like the king in the parable, God uses apparently ruthless measures to wean the soul from the love of the finite and to awaken in her the love of the eternal. According to Rumi, the measures the king uses may at times seem unjust or ruthless, but only a shallow person would really deem them as such, just like only a child would think that a healing operation is evil. While the child at the doctor cries with pain, the mother who takes her to the physician will be glad at heart. (2:244) Similarly, God's command to Abraham to slay his son seems cruel, but in reality it is only to benefit Abraham and his son by weaning them from their confused attachments. God is someone who "takes a half life and gives a hundred lives (in exchange): he gives that which enters not into your imagination" (2:246).

Here, Rumi connects the sacrifice story with another story in the Qur'an, that of the encounter between Moses and Khidr. The episode of Moses and Khidr narrated in Sura 18 (vv. 60–82) is unique in the Qur'an in that Moses has a divinely arranged appointment with a mysterious "servant of God," who takes him "behind the scenes," with the condition that he will not ask about anything until he gives an explanation. Moses promises to be patient, but he finds it very difficult to remain silent throughout the journey. They first get onto a boat and Khidr makes a hole in it. Moses protests, and rebukes him for endangering the life of the people in the ship. Khidr reminds him of his promise and Moses apologizes and asks for another chance. Next, Khidr does a favor to a people who were mean to them, which Moses does not find wise, and yet is reminded once again of his promise. Finally, Khidr kills a young boy, and Moses expresses his shock at it and the man announces that he and Moses cannot continue together any longer. Before they part ways, Khidr gives an explanation of how each of his apparently shocking acts actually served for an imminent benefit. For instance, he explains that "the boat belonged to some needy people who made their living from the sea and I damaged it because I knew that coming after them was a king who was seizing every [serviceable] boat by force" (Q. 18:79). Khidr says that he did not do any of these of his own accord; he was simply carrying out God's orders (Q. 18:72).

For Rumi, just as Moses, despite his prophetic light, did not have the right to judge Khidr's actions, the reader should also abstain from hastily judging Abraham's willingness to slay his son (2:235-6). For one should give due attention to *who* issued such a command; a command given with impure intentions and limited vision is not the same as the one given by the Absolute Mercy (2:243). If it is the former who is commanding it, it is simply an ugly plot. In contrast, if it is the Life-Giver speaking, then the situation is completely different. Hence, Rumi calls the believer to lay his head like Ishmael before Abraham: "Gladly and laughingly give up your soul before his dagger, in order that your soul may remain laughing unto eternity, like the pure soul of Ahmad [Muhammad] with the One [God]" (2:228).

Rumi's association of Abraham's near-sacrifice of his son with the Qur'anic story of Moses and Khidr opens up a very insightful interpretation of the sacrifice story. For it is clear that Moses' encounter with Khidr gives him a peek *behind* the scenes, but *not* a permission to change the guidelines for acting "on the scene," in everyday life. That is, the sacred law given to believers through Moses does not change because of Moses' encounter with Khidr. Moses does not come out of this encounter and announce that sometimes vandalism is good, or murder of a child is acceptable at certain times. Rather, what Moses has gained through this encounter is a deeper appreciation of the wisdom of events beyond human control. Connecting the Moses-Khidr narrative with Abraham's sacrifice, Rumi insightfully implies that just as Muslim tradition does not read the Khidr story as a legal text, the sacrifice story is also not to be read as such. Hence, the question whether the binding story justifies killing an innocent is simply out of question. Rather the text is about ushering a renewed sense of who God is and surrendering to God.

Rumi's reading of the sacrifice story as a story of submission is not unique in the Muslim tradition. What is remarkable, however, is that he fleshes out what that surrender may look like in everyday life as an *active* response to life situations. Submission to God in the face of calamity is not simply acquiescence to it; rather, it is turning the calamity into an opportunity to grow. Thus Rumi's understanding of submission to God cultivates an attitude that is the opposite of victim mentality, which gives up agency in the face of difficulty. In this interpretation, Ishmael/Isaac is *not* a victim, nor is the wise person who knows God. In sum, for Rumi, what is to be slaughtered is the illusions: the illusion that one is independent of the Creator, that the world is a resting place rather than a sign pointing to God, that things happen haphazardly and that we are victims of random forces of history and nature.

In the last section of this essay, we shall look at this understanding of "active" submission to God as it plays out in the pilgrimage rituals associated with the binding story.

Performance as Interpretation: Hajj and Abraham's Sacrifice

Hajj is one of the major practices of Islam where many believers from all over the world come to Mecca annually and worship together during the pilgrimage season, which lasts for around five days. At the heart of hajj lies the notion of surrender to the one and only God, and the rituals of hajj reenact the Abraham story as a commemoration of and recommitment to such surrender to God.

According to the Muslim tradition, hajj is a religious call that is to be answered by each and every adult Muslim (if she or he is financially and physically able) once in a lifetime. The rites that are undertaken during the stay in Mecca, outlined by the Qur'an and Muhammad's example, are crucially linked to Abraham. For the Kaaba, the ancient temple at the heart of Mecca, is believed to be the first temple to be dedicated to the worship of one God. There are traditions that narrate that Adam first raised it, and then Abraham and his son Ishmael re-erected it. The Qur'an skips much of the narrative detail as usual, and highlights Abraham and Ishmael's prayer:

> And when Abraham and Ishmael were raising the foundations of the Temple, [they prayed:] "O Our Sustainer! Accept Thou this from us: for verily, Thou alone are all-hearing, all-knowing! O Our Sustainer! Make us surrender ourselves unto Thee, make out of our offspring a community that shall surrender itself unto Thee, and show us our ways of worship, and accept our repentance: for, verily, Thou alone art the Acceptor of Repentance, the Dispenser of Grace!" (Q. 2:127)[46]

---

46. Here, I used Muhammad Asad's translation so as to bring forth the "surrender" emphasis in the verse (cf. Abdel Haleem who translated the same term *muslimīn* less literally, as "devoted.") Asad, *Message of the Qur'an*, 688.

Indeed, according to the Qur'an, Abraham is the "Muslim" (lit., "the one who surrenders") par excellence (Q. 22:78), and he is the one who also instituted the pilgrimage (Q. 22:26-28).

An often repeated collective chant throughout the pilgrimage is "Here I am Lord, Here I am, there is no god except You," which emphasizes the oneness of God and the act of answering to divine call. Two other important rituals in the hajj directly connect with the story of sacrifice, and thus offer a performative interpretation of the story of Abraham's sacrifice. The first is the ritual stoning of Satan, which consists of throwing small pebbles at three different stone pillars at Mina. The ritual represents renunciation of all evil and the believer's resolve to resist Satan's temptations. This ritual is traditionally linked with Abraham's and his family's temptation by Satan, when Abraham decided to sacrifice his son as an act of surrender to God.

The second rite of the hajj that connects with the sacrifice story is the one that concludes the hajj, which is the sacrifice of a sheep, ram, or a similar animal. The Muslim tradition has understood this ritual as a commemoration of Abraham's sacrifice of the ram as a "ransom" for his son (see Q. 37:107). The day of sacrifice in hajj constitutes the annual Festival of Sacrifice, *Eid al Aḍha*, which is celebrated not only by those who are in Mecca for hajj but also by Muslims worldwide. The Qur'anic command regarding animal sacrifice repeatedly highlights the concept of the oneness of God, and submission to him and gratitude for blessings (Q. 22:34ff.). In these passages, submission is glossed also in terms of one's attitude to life, and perhaps Rumi's emphasis on active submission was inspired by these:

> Your *God is the One and Only God*: hence, *surrender* yourselves unto Him. And give thou the glad tiding [of God's acceptance] unto all who are humble—all whose hearts tremble with awe whenever God is mentioned, and *all who patiently bear whatever ill befalls them, and all who are constant in prayer and spend on others out of what We provide for them as sustenance.* (Q. 22:34-35).[47]

The cattle is to be sacrificed by declaring God's name on it, and the meat is eaten and also distributed to the poor and the neighbors (Q. 22:36). Since the number of pilgrims has increased significantly over the centuries, reaching to over two millions, today during hajj season refrigerated planes fly out of Saudi Arabia to Africa in order to distribute the meat to the needy.[48] It is noteworthy

---

47. Asad, *Message of the Qur'an* 511 (italics added).

48. Sherwood, "Binding–Unbinding," 844.

that the Qur'an explicitly notes the symbolic value of the sacrifice: "It is neither their meat nor their blood that reaches God but your piety" (Q. 22:36). Thus the annual sacrifice ritual brings out the symbolic implication of the story: just as Abraham was not meant to sacrifice his son, the meat of the sacrificed animal is not meant to reach God. Rather, it is Abraham's and his son's surrender as well as the common believer's attitude toward God that matters.

Ali Shariati (1933–1977), an influential Muslim intellectual of the modern era, offers reflections on pilgrimage rites in this vein. Shariati sought to recover the importance of *tawhid*, the oneness of God, in contemporary Muslim life, which he considered to be obscured under contemporary religious establishment as well as unfair distribution of wealth. He explains how each step of pilgrimage rituals as prepares the pilgrim for a deeper connection with the One. For instance, when the pilgrim reaches Kaaba, the cubic structure that is empty inside, she realizes that Kaaba itself is not the aim itself but a signpost; the real goal is God.[49]

According to Shariati, the act of sacrifice in hajj is also a performative reiteration of the oneness of God. It is to affirm that nothing else is worthy of worship, and all idols are to be discarded. For him, Abraham's test of sacrificing his son is a test that is most touching, challenging, and most profound. The divine command to sacrifice Ishmael was meant to elevate Abraham to the full freedom of worship of God alone.[50] Shariati imagines and dwells on Abraham's pain at length. Abraham must have felt a deep pain, "beyond tolerance or imagination! Ibrahim [Abraham], the most humble servant of God and the famous rebel of human history, started to shake as if he were falling apart and the great invincible of history was breaking to pieces."[51] This was an internal battle for Abraham: he had to choose between God and Ishmael, between serving his instincts and God.[52] Thus, in reenacting the sacrifice, the pilgrim must keep this awareness of personal idols in mind:

> Who is your Ismail [Ishmael]—Your position? Your honor? Profession? Money? House? Farm? Car? Love? Family? Knowledge? Social class? Art? Dress? Name? Your life? Your youth? Your beauty . . . ? How do I know? But you know it yourself whoever and whatever, *you should have brought it with you* to sacrifice here. . . .[53]

49. Ali Shariati, *Hajj*, (USA: Filinc, 1978), 21–22.

50. Ibid., 95.

51. Ibid., 86.

52. Ibid., 86.

53. Ibid., 84 (italics added).

Shariati goes on to give clues to help discover one's Ishmael—or rather, an idolized attachment to your Ishmael: anything that stands between you and an honest recognition of truth, anything that makes you escape your responsibilities, and "whatever causes you to rationalize for the sake of convenience." [54] The act of submission is, again, interpreted as an active response; it is to be willing to attend to truth and take responsibility, even if it is inconvenient to the ego.

Thus, for Shariati, the son before the sacrifice attempt represents that which the believer idolizes other than the One.[55] The sacrifice is there to abolish such idolatry, and the son after the sacrifice is the son received as a gift of God, and not as an alternative to God. It is thus very meaningful for Shariati that Ishmael does not get hurt at all in the process: for the target was not him per se, but an idolized attachment to him.[56] Shariati basks in the ending of the story as well as the pilgrimage rite of sacrifice:

> A lesson was taught by the Almighty God—from now on there would be *no more sacrifice* of man for God. . . In Ibrahim's religion, sheep are sacrificed and not man! . . . This is Ibrahim's faith (Islam) and not the story of bloodthirsty gods, masochists or human torturers. It is a story of man's perfection and his freedom from selfishness and animalistic desires. . . . This is what Almighty God requested at the end of this greatest human tragedy—to sacrifice a sheep to feed a few hungry people.[57]

To be sure, the pilgrim, unlike Abraham, knows the end of the story: that Ishmael will not be hurt and it is a ram that is sacrificed. This foreknowledge both nuances and complicates the reenactment. It nuances in that the fact that Ishmael does not get sacrificed shows that the point is about changing how one *relates* to the "things" (including to one's spouse, child, possessions, and oneself) rather than destroying the things out there. Yet, it also makes the enactment of the story complicated, for one may think that nothing really changes, Abraham and Ishmael remain the same: they are alive before and after the sacrifice. Thus, Shariati cautions the pilgrim to be receptive to a genuine cleansing of his soul from idolatry: "do not choose the sheep (ransom) yourself; let the Almighty help and present it to you as a gift." That is, in the act of sacrificing the animal,

54. Ibid.
55. Ibid., 95.
56. Ibid., 97.
57. Ibid., (italics added).

the pilgrim should genuinely intend to give up his idols without any bargain, and beware of doing the sacrifice as an end in itself. A sacrifice of a sheep is meaningful only if it replaces your idolized attachment to Ishmael, otherwise sacrificing the animal is pure "butchery"![58]

Conclusion

In her comparative study of the reception of Abraham's "near-sacrifice" of his son in three Abrahamic traditions, Sherwood argues that there is a scary "parenthetical qualification" that haunts the biblical command not to kill: "Thou shalt not kill a human being (although you should be prepared to offer a family member as a burnt offering if God tells you to.)"[59] She shows how each tradition both sensed and resisted that qualification in compelling ways. She also suggests how the Qur'anic story seems to ease the tension by omitting much of the graphic physical detail, so that "there is no fire, no knife, no firewood" mentioned. Moreover, the son's consent to the sacrifice in the Qur'anic account "effectively pours salve on the major ethical wound in the biblical narrative."[60] Moreover, the text announces that this was *clearly* a test, and Abraham's submission is presented in this Qur'anic chapter as part of a "long chain of surrender that stretches through Noah, Moses and Aaron, Elijah (Ilyas), Lot and Jonah."[61]

This essay further illustrated how Muslim interpreters across the ages read the story as suggesting something completely different from doing violence to your innocent beloved. As we have seen, the narrative detailing and embellishment of the Qur'anic story acknowledged the counter-intuitiveness of the divine command. The theological discussions about whether sacrifice of the son was indeed a divine command further assured that the story was not meant to disrupt human reasoning, common sense, and the sacred law. Razi insisted that it was a divine command, but one that was not meant to be carried out, while his opponents insisted that the sacrifice of the son was not part of God's command to Abraham at all. Furthermore, Ibn Hazm clearly noted how the same action under any other circumstance would be an act of extreme insanity or cruelty. All of these are ways in which the tradition simply rejected the idea that one should be prepared to act insane for God's sake. Instead, the story was to be read as calling to a different type of praxis.

58. Ibid., 98.
59. Sherwood, "Binding–Unbinding," 843.
60. Ibid., 842.
61. Ibid., 841.

Indeed, among the best interpreters of the sacrifice story in the Muslim tradition have been the ones who focused on self-formation. For they read it as potentially having a meaningful implication for *anyone*. Theirs was also the most consistent within the Qur'anic framework in that the Qur'an explicitly presents prophets as exemplary models. Thus, Ibn 'Arabi noted how Abraham's attempt at interpreting the dream is a "bridge" to be crossed by each reader. Abraham's test teaches us a lesson in the interpretation of signs in life's journey to God. Ibn 'Arabi affirmed the role of reason in discerning the correct implications of images and inspirations that one receives, and also qualified his reference to reason by noting that it should be enlightened by a proper vision of "Reality."

Similarly, Rumi took the story as applying to each human being in her life journey. He called the reader to be an Ishmael, and to be open to receive God's mercy and wisdom even in the most painful circumstances. Becoming an Ishmael before Abraham's knife is every believer's call: anyone who is willing can unconditionally surrender to the King of Love, and be liberated from being a victim of the random forces of nature, ego, and history. What is to be slaughtered is the attitude of unconsciousness, of forgetting who the Lord is and that all that comes from the Lord is meaningful.

Finally, annual pilgrimage offers a performative communal reading of the story. The pilgrims commemorate Abraham's story by confronting Satan in stoning ritual and through animal sacrifice. The sacrifice meat is distributed to the poor, and it is clear that just as Abraham was not meant to sacrifice his son, the meat of the sacrificed animal is not meant to reach God. What is meant in this performance, as Shariati noted, is liberation from worshipping idols: the act of sacrifice is an exercise of freedom from idolatrous relationships. If Rumi focused on how to act like Abraham's son, Shariati focused on how to act like Abraham: to receive our Ishmaels and Isaacs, our beloveds—including our own selves—as gifts from God, and face our responsibility honestly even at the face of convenient excuses.

To my mind, the reception of the sacrifice story in the Muslim tradition—not unlike Christian and Jewish traditions—is an example of how the Qur'anic text, or more broadly a scriptural text, may have a deeper meaning than what may first meet the eye. A text that seems so strange and apparently so vulnerable to misunderstanding may in fact be disclosing a most valuable lesson for the reader. This does not mean that the texts can never be abused, but it strongly suggests that we should not readily dismiss apparently strange stories in sacred scriptures—lest we are deprived of profound messages dressed in provocative garb.

PART II

Modern Readings

4

KANT

The Attack on Abraham

Ronald Green

For two thousand years Abraham had been hailed as the "father of faith." Among Jews, Christians, and Muslims, in sacred Scriptures and commentaries, his willingness to sacrifice his beloved son Isaac was taken as the epitome of faithful obedience to God.[1] Even philosophers worked to reconcile the events in Genesis 22 with reason and divine justice. In his *Summa of Theology*, Thomas Aquinas argued that because Isaac had incurred the penalty for sin due to all of Adam's descendants, the command to kill him did not violate the natural moral law.[2] Here and elsewhere, the presumption was that God's command was just and Abraham's obedience heroic.

Against this background we can appreciate the strikingly discordant note sounded by Immanuel Kant in works written near the end of his career. At three places in his mature writings—two in his *Religion within the Boundaries of Mere Reason* (1793) and a third in *The Conflict of the Faculties* (1798)—Kant openly criticized Abraham (or anyone like him) who would obey an alleged divine command to kill an innocent child. The most stinging rebuke appears in *The Conflict of the Faculties*, in connection with a discussion of the difficulty of understanding any command as coming from God. "It is quite impossible," says Kant, "for a human being to apprehend the infinite by his senses." But "the human being can be sure that the voice one hears is *not* God's" if it "commands

---

1. For discussions of classical Jewish and Christian treatments of Abraham, see my *Religion and Moral Reason* (New York: Oxford University Press, 1988), chs. 4 and 5.

2. *Summa Theologiae*, Ia IIae, Q. 94, Art. 5.

him to do something contrary to the moral law." Even if such a voice "may seem to surpass the whole of nature," Kant concludes, "he must consider it an illusion." Kant then adds the following footnote:

> We can use, as an example, the myth of the sacrifice that Abraham was going to make by butchering and burning his only son at God's command (the poor child, without knowing it, even brought the wood for the fire). Abraham should have replied to this supposedly divine voice: "That I ought not to kill my good son is quite certain. But that you, this apparition, are God—of that I am not certain, and never can be, not even if this voice rings down to me from (visible) heaven."[3]

In the *Religion*, the same estimate of Abraham's conduct is anticipated in a remark not directly mentioning the patriarch:

> [A]s regards the *theistic* miracles, reason can at least have a negative criterion at its disposal, namely, if something is represented as commanded by God in a direct manifestation of him yet is directly in conflict with morality, it cannot be a divine miracle despite every appearance of being one (e.g. if a father were ordered to kill his son who, so far as he knows, is totally innocent).[4]

The third critical passage appears much later in the same work. It is set within a discussion of the meaning of conscience. Kant offers the example of an "inquisitor" who, following what he believes to be a "supernaturally revealed Divine Will," condemns to death on the grounds of heresy an otherwise good citizen. This inquisitor, says Kant, can be accused of "plain *lack of conscience*" (emphasis original). Explaining this judgment, Kant adds:

> That to take a human being's life because of his religious faith is wrong is certain, unless (to allow the most extreme possibility) a divine will, made known to the inquisitor in some extraordinary way, has decreed otherwise. But that God has ever manifested this awful will is a matter of historical documentation and never apodictically certain. After all, the revelation reached the inquisitor

---

3. *The Conflict of the Faculties* in *Religion and Rational Theology*, ed. and trans. Allen Wood and George Di Giovanni (Cambridge: Cambridge University Press, 1996), 283.

4. Immanuel Kant, *Religion within the Boundaries of Mere Reason* in *Religion and Rational Theology*, 124. Emphasis in original.

only through the intermediary of human beings and their interpretation, and even if it were to appear to him to have come from God himself (like the command issued to Abraham to slaughter his own son like a sheep), yet it is at least possible that on this point error has prevailed. But then the inquisitor would risk the danger of doing something which would be to the highest degree wrong, and on this score he acts unconscientiously.[5]

Readers familiar with Kant's philosophy will recognize here some of the most important ideas of his epistemology and ethics. That God cannot be made the object of sense experience follows from the understanding developed at length in the *Critique of Pure Reason* that God belongs to noumenal reality, "the thing-in-itself," and exists outside of the phenomenal realm of time and space. Human knowledge is confined to phenomena, the world of sense experience. We participate in noumenal reality in only one way: through our experience of moral obligation (and the conviction of freedom that accompanies it). In the "ought" of duty we may intimate a divine reality, but we can never *know* God or receive sensory knowledge about him. It follows that no visual or auditory communications from God are reliable.

What are certain, however, are the commands of duty. These are logical conclusions that follow from the application of duty's supreme principle, the categorical imperative: "Act only according to that maxim by which you can at the same time will that it might become a universal law."[6] This principle inheres in human reason and is all we need to distinguish right from wrong. It is the necessary and sufficient basis for human moral knowledge. Resort to other sources of guidance, unless these conform absolutely to the dictates of the imperative, is forbidden. This is the basis of Kant's distinction in the *Foundations of the Metaphysics of Morals* between moral autonomy and heteronomy. The former requires that a human being be seen as "subject only to his own, yet universal, legislation." Heteronomy, in contrast, binds man to a law not of his own rational willing but imposed from without and obeyed because of an incentive (fear or hope for reward) that is alien to morality.[7]

5. Ibid., 203–4. There appears to be a typographical error in this quote, with "doing" rendered as "dong."

6. Immanuel Kant, *Grundlegung zur Metaphysik der Sitten*, s. 421. The translation here is my own since I believe the standard translations by Beck and Paton are misleading. For a discussion of this matter, see my "The First Formulation of the Categorical Imperative as Literally a 'Legislative' Metaphor," *History of Philosophy Quarterly* 8, no. 2 (April 1991): 163–79. This is reprinted in my *Kant and Kierkegaard on Time and Eternity* (Macon, GA: Mercer University Press, 2011), ch. 1.

From this conceptual framework, we can see that Kant's animus against Abraham is not just a reflection of some possible anti-religious bias, but rests on the main pillars of his philosophy. The purported divine command itself is unethical: an unexplained command to kill an innocent person that cannot be justified within the universalizing constraints of the categorical imperative. Abraham's obedience, whether motivated by fear or love of God (or some combination of the two), inverts the priority that reasoned willing must have before any personal incentive for conduct, however pressing or lofty that incentive may be. The patriarch's obedience is thus a consummate expression of heteronomy. Finally, the claim that this command can in any way be perceived as such defies our epistemological constraints. God cannot be known through sense experience, but only through the inner voice of conscience. Here, that inner voice condemns an auditory command, which it can only judge on both epistemological and ethical grounds to be a dangerous illusion.

It would seem that little more is needed to appreciate Kant's attacks on the patriarch than an understanding of the ways that Abraham's willingness to sacrifice Isaac violates moral and epistemological constraints. However, Kant's treatments of Abraham cannot be separated from his broader discussions of religion in these two mature writings. Within their contexts, these treatments point to a much deeper question that Kant is addressing. That question concerns the role of historical events in human moral salvation. It involves further questions about the depths of human sinfulness and the appropriate remedy for human moral failure. Borrowing the epigraph from Kierkegaard's *Philosophical Fragments*, the chief question is: "Can a historical point of departure be given for an eternal consciousness; how can such a point of departure be of more than historical interest; can an eternal happiness be built on historical knowledge?"[8] Kant's answer to all these questions is "no," and Abraham represents the dangers of relying on historical information (and with that any form of ecclesiastical dogma) as the basis for one's moral and spiritual salvation.

This larger issue is already evident in the *Religion*. Abraham emerges, we saw, in the context of a discussion of an inquisitor who relies on a historically mediated command from God to persecute heretics. At issue is the question of the extent to which one may conscientiously rely on historical religious teachings when making crucial moral decisions. However, this question itself is set within a prolonged consideration occupying most of the *Religion* of how we

---

7. Kant, *Grundlegung zur Metaphysik der Sitten*, s. 432–33.

8. Søren Kierkegaard, *Philosophical Fragments, Johannes Climacus*, ed. and trans. Howard V. Hong and Edna H. Hong (Princeton: Princeton University Press, 1985), 1.

may respond to the discovery of our profound inner moral unworthiness, what Kant chooses to call human "radical evil."

I use the word "discovery" here in two senses. First, it describes each individual's encounter with the possibly deep corruption inhabiting his or her moral willing. This corruption leads to the judgment that the human will is "radically evil," evil at its root, and it prompts the question of whether it is possible to escape total moral despair and self-condemnation. "Discovery" also describes the prolonged intellectual process that led Kant himself to understand the necessity of this harsh self-judgment. That process began with the elucidation of the moral law in the *Foundations of the Metaphysics of Morals* (1785) and the second *Critique*, the *Critique of Practical Reason* (1788). In the latter work, Kant dwelled on the fact that the absolute priority that must always be accorded the categorical imperative means that morality can sometimes require the irrevocable sacrifice of one's personal well-being. Unlike Greek ethics, which always sought to connect virtue to happiness (*eudaimonia*), Kant's demanding law-based ethic of duty raised the question of whether happiness or virtue can ever be reunited. Recognizing the salience of personal well-being in all human willing, Kant addressed this question at the end of the second *Critique*. There he offered the idea of moral faith: belief in a supreme governor and creator of the universe who can proportion virtue to happiness to us as moral or noumenal beings, perhaps in some form of immortal existence.[9] This moral faith, Kant was careful to observe, is not knowledge, since it involves the postulation of noumenal possibilities beyond the range of our cognition. Nor does this argument amount to any kind of logical "proof" of God's existence. Rather, it represents an effort by an individual earnestly wishing to maintain the strict priority of duty to resolve the conflict between duty and happiness. As such it is "a voluntary decision of our judgment . . . itself not commanded" by reason.[10]

Even as it "solved" some of the conceptual problems posed by his duty-based ethic, Kant's discussion at the end of the second *Critique* exposed others. Foremost among these was the degree of human *rational* freedom before the moral law. This freedom results from the fact that when duty conflicts with happiness, obedience to duty cannot be shown to be rationally necessary. In all such cases of conflict the question is "Why should I choose to respect morality's transpersonal, objective standpoint if that standpoint imperils me as a subject?"

9. In this respect, we can see that Kant had rediscovered the need for an "afterlife" already arrived at in the law-based biblical religious traditions.

10. *Critique of Practical Reason*, trans. Lewis White Beck (Indianapolis: Bobbs-Merrill, 1956), 151.

Kant saw that it only begs this question to reply that one would advocate moral obedience if one looked at the matter rationally by adopting a transpersonal, objective standpoint, for why one should adopt that standpoint is just what is being asked. By means of this analysis in the second *Critique*, Kant had discovered that while morality is a product of reason, human moral obedience cannot always be rationally justified. Nor can the religious beliefs needed to heal the breach between duty and happiness be shown to be necessary. Thus, the supremely important feature of human existence, obedience to the moral law, is shown to rest on voluntary commitments of the heart, mind, and will.

What is voluntary can be forsworn. Not surprisingly, therefore, Kant begins the next work in the progression of his ethical-religious thought, the *Religion*, with a discussion of the radical evil in human nature. The gist of the argument is that no human being can vouchsafe that he or she possesses unwavering inner moral commitment to the supremacy of moral willing over "self-love." Each human being, Kant says, recognizes the force of the moral law, which impresses itself "irresistibly, because of his moral predisposition."[11]

If there were no other incentive than this, human beings would be morally good. But each person also possesses the "equally innocent natural predisposition" to be moved by the "incentives of his sensuous nature," which, "according to the subjective principle of self-love" he adopts into the basic rule governing all his willing (what Kant calls his "maxim").[12] Thus, each of us has two principles moving our will: morality and self-love.

In view of this, it might be thought that human beings are neither good nor bad, but rather *both* good and evil. However, Kant rules this option out. Morality requires that in each and every act of willing we prioritize its dictates. Someone who reserves the right to *occasionally* act on self-love cannot be moral (anymore than a promise made with the reservation to occasionally break it is no promise). The presence of this unresolved conflict between the conflicting motives or morality and self-love forces each of us to question the inner purity of our supreme underlying maxim of willing and, hence, the integrity of our will. Furthermore, within this context, even a single act of wrong willing is fatal. This is so because I am always free to choose morality over self-love. If I have even once freely and without necessitation chosen to reverse this priority, how can I be confident that I will not do so again and again and again? How can I be sure that my underlying maxim is stable? But it is precisely confidence in this stability that is necessary for any positive self-judgment of moral worth.

---

11. *Religion within the Boundaries of Mere Reason*, 82.

12. Ibid., 82–83.

Since no one, reviewing his own history of moral willing or the experience of others, can fail to perceive instances of immoral self-love, no one can vouchsafe the unerring future commitment to obeying the moral law, and we must each confess our moral unworthiness and guilt. Furthermore, no gradations in worth are available to us here. Since even one act of moral disobedience is of enduring significance and portends violations that are qualitatively limitless in their potential for evil, we must judge ourselves to bearing an "*infinity* of guilt" and meriting "*infinite* punishment and exclusion from the Kingdom of God."[13]

Can we ever achieve the state of enduring moral commitment that morality requires for our sense of positive self-regard? While the opening chapters of the *Religion* lay out the problem, subsequent chapters tentatively propose a solution. As with the problem of moral commitment explored at the end of the second *Critique*, that solution amounts to the voluntary adoption of a religious belief. In this case, it is the belief that someone who rededicates himself to "the holy intention of leading a life well-pleasing to God," may suppose that "God's love for humankind . . . will somehow make up, in consideration of that honest intention," for that individual's "deficiency in action."[14] In other words, so long as one begins with renewed moral striving, one may rely on all-seeing divine omniscience and divine grace to overcome the acknowledged problems in one's moral self-estimate.

To his credit, Kant recognized the problems with this solution, and much of the rest of the *Religion* is devoted to addressing them. One concerns the difficulty of reconciling our freedom with any kind of divine intervention. How can I credit myself as morally worthy if my improved performance is in any way attributable to God's help? Kant's response to this question draws on both his epistemology and ethics. Although we are situated in the world of causal determination, we are also morally free. We cannot know how this is so, since doing so would require us to rise above phenomenal knowledge and have a full understanding of the relation between phenomenal and noumenal reality. But we cannot *know* how freedom is compatible with causal determination. Neither do the limits of our knowledge permit us to deny that possibility, and what is true of phenomenal causation may also be true of noumenal causation. An act of divine grace that shapes our will while preserving our freedom is not impossible, although for practical purposes, what *we* must attend to is not discerning how this is so but in properly exercising our will.

13. Ibid., 113. Emphasis in original.
14. Ibid., 150.

Another challenge is moral. If I have once done wrong, how can I make up for that? Even a single act of wrong willing, we saw, amounts to total defection from the moral law and merits limitless punishment. In Kant's words, no matter what a person now resolves, "*he nevertheless started from evil, and this is a debt which is impossible for him to wipe out.*"[15] Kant attempts to solve this problem by arguing that the suffering undergone by the penitent individual, a suffering justly incurred by the old self but experienced by the reformed and "innocent" new self, may be regarded as an acceptable repayment to God for the violation of His holy moral law. Although Kant will not accept the idea that one person can make up for another's faults, and hence rejects the traditional Christian idea of vicarious atonement, he sees this moralized and internalized conception of transferred suffering as containing the underlying moral logic of the traditional Christian doctrine.

Kant's philosophical discovery of human sinfulness and his attempts to address it are groundbreaking. They merit continued respect and attention from philosophical theologians and moral philosophers. But they can also be seen as filled with problems and not fully capable of addressing the challenges they present. This is clear in connection with the problem of overcoming past sin, for how can I assume that the penitent suffering I experience in my new self is adequate to make up for the wrong I have done? How am I allowed to balance my anguish against the potentially limitless harm to others I might have willed? Again, is it not presumptuous of me to believe that God's love will "make good" for my prior deficiencies? Above all, how dare I believe that my confidence in grace is warranted and not just another sinful, self-deceiving evasion of responsibility and blame? If so, how can I escape the quicksand of moral despair into which Kant's own rigorous and unsparing analysis of moral obligation and moral failure has cast me?

In *The Conflict of the Faculties* Kant continues to wrestle with these issues and challenges. In a remarkable series of passages, Kant offers what he terms reason's "own objections" to the understanding of grace he has developed in the *Religion* and now reiterates in *The Conflict of the Faculties.*

> *Objection:* To believe that God, by an act of kindness, will in some unknown way fill what is lacking to our justification is to assume gratuitously a cause that will satisfy the need we feel (it is to commit a *petitio principii*); for when we expect something by the grace of a superior, we cannot assume that we must get it as a matter of

---

15. Ibid., 112. Emphasis in original.

course; we can expect it only if it was actually promised to us, and hence only by acceptance of a definite promise made to us, as in a formal contract. So it seems that we can hope for that supplement and assume that we shall get it only insofar as it has been actually pledged through divine *revelation*, not as a stroke of luck.

To this objection, Kant now endeavors a reply:

> *Reply*: A direct revelation from God embodied in the comforting statement "Your sins are forgiven you" would be a supersensible experience, and this is impossible. But it is also unnecessary with regard to what (like religion) is based on moral principles of reason and is therefore certain a priori, at least for practical purposes. There is no other way we can conceive the decrees of a holy and benevolent lawgiver with regard to frail creatures who are yet striving with all their might to fulfill whatever they recognize as their duty; and if, without the aid of a definite, empirically given promise, we have a rational faith and trust in his help, we show better evidence of a pure moral attitude and so of our receptivity to the manifestation of grace we hope for than we could by empirical belief.[16]

I have developed elsewhere the problems in Kant's reply here.[17] He is mistaken, for example, to say that a direct revelation concerning our forgiveness is "impossible," when what he means to say, in keeping with his own epistemology, is that it is impossible for us to *know* that such a revelation is of God. It is not impossible, however, that God has delivered such a revelation, or that a phenomenal event, such as the crucifixion of a saintly innocent man, may contain that revelation. Nor does it really answer reason's objection concerning the presumptuousness of assuming grace merely to re-affirm our need for it, especially when that need is accompanied by a sense of near certitude of our moral unworthiness.

But we do not have to become embroiled in the details of Kant's inner argument here to begin to see its pertinence to his discussion of Abraham in both *The Conflict of the Faculties* and the *Religion*. For what is clearly on Kant's

---

16. *The Conflict of the Faculties*, 271.

17. See my *Kierkegaard and Kant: The Hidden Debt* (Albany: State University of New York Press, 1992), ch. 4; my *Kant and Kierkegaard on Time and Eternity*, ch. 4; and "Kant: A Debt both Obscure and Enormous," in *Kierkegaard and His German Contemporaries, Tome 1: Philosophy*, ed. Jon Stewart, in the series Kierkegaard Research: Sources, Reception and Resources (London: Ashgate, 2007), 179–210.

mind is whether there is need for what he calls "a definite, empirically given promise" concerning the bestowal of divine grace. Both here in *The Conflict of the Faculties* and in the related section of the *Religion*, what Kant is arguing against is the need for reliance on any historically mediated or "revealed" truths in the process of our moral redemption. And just as he has argued against resort to heteronomous moral teachings when autonomous moral reason must take priority, so Kant is deeply uncomfortable with any suggestion that we need to rely on historically mediated information for our moral redemption. Against this, he wants to affirm that we possess within ourselves all the resources we need to escape even the most negative moral self-judgment. Affirming our need for God's grace and renewing our moral efforts suffice. Grace, yes, but no active intervention by God in time that we must acknowledge as crucial for our moral progress.

Abraham here becomes a central symbol of the debate. It is not simply the ethics of his (and God's) conduct that is at issue, but the worth and reliability of historical testimonies where our moral salvation is involved. As Abraham was wrong to heed a divine voice, as an inquisitor would be wrong to persecute someone based on commands received in the past and handed down, so it would be mistaken to make our moral reform depend in any way on prior acts by God.

It is important to note that Kant is not opposed to much that Christian teaching says about Jesus Christ. In the *Religion*, without naming Jesus, he discusses at length the idea of the "only begotten Son" of God presented in scripture. He expresses admiration for the purity of the moral teachings associated with this figure, and presents him as conforming to an "archetype" of reason representing an "ideal of a humanity pleasing to God." This Son of God, Kant tells us, is "the idea of a human being willing not only to execute in person all human duties, . . . but also, though tempted by the greatest temptation, to take upon himself all sufferings, up to the most ignominious death, for the good of the world and even for his enemies."[18]

But this person is only an idea, resident within our reason, of what each of us can become, one that we can use to further our moral redemption. He must not be thought of as an actual supernatural individual whose life and death are efficacious for our salvation. "There is no need, therefore, of any example from experience to make the idea of a human being morally pleasing to God a model to us."[19] Indeed, to confer objective reality on this idea, to think of the Son of

18. *Religion within the Boundaries of Mere Reason,* 104.
19. Ibid., 105.

God as a supernaturally empowered person sent for our salvation has the most "injurious consequences."[20] This is so because "on the contrary, the elevation of such a Holy One above every frailty of human nature would rather, from all that we can see, stand in the way of the practical adoption of the idea of such a being for our imitation. . . . The consequent distance from the natural human being would then again become so infinitely great that the divine human being could no longer be held forth to the natural human being as *example*."[21]

One could dispute Kant's objections here to an incarnated divine savior. Certainly the New Testament account of Jesus' life, suffering, despair, and death do not present someone whose "distance from the natural human being" is "infinitely great."[22] This suggests that Kant's objections to a historically mediated salvation go deeper than this superficial moral objection. In *The Conflict of the Faculties* we see that this is the case. The first part of this book, a treatment of the conflict of the philosophy faculty with the theology faculty, is a prolonged defense of the philosophy faculty's right to interpret sacred scripture over that of the theology faculty. This right derives from the fact that only those aspects of scripture that support human beings' reasoned moral concepts and commitments merit the name of "pure religious faith." Philosophy interprets these elements. Everything else belongs to a lesser and non–rationally penetrable "ecclesiastical" faith that contains only teaching about alleged historical events or statutory laws (as in the Hebrew dietary and cultic laws). Because its content concerns matters not universally available to all rational persons, Kant insists, "history is not entitled to pass itself off as divine revelation."[23]

As Kant's discussion proceeds, we see that his criticisms of ecclesiastical faith center on one issue: whether a confession that we have received a bestowal of divine grace is necessary for and must precede our efforts at moral renewal. Kant examines the teachings of a variety of Protestant sects, from the Pietists to the Moravian Brethren who, in different ways and with different emphases, claim that the historical fact of God's redeeming grace is needed to initiate our moral redemption. But Kant disagrees with all such ecclesiastical positions, and sees in them a counsel to moral neglect:

20. Ibid., 107.

21. Ibid., 106. In *The Conflict of the Faculties*, 265, Kant makes the same point, saying, "since we cannot require ourselves to rival a God, we cannot take him as an example."

22. In *The Conflict of the Faculties*, 265–66, with an equally poor ear for religious subtleties, Kant errs in the opposite direction, taking Jesus' expression of despair on the cross as a sign of the failure of his messianic mission and as an internal textual refutation of the truth of the doctrine of resurrection.

23. *The Conflict of the Faculties*, 271.

> Action must be represented as issuing from the human being's own use of his moral powers, not as an effect [resulting] from the influence of an external, higher cause by whose activity the human being is passively healed. The interpretation of scriptural texts which, taken literally, seem to contain the latter view must therefore be deliberately directed toward making them consistent with the former view.[24]

Kant concludes his discussion of historical faith and divine grace with the pungent remark, "but it is superstition [*Aberglaube*] to hold that historical belief is a duty and essential to salvation."[25] A lengthy footnote appears here that begins by defining superstition as "the tendency to put greater trust in what is supposed to be non-natural than in what can be explained by laws of nature, whether in physical or in moral matters." The footnote continues with Kant asking whether biblical faith ("as empirical belief") or morality ("as pure rational and religious belief") should serve as one's guide. "In other words, is the teaching from God because it is in the Bible, or is it in the Bible because it is from God?" Replying, "Only the second proposition is acceptable," Kant then appears to offer this "example" of empirical faith:

> The disciples of the Mosaic-messianic faith saw their hopes, based on God's covenant with Abraham, fail completely after Jesus' death (we had hoped that he would deliver Israel); for their Bible promised salvation only to the children of Abraham. Now it happened that when the disciples were gathered at Pentecost, one of them hit upon the happy idea, in keeping with the subtle Jewish art of exegesis, that pagans (Greeks and Romans) could also be regarded as admitted into this covenant, if they believed in the sacrifice of his only son that Abraham was willing to offer God (as the symbol of the world-savior's own sacrifice): for then they would be children of Abraham in faith (at first subject to circumcision, but later even without it).—It is no wonder that this discovery which, in a great gathering of people, opened so immense a prospect, was received with the greatest rejoicing as if it had been the direct working of the Holy Spirit, and was considered a miracle and recorded as such in biblical (apostolic) history.[26]

24. Ibid., 267.
25. Ibid., 285.
26. Ibid., 285n.

Despite the ingenuity of this apostolic teaching Kant will have none of it. He concludes the footnote by stating "But religion does not require us to believe this as a fact, or obtrude this belief on natural human reason. Consequently, if a church commands us to believe such a dogma, as necessary for salvation, and we obey out of fear, our belief is superstition."[27]

Here, once again, is Abraham. What is striking, however, is that now, more clearly than ever, he appears fully in the midst of a treatment of the reliance on the historical teachings of faith and reports of God's saving grace in and through Christ. This is evident in Kant's evocation of a long Christian tradition, dating back to Hebrews 11:17-19, according to which Abraham's sacrifice of his son is proof of the resurrection of the body and a "type" or prefigurement of God's sacrifice of his own son.[28] Thus, the dogma that Kant rejects is one that holds belief in the historical reality of the death and resurrection of Jesus Christ as necessary for our salvation. Against this, Kant continues to insist on rededicated moral striving alone. Faith consists in trust in the perfected archetype of morality residing within our own reason, not belief in the reality or saving grace conveyed by the historically reported life and death of the historical Christ.

We began this exploration by noting Kant's animus against Abraham for prioritizing revelation above moral reason. We can now see that that these treatments of Abraham are actually surrogates for Kant's more pervasive opposition to reliance on any of the teachings of a historical or ecclesiastical faith, and especially for his discomfort with the belief that salvation from sin must begin with faith in the divine grace bestowed in Christ. For Kant everything we need for our moral salvation is found, not in history or the teachings of church traditions, but within our own reason. In multiple ways Abraham serves for him as an example of what religion should not be. No longer the "father of faith," Abraham has come to symbolize the multiple ways that religion can forfeit its moral vocation.

Understanding how the critique of Abraham is integrated into Kant's philosophy of religion has importance beyond Kant's work. Half a century after the publication of the *Religion* and *The Conflict with the Faculties*, Søren Kierkegaard offered a vigorous defense of Abraham in *Fear and Trembling*. For Kierkegaard, Abraham is a "knight of faith" who defies both ethics and reason in his singular devotion to God.

On the surface it might appear that Kierkegaard is simply rejecting Kant's moral criticism of Abraham. In fact, however, Kierkegaard's engagement with

27. Ibid.

28. David Lerch, *Isaaks Opferung christlich gedeutet* (Tübingen: J. C. B. Mohr, 1950).

Kant is extensive and reaches into Kant's entire philosophy of religion. We know that Kierkegaard was familiar with both of Kant's mature works.[29] He was clearly impressed by Kant's ethical rigorism and his discussion of radical evil. In the *Concept of Anxiety* and *Concluding Unscientific Postscript* he drew on these to buttress his conviction that the ultimate consequence of ethics is despair over one's sinfulness. Kierkegaard also seems to have been attentive to Kant's struggle to make room for grace in the economy of redemption without yielding to reliance on a prior saving act by God in history. But in the end, Kierkegaard rejected Kant's conclusions. Perceiving weaknesses in Kant's arguments—some made clear by Kant's own discussions of "reason's objections" to his positions—Kierkegaard built on the foundation Kant provided to offer a new defense of the role of history in moral redemption. Drawing on Kant's analysis of the decisive nature of free acts for our moral destiny, Kierkegaard concluded that sins incurred in time cannot be expiated by timeless rational concepts but require reliance on a decisive free act by God in time for their erasure.[30] To the questions that begin the *Philosophical Fragments*, "Can a historical point of departure be given for an eternal consciousness. . . . Can an eternal happiness be built on historical knowledge?" Kierkegaard answered with a resounding "yes." That Abraham plays such a central role in Kierkegaard's writings is no accident. Using Abraham, Kierkegaard hoped to finish the debate that Kant had begun.

---

29. See my *Kierkegaard and Kant: The Hidden Debt*, ch. 1.

30. See the introduction to my *Kant and Kierkegaard on Time and Eternity*.

5

HEGEL

Abductive Inference, Autonomy, and the Faith of Abraham

Preston Stovall

> *I do aver that I love my country, that I
> am proud of its institutions, that I have a
> feeling . . . which is the proudest thing in
> me, that there is no man above me—for
> my ruler is only myself, in the position
> of another, whose office I impose upon
> him—nor any below me.*
>
> —Nathaniel Hawthorne,
> *Dr. Grimshawe's Secret*

Any consideration of Hegel's interpretation of the faith exemplified in Abraham's willingness to sacrifice his son at God's command must bear in mind Johannes de silentio's criticism of Hegel on just this issue in Kierkegaard's *Fear and Trembling*.[1] But though Hegel forms the contrast against which each of the *problemata* of that work are framed, Johannes does not engage Hegel's interpretation of the religious significance of the faith of Abraham. Instead, as Jon Stewart shows in *Kierkegaard's Relations to Hegel Reconsidered*, the passages Johannes takes as his foil concern either issues in Hegel's politics, as in *problemata*

---

1. My thanks to Robert Brandom for discussion over an earlier version of this paper, and for providing so much of the framework within which it is situated. Søren Kierkegaard, *Fear and Trembling and The Book on Adler*, trans. Walter Lowrie (New York: Alfred A. Knopf, Inc., 1994).

1 and 3, or, as in *problema* 2, with aspects of Hegel's logic that have "nothing to do with Johannes de silentio's discussion."[2] As a result, Stewart concludes "Johannes de silentio and Hegel are talking about two different things."[3] But Hegel dealt with the religious import of Abraham's faith in a number of places throughout his career, and while Kierkegaard did not have access to the views on Abraham one finds in Hegel's *Early Theological Writings* (e.g. the first 20 pages of "The Spirit of Christianity and its Fate"),[4] an edition of Hegel's *Lectures on the Philosophy of Religion* was brought to press in 1832, the year following Hegel's death. Had Kierkegaard been interested to work through those lectures, de silentio could have engaged Hegel directly over the issue of the significance of faith for a people's identity. For it is to religion, not political philosophy, that one must turn if one is interested in Hegel's understanding of Abraham's trip to Mt. Moriah as the expression of a people's faith.

But Hegel's *Lectures on the Philosophy of Religion* were given at four different times over the last decade of his career (in 1821, 1824, 1827, and 1831), and the discussion of Judaism in particular undergoes revision over the course of that decade. This makes a direct contrast of Hegel's views with Johannes somewhat difficult. This difficulty is compounded by the need to read Hegel's discussion of Judaism in those lectures in the context of his philosophical system. This being so, rather than endeavor to address Johannes's critique of "Hegel" directly, the current paper aims to consider Hegel's discussion of the faith of Abraham within the context of his own views. In the process of tracing the contours of Hegel's position on these issues I hope to open the door to an appropriation of some of the rationalist and romantic elements animating the Hegelian project, in particular concerning his logic, metaphysics, and social philosophy.

---

2. Jon Stewart, *Kierkegaard's Relations to Hegel Reconsidered* (New York: Cambridge University Press, 2003), 326.

3. 331; see 315–16, 329–33. Stewart argues that Hegel and Johannes are talking "at cross purposes" (321 and 323) because Kierkegaard is interested in critiquing not Hegel, but some of the contemporary Danish Hegelians—in particular Johan Ludvig Heiberg, Hans Lassen Martensen, and Rasmus Nielsen (307–9, 327–35). Kierkegaard has Johannes address Hegel, on this reading, because Hegel is "a convenient target by means of which to set up [Kierkegaard's] own view and a convenient symbol that would have a clear significance to his contemporary Danish reader" (323).

4. G. W. F. Hegel, "The Spirit of Christianity and Its Fate," in *Early Theological Writings*, trans. T. M. Knox and Richard Kroner (Philadelphia: University of Pennsylvania Press, 1948), 182–301.

1. The Faith of Abraham in the *Lectures on the Philosophy of Religion*

Though the relationship between philosophy and religion is a central concern throughout Hegel's work, it was only after settling in at Berlin that he devoted himself to a systematic treatment of the philosophy of religion. Though there are large-scale structural features in common across the decade in which Hegel gives these lectures, much of the detail is revised substantially (Hodgson's editorial introductions to the three English volumes of the religion *Lectures*—itself a small book—offers an extensive treatment of these changes). Throughout all four lectures Hegel divides his treatment of religion into three stages: an examination of the concept of religion and the character of the social practices that realize that concept at any given time (published as Volume 1: *Introduction and the Concept of Religion*);[5] a consideration of various determinate religions in Western history as stages in the working out of humankind's understanding of its place in the world (Volume 2: *Determinate Religion*);[6] and a treatment of Christianity as the sociohistorical realization of the concept of religion at work in this process (Volume 3: *The Consummate Religion*).[7] In all four lectures Determinate Religion takes primitive natural religion as a starting point and Roman state religion as an end point. But the place of Judaism in the transition from primitive to Roman religion varies. This variation is not substantial, and most of the differences between earlier and later versions of Determinate Religion are the result of Hegel familiarizing himself with more foreign religions, particularly those of China and India, and endeavoring to understand their place in the West's intellectual development. One might wonder whether cultures with such little interaction with the sociohistorical development that Hegel is interested in tracing ought to be treated as moments in that development; I will bracket these concerns in most of what follows, aiming instead to focus on the metaphysics of personal identity that underwrites this philosophical anthropology. I begin with a brief survey.

5. Hegel, *Lectures on the Philosophy of Religion*, vol. 1: *Introduction and the Concept of Religion*, ed. Peter C. Hodgson, trans. R. F. Brown, P. C. Hodgson, J. M. Stewart, J. P. Fitzer, and H. S. Harris (Berkeley: University of California Press, 1984).

6. Hegel, *Lectures on the Philosophy of Religion*, vol. 2: *Determinate Religion*, ed. Peter C. Hodgson, trans. R. F. Brown, P. C. Hodgson, J. M. Stewart, and H. S. Harris (Berkeley: University of California Press, 1987).

7. Hegel, *Lectures on the Philosophy of Religion*, vol. 3: *The Consummate Religion*, ed. Peter C. Hodgson, trans. R. F. Brown, P. C. Hodgson, J. M. Stewart, and H. S. Harris (Berkeley: University of California Press, 1985).

With the exception of the 1824 lectures, Hegel divides *Determinate Religion* into three stages—primitive religion, the religions of spiritual individuality in ancient Judaism and ancient Greece, and the Roman state religion. The following from the end of the introduction to the 1827 lectures on Determinate Religion is representative of Hegel's view throughout the decade:

> So far as the historical development is concerned, nature religion is the religion of the East. The second form of religion, namely that in which the spiritual elevates itself above the natural, is in one aspect the religion of sublimity (that of the Jews) and in the other aspect the religion of beauty (that of the Greeks). . . . The third form, the religion of external purposiveness or expediency, is Roman religion . . . which constitutes the transition to absolute religion. (22:520–21)[8]

As we will see, the collective activities of a people, and the self-understanding that unites those activities under a set of shared purposes, is central to Hegel's theory of personal identity and sociohistorical development. One way of tracing a line of thought through Hegel's *Lectures on the Philosophy of Religion*, then, is to focus on his understanding of the purposive character of the practices surrounding a given religion's cultus. And one way of bringing this feature to light is to consider the general shape of his story of religious development in Determinate Religion, beginning with what Hegel calls "primitive religion."

According to Hegel, primitive religion represents the divine in a form fit for sensation and the immediate inclination of a sapience just emerging from sentient life. Here the purposes that unite a people are pre-reflective desire and aversion with regard to natural events (2 2:518–19 [1827]).[9] Hegel sees the emergence of socially self-conscious communities out of this primitive religion occurring in two moments—in the development of the city-states of ancient Greece and in the religious conviction of ancient Judaism. Hegel characterizes this as the birth of *spiritual individuality*. The transition from primitive natural religion to the Jewish religion of spiritual individuality is a transition from the pursuit of purposes associated haphazardly with pre-reflective inclination and a desire to gain control over capricious divinized nature, to a religion where the divine is conceptualized as an agent, a locus of power and subjectivity with control over nature, whose purposes are immutable and universal (2:134–35,

---

8. See also the selection from the 1831 lectures on this point at 2:514n.

9. When referencing the *Lectures on the Philosophy of Religion* I will include in square brackets the year in which the referenced passage occurs as part of Hegel's lectures, unless the year is already clear from my discussion.

139, 152–54 [1821]; 444–48 [1824]; 674–75 [1827]). This universality occurs only on the side of these purposes' origin in the absolute subject of God, however—as pursued within the community they are not truly universal, for despite God's identity as the sole power and source of these laws and values the Jewish people conceived of themselves as a *privileged* people, as one that bore a unique relationship to the divine (2:157–59 [1821]; 434–36 [1824]; 683ff [1827]; 683–85n [1831]) Additionally, Hegel thinks ancient Judaism's purposes are externally imposed upon the people in a way that does not express the proper relationship between a society and its customs. As we will see, the story of God's command that Abraham sacrifice his son is representative of the external character of these purposes.

The second element of Determinate Religion at the stage of spiritual individuality is the religion of ancient Greece. In contrast with the ancient Jewish conception of the divine as a single absolute power, the Greek gods form a community, each with his or her own sphere of influence and relation to the other gods. Hegel praises the Greek cultus for its ability to permeate communal life with the ideals these gods represent, but they as yet remain ideals of human character—strength, wisdom, beauty, fidelity, family, and so on (2:387–89 [1824]; 642–44, 662–64 [1827]). Despite raising individuals up to a level where they recognize themselves as a community, the purposes that animate Greek religious worship do not unite the members of these communities under one common self-conception or aim. But in the Roman religion this panoply of gods is unified around the purposes of the Roman state, and thereby the disparate cultic practices of the people are associated with the ongoing life of the empire (2:388–89 [1824]). Nevertheless, Roman purposes remain external to spirit's development; they do not represent the self-expression of self-consciousness as such (2:406–7 [1824]; 521 [1827]). It would take the infusion of the Judaic conception of God, wedded to a new view of the relationship between the divine and the individual, to effect the emergence of a truly universal purpose out of the ancient Roman cultus. As Hegel sees Christianity, then, it unites the truly universal *concept* of God found in Judaism with the properly universal cultic *practices* that come out of the Greco-Roman religious tradition (I will have more to say about Hegel's views on Christianity below).

Throughout the lectures, Hegel takes the faith of Abraham and Job to be emblematic of the Jewish relationship to the divine.[10] Nevertheless, his

---

10. One of the major changes throughout these lectures is the place of the discussion of the different proofs for the existence of God, which Hegel correlates to different religious standpoints. I will ignore this issue in what follows, as it does not directly bear on the treatment of classical Judaism itself.

interpretation of Judaism evolves over the decade in which he gives the lectures, with the most striking development occurring at the start, between the 1821 and 1824 lectures.[11] The 1821 treatment of the world-historical significance of Jewish conceptions of the divine differs little from the view Hegel came to in the years prior to the writing of the *Phenomenology of Spirit*[12] (published in 1807), typified by the discussion of Judaism at the start of "The Spirit of Christianity and Its Fate."[13] Here the emphasis lies on God as Lord and his people as his servants; fear of God and submission to his will is the definitive mark of classical Jewish religion in the early lectures: "The relationship [is that] of servant to a Lord; the fear of the Lord is what defines it" (2:156; bracketed remarks preserved from the translation). Though Hegel celebrates ancient Judaism for its religious conviction that the divine is not a natural or animistic force and is instead a self-conscious subject and seat of universal power, wisdom, and justice, his view of the religion in 1821—and of the faith that Abraham exemplifies in it—remains primarily critical: "God's people is the one that he has accepted on condition that they shall fear him, and have the basic feeling of their dependence, i.e., of their servitude" (2:158). Crucially for Hegel, the purposes of God in ancient Judaism are external to the will of the worshipper—they are not the purposes of a community of autonomous actors. Instead, they are to be followed simply in virtue of the fact that God has willed them: "Virtue or piety would be a purpose in and for itself, [whereas] in fact it is only fear of the Lord, only absolute submission [to his will] that is valid—submission itself is the goal, is what counts" (2:139; bracketed remarks preserved from the translation).

But the 1824 lectures develop a more favorable treatment of ancient Jewish faith, and the contour of this treatment would remain more or less constant through 1831. In contrast with the earlier writings' emphasis on Judaism as a religion of servitude, in the 1824 lectures Judaism is taken to be a religion of *liberation*, of freedom from the contingencies of worldly dependence exemplified in primitive natural religion, a liberation effected by making oneself wholly dependent upon the divine. Because God is conceived as an absolute

11. Despite the apparent continuity in Hegel's views of Abraham between the early writings and the 1821 lectures, there is evidence that Hegel's reading in the later period is in flux from the very start. There are three sections of *Determinate Religion* from 1821 that received somewhat different formulations in that year; two of the three of these sections occur in the material on the Jewish religion (2:134–35n.).

12. *Hegel's Phenomenology of Spirit*, trans. A. V. Miller (New York: Oxford University Press, 1977).

13. Published in the *Early Theological Writings*. This translation is a pastiche of a number of Hegel's early writings; see H. S. Harris, *Hegel's Development: Toward the Sunlight, 1770–1801* (Oxford: Oxford University Press, 1972), 330ff for a discussion.

power governing nature, nature is conceived to be wholly dependent upon God; by submitting their will to the Lord, the Jewish people thereby acquire a kind of independence from nature through a total dependence on the Lord (2:384). Fear of the Lord is still an emblem of this religious faith, but now that fear, and the submission it elicits, is associated with freedom from worldly concern (2:443–44). The faith in God that follows one's fear of the Lord is typified not as servitude, but as "liberation, being free from all dependence" (2:444). "It is this trust, this faith of Abraham's, that causes the history of this people to carry on; it also constitutes the turning point in the book of Job" (2:446). Yet this mindset affords liberation only from nature, and God in this religion "will not tolerate anything that possesses autonomy" (2:387). Though after 1821 Hegel is willing to emphasize the progressiveness of the Jewish conception of the divine as against primitive natural religion, this interpretation of the faith of Judaism as submission to an externally authoritative Lord who is master over his people remains constant throughout the lectures.[14] And so it is to *autonomy* that we must turn if we are to understand why Hegel finds classical Jewish faith problematic.

14. In terms of changes in substance, in 1827 Judaism is "elevated" above Greek religion as a religion of spiritual individuality (2:641–42, 669). Both religions still represent transitions out of the sensuous immediacy of primitive natural religion, but the Jewish religion is supposed to have effected this transition by conceiving the divine as something to be grasped in thought rather than through sensuous representation, as in the Greek religion—the Jewish religion of sublimity conceives of spirit as "elevating itself . . . beyond naturalness and finitude, and is no longer afflicted with and clouded by the external (as is still the case with the form of beauty)" (2:642). The only major change with regard to Judaism in the 1824 lectures that is not carried through to later lectures concerns the structure of the 1824 presentation, not its substance. While in 1821 Judaism is grouped together with Greek religion as a middle step between natural religion and Roman state religion, with Christianity treated as a new moment, in 1824 Judaism and the ancient Greek religion are grouped together with Roman religion as an intermediate point between natural religion and Christianity. In 1827 Hegel reverts to the 1821 division, and in 1831 Determinate Religion is reorganized again. Hegel in 1831 still conceives of Determinate Religion in three stages—primitive natural religion, a stage where the spiritual is set over against the natural, and the religion of freedom or self-determined purpose. But the second stage, conceived as a religion of "cleavage" (2:516n) or the "internal rupture of religious consciousness" (2:725) is understood to include Chinese, Hindu, and Buddhist religions—the religions of the East, which in previous lectures were associated either with primitive natural religion or as transition points between natural religion and the religions of spiritual individuality. Now, however, Judaism is grouped together with Phoenician religion (the religion of anguish) and Egyptian religion (the religion of ferment) as a transitional religion at the start of the third stage of Determinate Religion, the religion of freedom. The second two moments of the religion of freedom are now the religions of ancient Greece and Rome (2:736–60).

2. Conceptual Determinacy and the Metaphysics of Kinds and Properties

It does not take a great stretch of one's imagination to think of Abraham's trip to Mount Moriah, and the faith exemplified in his willingness to sacrifice his son there, as an expression of servitude to a Lord who commands submission to his will simply because it is his will. But to understand why Hegel takes this servitude to offer a defective conception of self-consciousness, one must understand Hegel's views on the faith emblematic of Christian conceptions of humanity's relation to the divine.[15] And to understand Hegel on Christianity one must understand some of his logic and metaphysics. Rather than imagining a transcendental canon for reason, judgment, and understanding that could be given by attending to the categorial structure of thought fixed once and for all, Hegel believed that to understand the nature of our discursiveness we have to understand the way our concepts—and the categories that delimit them—undergo development over the course of their use in reasoning. At the same time, he thought that some things in the world were themselves undergoing processes of conceptual self-determination—in particular, persons and societies. By tracing the genealogies of some of the concepts he found most important (including those for God, the state, and personal identity) Hegel proposed to show that historical change itself could be understood as the working out, the revision and development, of a single concept. The concept he thought he saw taking shape in the development of these other concepts was the concept of conceptual determinacy itself—the better we have been able to think the various determinate things we think, the better have we understood the nature of determinate thought itself, Hegel argues. Here Hegel was driven by his views on logic, specifically on the understanding we acquire of the concepts falling under categories of individuality, particularity, and universality when we conceive them via the roles they play in different sorts of syllogistic inference. It is in the first three chapters of the Subjective Logic—those on the concept, the judgment, and the syllogism (*Science of Logic* 600–704, discussed in the *Encyclopedia Logic* 223–59)—that these views are worked out.[16]

As was common practice in logic texts of the period, Hegel in this section begins with a discussion of concepts, proceeds to a consideration of judgment,

---

15. One might also look to the discussion of the Lord and Bondsman in the Self-Consciousness chapter of the *Phenomenology of Spirit* for an understanding of why Hegel views this sort of relationship as defective, of course.

16. *Hegel's Science of Logic*, trans. A. V. Miller (New York: Humanity Books, 1969), and *Hegel's Logic: Being Part One of the Encyclopedia of the Philosophical Sciences (1830)*, trans. William Wallace (Oxford: Oxford University Press, 1975).

and finishes with a treatment of syllogistic inference. The concepts Hegel takes as basic are those occurring in categories of individuality, particularity, and universality. Though some of what follows will require modifying this slightly, for now think of the linguistic analogues of these categories as singular terms, common nouns, and predications, denoting objects, kinds, and properties (Hegel habitually speaks of individuality, particularity, and universality in what we today would call both the formal or linguistic and material or world-denoting modes). Though what we would regiment as common nouns and predicates can occur on both sides of the particularity/universality divide, I will be concerned mostly with particulars as common nouns and universals as predicates (this will be modified slightly when concerning genus/species relations below). The aim is to come to some understanding of Hegel's view of persons (individuals) as members of cultural groups (particulars) unified by having in common a set of properties (universals) definitive of their sociohistorical communities.

For each category there are two kinds of relations that concepts may stand in with regard to the other categories, one with each. This results in three forms of judgment. A universal (conducting electricity) can subsume an individual (this rod) as in the judgment "This rod conducts electricity," or that universal can subordinate a particular (being metal) as in "All metal conducts electricity."[17] Particulars, in addition to being subordinated to universals, can also subsume individuals: "This rod is metal." Finally, individuals can be subsumed by particulars and by universals (as in the first and the third of these sentences).[18] The categories of individuality, particularity, and universality, and the basic forms of judgments they stand in, were in turn individuated by Hegel according to three syllogistic figures.[19] For it is Hegel's contention that we do not understand these categories, or the judgments their concepts enter into, until we understand the role such concepts play as middle terms in, respectively, inductive, deductive, and abductive inference. In his "Deduction, Induction, and Hypothesis," the last of six essays written for *Popular Science Monthly* between 1877 and 1878, Peirce makes the same division of syllogistic figures

17. Hegel does not use "subsumption" and "subordination" in this way; I adopt it for ease of exposition. See his discussion of subsumption and inherence (*Subsumtion* and *Inhärence*) at 645–50 of the *Science of Logic.*

18. Whether a concept is a particular or a universal will be a matter of context, of course—in "these shoes are white" the term "white" functions as a universal; but in the context of the judgment "to be white is to be colored," it is a particularization of the more universal concept "being colored."

19. "The relationship of individuality, particularity and universality is . . . the *necessary and essential form-relationship* of the determinations of the syllogism" (*Science of Logic* 667, emphasis in the original).

that Hegel makes in the *Science of Logic*.[20] Using the instances of individuals, particulars, and universals introduced above, we can represent Hegel's figures as follows (I include Peirce's examples as well):

20. Charles Sanders Peirce, "Deduction, Induction, and Hypothesis," in *The Essential Peirce: Selected Philosophical Writings, Vol. 1 (1867–1893)*, ed. Nathan Houser and Christian Kloesel (Bloomington: Indiana University Press, 1992), 186–199. Peirce already made this distinction in lectures given at the Lowell Institute in Boston in 1866, published as "On The Natural Classification of Arguments," *Proceedings of the American Academy of Arts and Sciences*, 7 (May, 1865–May, 1868): 261–87, and in 1867 Peirce presented a paper to the American Academy of Arts and Sciences that distinguishes different ways of thinking about the content of our concepts: "Upon Logical Comprehension and Extension," *Proceedings of the American Academy of Arts and Sciences*, 7 (May, 1865–May 1868): 416–432. As we will see, these latter distinctions help track the function that those different forms of syllogistic inference play in the revision of conceptual content over the process of inquiry. But Peirce does not mention Hegel in any of these papers, and I do not know whether Peirce developed this classification independently of Hegel—the use of Peirce I put to making sense of Hegel's logic is my own. Regardless of direct influence, Peirce and Hegel end up saying rather similar things, particularly concerning what Peirce will call "abduction," "hypothesis" or "retroduction," in Hegel's third figure syllogism. See Paul Redding, "Hegel and Peircean Abduction," *European Journal of Philosophy* 11, no.3 (December 2003): 295–313. Redding argues that Peirce's theory of abduction is influenced by Hegel's attempt to make sense of Kant's idea of reflective judgment, on which we are presented with a particular and then search for a universal to understand it. Interestingly, Hegel's third-figure inference, corresponding to what Peirce called "abduction," is the syllogistic inference that takes a universal as a middle term. In the *Logic* this inference is associated with analogy (which will be a focus of discussion below) and at this point another clue to the ancestry of these ideas comes into view. For in September of 1831, just two months before Hegel's death, Francis Wayland, president of Brown University, gave an address to the Phi Beta Kappa Society of Rhode Island entitled "A Discourse on the Philosophy of Analogy," (Boston: Hilliard, Gray, Little, and Wilkins, 1831). Wayland opens his talk by saying it is a subject that "so far as I have been able to discover, has not yet attracted the notice of any writer in our language" (4). He then proceeds to argue that in addition to inductive inference and demonstrative (or deductive—see 21) inference, the development of the sciences requires a theory of analogical inference, for "demonstration and induction never discover a law of nature" (12) and "the use of the instruments of proof can never . . . of itself, insure the progress of discovery." One versed in Hegel and Peirce will find Wayland's discourse resonant with themes in both philosophers' works, but Wayland does not mention Hegel. Nor does Peirce, so far as I know, ever mention Wayland. Nevertheless, the talk was published in pamphlet form in 1831, so Peirce could have had access to it before the Lowell Institute lecture of 1866, and it stands as another suggestive link between Hegel's third figure inference as analogy, its apparent roots in Kant's notion of reflective judgment, and Peirce's theory of abduction or hypothesis (on which see Redding's paper). But I am as yet unaware of whether there is anything more than suggestion to any of these links.

Table 1. Deduction: Hegel's First Figure (IPU) Peirce's Example

1) IP	1) This rod is metal.	1) This ball is from the urn.
2) PU	2) All metal conducts electricity.	2) All the balls in the urn are red.
3) IU	3) This rod conducts electricity.	3) This ball is red.

This inference is deductive: the judgment that an individual thing is subsumed by a particular, together with the judgment that that particular is subordinated to a universal, licenses an inference to the judgment that the individual is subsumed by the universal. In a deductive syllogism the particularity of a concept—its subordination under another universal—makes it fit for use as a middle term mediating that universal with an individual thing. The conclusion (IU) is the judgment that results from that mediation of particularity (P). Once this structure of the syllogism is made out, it takes only a simple permutation of sentences to derive the other two figures.[21] But whereas the conclusion of a first figure inference is deductively ensured, the conclusions of the other two are not. The second figure inference corresponds to induction:

Table 2. Induction: Hegel's Second Figure (PIU) Peirce's Example

1) IP	1) This rod is metal.	1) This ball is from the urn.
2) IU	2) This rod conducts electricity.	2) This ball is red.
3) PU	3) All metal conducts electricity.	3) All the balls in the urn are red.

Here individuality mediates a relation of subordination between a particular and a universal, in virtue of the observation that the individual (or a set of them) is subsumed by both the particular and the universal. Finally, taking a universal concept as a middle term we have the third figure, which Peirce will call "abduction," "hypothesis," or "retroduction," and which later philosophers will call "inference to the best explanation."

---

21. See the *zusatze* to §181 of the *Encyclopedia Logic,* and compare Peirce at 187–88 of "Deduction, Induction, and Hypothesis."

Table 3. Abduction: Hegel's Third Figure (IUP) Peirce's Example

1) IU	1) This rod conducts electricity.	1) This ball is red.
2) UP	2) All metal conducts electricity.	2) All the balls in the urn are red.
3) IP	3) This rod is metal.	3) This ball is from the urn.

This inference is a case of hypothesizing that a thing that one knows to fall under a universal (exhibits a property) also falls under a particular (is a member of a kind) because, in the context of a commitment that the universal subordinates that particular (that those kinds exhibit those properties), this would explain why the thing falls under that universal.[22] It is worth noting that whereas philosophers have historically considered deductive inference to be the apex of rational cognition, Hegel gives third figure inference pride of place in his logical system. For it is with this inference that we express our rational grasp of universals in mediating the relationship between individuals and particulars.

In the course of working out this line of thought Hegel applies these divisions to a wide range of logical distinctions. In particular, Hegel treats of both non-essential subject/predicate relations, like the color of a rose, and relations holding between natural kinds and their essential properties. Peirce's examples, by contrast, deal with non-lawlike statistical generalizations. It is important to note, then, that these forms of inference range over a variety of individual/particular/universal relations (and what stands in for particularity in Peirce's case—being from an urn—is not happily thought of as a common noun). But with the exception of the association between the third figure syllogism and inference by analogy, to be considered below, I will focus on the particularity/universality complex that shows up in the relation between kinds and their essential properties (common nouns and modally robust predications), and that between species and the genera that subordinate them (classes of common nouns standing in hierarchical relations).

We can see that the *Schlusspiel* marked out by Hegel's syllogism affects the extension and comprehension of the terms falling under the categories of individuality, particularity, and universality in three distinct ways. Call the

22. Notice that, on the usual translation of Aristotelian syllogistic into predicate logic, this inference is formally a case of the fallacy of affirming the consequent. Thus, it is essential that we understand an abductive inference as an inference whose goodness is material and not formal. This point is of course central to Hegel's claim that by making logic a matter of merely formal inferential transitions philosophers have misunderstood the nature of our discursiveness; see, e.g., discussion of "The Notion in General" at the start of Volume II of *The Science of Logic*, 577–95.

"extension" of a term the objects it refers to on some interpretation. Call its "comprehension" the array of entailments that are implicated by the use of the term on some interpretation. Let "content" be the genus of which extension and comprehension are species. In a paper presented to the American Academy of Arts and Sciences in 1867 entitled "Upon Logical Comprehension and Extension," Peirce uses this distinction to mark some of the different ways a term's content can change over the course of inquiry (Peirce replaces "comprehension" and "extension" with "depth" and "breadth" in that paper, but I will use the more traditional terms). Peirce's distinction between the *informed* comprehension and extension of a term and its *substantial* comprehension and extension can be used to shed light on Hegel's account of the syllogism. The former is meant to capture the implication relations and referents of our terms at a particular time, and the latter is an ideal "state in which the information would amount to an absolute intuition of all there is, so that the things we should know would be the vey substances themselves, and the qualities we should know would be the very concrete forms themselves" ("Upon Logical Comprehension and Extension," 426).

For those of us used to working in an extensional predicate calculus, it can seem odd to talk of a term's content *changing* from one informed state to the next. After all, the model by which we interpret the language fixes the content of the terms and predicates once and for all, and on that basis computes the truth-values of sentences. On such a view of logic there is no sense in talking about a term changing its content except insofar as one uses the term under a different model. But if we are instead working with a theory of meaning that takes inferential relations as basic and computes the content of terms on that basis, and if further this theory is meant to apply to our actual practices of reasoning about and so coming to understand the world, then it becomes reasonable to allow that a term's content can change while working within one and the same model for the language. The suggestion, then, is to think of different inferences as functions that, over the course of inquiry, take us from one interpretation of our terms to successive ones.

By these lights, deductive inference has the function of explicating the comprehension of a singular term implicit in the subsumption of that singular term under a common noun. It does so by deriving as a conclusion the subsumption of that singular term under a predicate that is part of the pre-existing comprehension of (i.e. is subordinated to) the common noun. In this regard deductive inference does not affect the content of our concepts so much as make explicit what was implicit in a preexisting set of judgments. Inductive and abductive inference are otherwise, however. For an inductive inference increases the comprehension of a kind-term (a common noun); by accepting an inductive link between a property and a kind one is licensing the predication of that property to any singular term subsumed under the corresponding kind-term. Indirectly, then, inductive inference will also affect the comprehension of all the singular terms in the extension of that common noun. Abduction, meanwhile, both increases the extension of a kind-term and increases the comprehension of a singular term. By classifying this rod as metal on the basis of its disposition to conduct electricity, I both increase the extension of the kind-term "metal" and increase the comprehension of the singular term, the understanding we in the language now have of the object denoted by that singular term (I am eliding difficult issues regarding when abductive and inductive inference are warranted, of course, and concerning the more distal implication relations that are affected by changes in comprehension). This understanding is facilitated by the fact that the subsumption of a singular term under a common noun implicitly predicates of the singular term all of the concepts contained in the comprehension of that common noun. And deductive inference, as we have seen, allows us to make these implications explicit.

In the canonical form of Hegel's third figure inference, we reason with a universal so as to classify an individual as a member of particular kind. In this way we explain a given property on the basis of a kind-identity, with the comprehension of that kind-identity remaining unaffected. But Hegel also discusses the third figure as analogical inference at 692–95 of the *Science of Logic* and 252–54 of the *Encyclopedia Logic,* and here we see a process that enriches a kind-term's comprehension by (potentially) increasing its inferential application, the predicates implicated by the employment of that kind-term. In both the *Science of Logic* and the *Encyclopedia* Hegel gives the following as an example of analogical inference:

> The earth is inhabited
> The moon is an earth;
> Therefore the moon is inhabited.

In both cases he writes that the middle term is an individual thing (the earth) that is understood in terms of its kind-identity; it is "taken as a concrete that in its truth is as much a universal nature or genus as an individual" (*Science of Logic*

693–94; cf. *Encyclopedia Logic* 252). This is what Hegel has to say about analogy in the *zusatze* to §190 of the *Encyclopedia Logic*:

> In the syllogism of Analogy we conclude from the fact that some things of a certain kind possess a certain quality, that the same quality is possessed by other things of the same kind. . . . Analogy is the instinct of reason,[23] creating an anticipation that this or that characteristic, which experience has discovered, has its root in the inner nature or kind of an object, and arguing on the faith of that anticipation. (254)

It is clear that kinds and properties are playing different roles in these two sorts of third figure inferences. In the first inference a single *property* (conducting electricity) is used to infer a *kind-identity* (being metal). But in the inference concerning the earth and the moon, the *kind-identity* (being a planet; an "earth") is used to infer that some one thing of that kind has some *property* had by another thing of that kind—in this case, being inhabited. Call the first inference *an abduction of a kind on the basis of a property* and the second *an abduction of a property on the basis of a kind*. Each of these forms of inference contribute to the determination of conceptual content in different ways. While the abduction of a kind on the basis of a property has the effect of enlarging a kind-term's sphere of extension (the individuals it ranges over) and so potentially explaining some property that an individual exhibits, it does not tell us anything new about the inferential link between the kind and the property in question. After all, we must rely on that link as a rule uniting the kind and the property if we are to infer the kind-identity on the basis of the property.

Things are otherwise with the abduction of a property on the basis of a kind, however. For the conclusion of an analogical inference is a hypothesis that, if verified in a range of cases, permits one to make an induction over those cases to the *establishment* of a rule or generalization that links the property and the kind together.[24] The abduction of a kind on the basis of a property expands a kind-term's extension but does not change its inferential role, for that sort of inference depends upon an antecedent grasp of a rule linking a kind and a property (it does change the inferential role of the singular term, of course). But the abduction of a property on the basis of a kind is (potentially) a stage in a

---

23. Wallace has "instinct or reason," but the German is *der Instinkt der Vernuft*. My thanks to Robert Brandom for bringing this to my attention.

24. In many cases we are not content unless we also have some causal story linking the kind and the property in question, but I leave this to the side.

process that would institute such a rule, and thereby enrich our understanding of what it means to be a member of that kind.[25] Though Hegel does not make this distinction explicitly, we will see that it corresponds to two different ways in which persons exert control over their social and individual identities, so that to understand what it is for persons to be *autonomous* one must understand what it is for them to engage in these kinds of inferential practices.[26]

We need one further distinction from Hegel's logic to see how this works—like the others, it encodes a corresponding metaphysical commitment. Thus far I have focused on Hegel's treatment of universality and particularity in terms of property and kind relations (cf. *Encyclopedia Logic* 232; *Science of Logic* 602, 638–40). But Hegel also speaks of particularity and universality as conceptual containment relations marking off species/genus classifications (cf. *Encyclopedia Logic* 229; *Science of Logic* 605–6, 620, 701–2).[27] With particularity

25. Of course, if the right property/kind relations obtain one can also *deduce* a kind on the basis of a property (only mammals produce milk; this animal produces milk; therefore this animal is a mammal) or a property on the basis of a kind (that this is copper means that it conducts electricity). But these deductions depend upon already having the rule or generalization linking the property and kind in question.

26. Peirce does appear to mark the distinction, however. In "Deduction, Induction, and Hypothesis," Peirce writes about abduction (hypothesis) that it is "where we find some very curious circumstance, which would be explained by a general rule, and thereupon adopt that supposition. Or, where we find that in certain respects two objects have a strong resemblance, and infer that they resemble one another strongly in other respects" (189). The first of these criteria corresponds to the inference of a kind on the basis of a property; the second of a property on the basis of a kind (reading resemblance as a classification). He also writes that "hypothesis substitutes, for a complicated tangle of predicates attached to one subject, a single conception" (198). This would be a characterization of the inferring of a kind on the basis of a property—or a "tangle" of properties. Peirce does not call the abduction of a property on the basis of a kind *analogical* inference, however, as he understands by "'analogy" a process of drawing deductive consequences from a combination of inductive and abductive inferences; 285–86 of "On the Natural Classification of Arguments."

27. Hegel marks a transition from property-talk to genus/species talk at the transition from the Judgment of Reflection to the Judgment of Necessity in the *Science of Logic*, 649–50. Hegel will also sometimes speak both of property/kind and species/genus relations within the context of a single discussion of particularity/universality; cf. *Encyclopedia Logic* 241–42 and *Science of Logic* 649–57. He does this for methodological reasons, as he rejects a treatment of conceptual content on which a given set of categories is fixed once and for all. In his discussion in the *Science of Logic* of the difference between the coordination of different species as particularizations under a genus and the subordination of a given particularization to a universal, Hegel characterizes as "sterile" the things logicians are led into saying when they conceive of subordination and coordination as "completely rigid relationships" (*Science of Logic* 616; see also the disparaging remarks about the prospect for a Leibnizian universal characteristic at 685). He believes that by the time he is dealing with the logic of the notion, he has already entitled himself to use these categories to talk about being and essence—the focus of discussion in the first two

we can discriminate a wider range of specificity—to be able to see the world as containing copper, gold, and silver, and not merely metal, is to be able to see the world more determinately, to avail oneself of a greater comprehension of it. And with universality we can bundle together and understand in common a wider range of particular individuals. Knowing that copper, gold, and silver are kinds of metals lets us classify the world and pick out regularities. With greater precision in discriminating particularity we gain a greater comprehension of the individuals that populate the world; with a greater precision in discriminating universality we gain a greater comprehension of the organization of the world's manifold variety. Notice that in the context of the subordination of a specific kind of metal (e.g. copper) under the kind-term "metal" we now classify "metal" as a universal rather than a particular. Unlike the distinction between common nouns and predicates, the distinction between universals and particulars can vary with inferential context.[28]

According to the first way of thinking about universality and particularity, a set of properties (universals) differentiates a kind from other kinds (a particular from other particulars) in virtue of the relations that those properties stand in to other kinds and their properties. But a further level of kind fine-structure comes into view when we consider properties that relate a kind to other kinds as species of a common genus. The former distinction enables us to comprehend individual things as particulars related to different particular things, while the second places a particularized individual in community with other individuals under a common kind.

sections of the *Science of Logic* to which the notion is the third (cf. *Science of Logic* 591 and 596). In the introductory chapter of the logic of the notion, entitled "The Notion in General," Hegel contrasts his approach toward logic and the content of thought with the approaches of others, emphasizing that his view requires us to consider conceptual relations not just in virtue of logical form, but also in terms of a concept's "specific determinateness" (589), writing that "this formal science must be regarded as possessing richer determinations and a richer content . . . than is usually supposed" (594).

28. I do not have the space to enter into this here, but there are concerns that ought to be raised with Hegel's willingness to apply these categories across the subject/predicate distinction. A substantial line of thought that emerged in twentieth century philosophy of language argued that kind-terms (common nouns) should not be thought of as predicates. Background for this development can be found in Peter Geach's attack on Aristotelian and medieval theories of logic and language in *Reference and Generality: An Examination of Some Medieval and Modern Theories*, 3rd ed. (Ithaca: Cornell University Press, 1980; 1st ed., 1962) and "History of the Corruptions of Logic," in *Logic Matters* (Oxford: Basil Blackwell, 1972): 44–61, and in Willard Van Orman Quine, *Word and Object* (Cambridge: The MIT Press, 1960). More recent instances along this line of thought include Anil Gupta, *The Logic of Common Nouns: An Investigation in Quantified Modal Logic* (New Haven: Yale University Press, 1980), and Michael Durrant, *Sortals and the Subject-Predicate Distinction*, ed. Stephen Horton (Burlington, VT: Ashgate, 2001).

3. Inanimate Nature and the Self-Determination of Persons

As Robert Brandom has convincingly argued, Hegel's discussion of mediation and negation can be helpfully recast in terms of material implication and incompatibility.[29] Objects on this metaphysics–cum–logic are individuated in thought by tracking the material implication and incompatibility relations that express the paradigmatically causal relations that the object's properties stand in to other individuals, other instances of particularized universals. Knowing that some individual thing is made of metal suffices, so long as one comprehends the kind-term "metal," to know that it bears the property of electrical conductivity; in the formal mode, that this kind-term implicates that predicate. Thus, to comprehend an individual as a member of a kind (to subsume it under a particular) is to know the properties it bears as a member of that kind (so long as one comprehends the kind-term, of course). On the logical side these predicates stand in implication and incompatibility relations with other predicates implicated by different kind-terms and situational contexts. And in terms of the metaphysical side of this point, the properties that objects have are only properties insofar as they stand in determinate (often causal) relation to other properties and objects, with kinds as determinate loci of regular property possession.[30] Thus, to be given an individual's kind is to be given a comprehension of that individual as an object in community with other objects. That comprehension, on the side of the thinking subject, stands in a space of reasons carved out by the modal web with which we think its kind-specific predications. On the side of nature that comprehension is represented in the essential properties the object has as a member of its kind, the universals that the particular individual evokes as it interacts with other universally-implicating particular individuals. But there is an important asymmetry between the way these relations are determined among the inanimate natural world and the way they are determined among persons in a community of other persons. Understanding this asymmetry is a condition on understanding Hegel's theory of modernity as autonomy, itself the key to his views on the sociohistorical significance of different religious traditions.

That acids corrode metals and are neutralized by bases; that magnesium is flammable while gold is not, yet both, being metal, are malleable; these

---

29. Robert Brandom, "Holism and Idealism in Hegel's *Phenomenology*," in *Tales of the Mighty Dead: Historical Essays in the Metaphysics of Intentionality* (Cambridge: Harvard University Press, 2002), 178–209.

30. "[Properties] are only determinate in so far as they *differentiate* themselves from one another, and *relate* themselves *to others* as to their opposites," *Phenomenology of Spirit*, §114, p.69; emphasis in the original.

are facts about property/kind and genus/species relations, facts that specify a community of interacting objects and determine the nature of the individuals in that community, without any participation on the part of the individual things in specifying which facts will determine their identities. But on the side of spirit the identities of the individuals in question, while likewise governed by patterns of kind-identity and property implication, are determined by the activities of those individuals.[31] For persons are individuals whose particularity is in part self-determined. That a bit of hard stuff is copper, and that it thereby is metal, conducts electricity, is malleable, and stands in various relations with other natural objects and their properties, is a matter of the agent-independent operations of causal law. But that any one of us is, say, a professional, a good friend, or a political activist—and just what it means to be such things in our community—is at least in part a function of these individuals' self-determination. Unlike the properties and kind-identities that individuate inanimate natural things, the properties and kinds that determine the identity of persons are themselves shaped by historical development.

Just as is the case with natural properties and kinds, some properties and kind-identities of the social sphere will be incompatible with other properties and kind-identities under a common universal, a kind that unites a group as a people. But here these incompatibilities are subject to two sorts of control on the part of the individuals within their extension—first, persons can sacrifice various particular desires and inclinations in the interest of determining their individual identities (as we educate our children to be tolerant of others, or as the student gives up a chance to socialize so that she can do well in school); and second, we can set up our social institutions so as to allow that two forms of identity are jointly permitted that otherwise might be regarded as incompatible (as, say, being a woman and being a head of state)—"just as the former exhibits the power of Spirit over its actual existence, so does the other exhibit the power of Spirit over the specific Notion of itself" (*Phenomenology of Spirit* §669, 407). This power that spirit has over itself is the power to self-consciously determine a community of persons and their identities, a power one does not find in the inanimate natural world. It is a power of defining a universal that comes to subsume us all—a kind-identity for the community of we who say "we" to one another.

These processes come to be represented in thought by the two sorts of abductive inference discussed in part 2—the first is the abduction of a kind on the basis of a property, and the second is the abduction of a property on

---

31. That the self-regulating activity of living things is an important bridge category between inanimate nature and spirit is a point I pass over here mostly in silence.

the basis of a kind. By the first process we individually enlarge a social kind-concept's extension by conforming ourselves to its rules, thereby determining the comprehension of oneself as an individual; and by the second we collectively determine the content of that kind-concept, its comprehension, as the spirit that unites us. But because persons are self-determining things, the sort of abduction at work here is not the sort at work in our thought about inanimate nature. For the particular/universal relations of nature are fixed independent of human activity, and there our thought is obliged to conform itself to the implication and incompatibility relations that exist independent of us. In our thought about inanimate nature we reason according to structures of *heteronomous* abductive inference. But we have two degrees of autonomy in determining our identities as persons—individually we can decide how to exist as particulars within our communities, and collectively we can determine what sorts of norms will govern our communal practices. These are *autonomous* abductive inferences. Whereas we are forced to conform our thought to the property/kind and genus/species relations of nature, spirit is the realm of self-determination.

In contrast to the story that one could tell of the development of our concepts of inanimate nature, the genealogy of a social universal is not just the story of our uncovering the independent individuality of the things that fall under it. Instead, the history of the development of a people's self-conception *just is* the working out of whatever kind of people they are, individually and collectively. This process is driven by the activities of the individuals within that community, though coming to a historical realization of this fact in institutions capable of sustaining its expression is long and arduous. Hegel sees modernity as the blossoming of that realization. From the *Phenomenology of Spirit*:

> §351 The *labour* of the individual for his own needs is just as much a satisfaction of the needs of others as of his own, and the satisfaction of his own needs he obtains only through the labour of others. As the individual in his *individual* work already *unconsciously* performs a *universal* work, so again he also performs the universal work as his *conscious* object; the whole becomes, as *a* whole, his own work, for which he sacrifices himself and precisely in so doing receives back from it his own self. (213, emphasis original)

To see what Hegel is on about here, we have to understand his interpretation of the story of divine death and resurrection. We will then be in a position to appreciate why Hegel believes that the institutional frameworks and capacities for self-expression that best exemplify what he takes to be the theme of that story, a theme of autonomy, are modern frameworks. This will prepare us for some closing thoughts on the role of religious practice as the expression of that autonomous power peculiar to spirit in nature.

4. Religious Allegory and a People's Self-Conception

Throughout his youth Hegel struggled for a universal sufficient to subordinate as great a range of particularity among individual things as possible, and so of a particular kind of thing that we and the world are for which this universal denotes an essential property or a subordinating genus-kind. This struggle was driven by his urge to see the world not as some haphazard collection of indiscriminate particular things bumping about disconnectedly, but as a unified whole whose doings were intelligible given the kind of thing that it is. In this Hegel was a paragon of eighteenth-century rationalism. But Hegel was also immersed in the romanticism of the nineteenth century, and he believed that whatever prospect there was for comprehending human beings under a universal sufficient to integrate the range of their particularity would have to take seriously their embodied, lived existence, particularly in its sociohistorical (and its organic) aspects.[32] Early on, he began to focus on the processes of organic genesis and growth as a categorial frame for logic and metaphysics, and he came to believe that human societies develop in ways that are structurally similar to the development of organic things.[33] He also believed that concepts themselves undergo a kind of developmental process, a gradual determination of content through use in human activity, according to a process akin to organic growth, the development of social institutions, and the maturation of a person's self-identity.[34] Religious worship is a place where Hegel applies these cross-

32. Hegel's early works on love and mythmaking are a testament to the influence this had on Hegel from the beginning; Peirce's discussion of love as the driving force behind the cosmos bears comparison with Hegel in this regard, as does a consideration of how Peirce's tychism about the laws of nature might be used to revise the account given in the previous two sections of this paper.

33. See Richard Kroner's introduction to Hegel's *Early Theological Writings,* 15–17, 27–31, 52–53; and H. S. Harris in *Hegel's Development: Toward the Sunlight* 101–4, and *Hegel's Development: Night Thoughts, 1801–1806* (New York: Oxford University Press, 1983), 381 and 441ff. At 523–44 of *Hegel's Development: Night Thoughts,* Harris offers an illuminating analysis of a marginal diagram Hegel drew depicting spirit as an organism in the years just before the *Phenomenology* was published.

34. See Robert Brandom's "Some Pragmatist Themes in Hegel's Idealism: Negotiation and Administration in Hegel's Account of the Structure and Content of Conceptual Norms," *European Journal of Philosophy* 7, no. 2 (August 1999): 164–89 for the argument that selves, actions, and concepts all have the same structure and unity by the lights of the *Phenomenology of Spirit.* I take it that Hegel believes

categorial modalities with abandon, and even from his time as a *gymnasium* student he was tracing the development of different religious traditions in the context of this organic holism.[35]

These early works are marked by oscillations between religious experience and philosophical reflection as the mode under which to unite the world's particularities. But in the first years of the nineteenth century Hegel began to fix their respective places in what would become his system of knowledge, and by the publication of the *Phenomenology of Spirit* in 1807 his mature view was in shape. At the center of this breakthrough stands the philosophical interpretation Hegel gives the story of the incarnation of God in the Revealed Religion (paradigmatically, in Christianity). In the *Phenomenology* and afterward, Hegel interprets the story of the God-man's death, resurrection, and return to the community in spirit both as a model for the relationship between social organization and personal identity, and an allegory for how conceptual content is made determinate by a process of continuous revision through inquiry. On Hegel's reading, the story of Christ's incarnation, sacrifice, and return in spirit represents a view of persons as individual things that acquire their particular identities within their societies only in virtue of their willingness to sacrifice those identities that are incompatible with that which they wish to be, while this very practice of sacrifice collectively articulates whatever social order they come to have, and so whatever people they collectively are. This abstract idea was, Hegel thought, made concrete in the practices surrounding Christian worship. In the society-wide identification of the individuals of the Christian community with Christ's sacrifice of particularity for universality—the sacrifice of his mortal coil for the salvation of humanity—the members of that community come to identify themselves, individually and collectively, with those expressions of value supposed to be universal and collectively pursued, not simply as something imposed upon them by an external authority, but as something they understand as an expression of their own identities.[36]

that the processes governing organic growth and institutional change share the same categorial affinities as do those Brandom argues govern the development of personal identity, purposive action, and the determination of conceptual content (these are lessons I take away from the Observing Reason and Religion sections of the *Phenomenology*).

35. *Hegel's Development: Toward the Sunlight*, 3–7

36. *Phenomenology*, §784: "The *death* of the divine Man, *as death*, is *abstract* negativity, the immediate result of the movement which ends only in *natural* universality. Death loses this natural meaning in spiritual self-consciousness, i.e. it comes to be its just stated Notion; death becomes transfigured from its immediate meaning, viz. the non-being of this *particular* individual, into the *universality* of the Spirit who dwells in His community, dies in it every day, and is daily resurrected." (p. 475, emphasis original) The individual sacrifice and identification of the community members with Christ so as to receive a share in

Hegel's breakthrough, achieved around the time of the writing of the *Phenomenology*, was to see that this picture-thinking representation could be plumbed for a conceptual content suitable for thinking across a range of categorial modes—that this story of God might at once be the story of sociality, personal identity, and conceptual content itself. And so with the writing of the *Phenomenology* Hegel made philosophical cognition definitively preeminent over religious worship.

> §785 This self-consciousness therefore does not actually *die*, as the particular self-consciousness is pictured as being actually dead, but its particularity dies away in its universality, i.e. in its knowledge, which is essential Being reconciling itself with itself. The immediately preceding element of picture-thinking is, therefore, here explicitly set aside, or it has returned into the Self, into its Notion. (475)

Hegel came to see the story of God's incarnation, death, and resurrection as a story about any determinate identity whatsoever: "Everything is a *syllogism*, a universal that through particularity is united with individuality" (*Science of Logic* 669). With this he was prepared to fix the relation between religious worship and philosophical reflection. Religion throughout the ages teaches in picture-thinking form a truth about a people's identity, but philosophical reflection is required to take that truth out of its religious representation and cast it in the guise of thought (cf. *Phenomenology* §788, 479).

5. Autonomy and Modernity

Genuine freedom is for Hegel, as for Kant, autonomy rather than anomalousness. We are free not when our actions are undetermined, but when our actions are determined by a rule we recognize as self-legislated. Hegel also shares Kant's view of the Enlightenment as a project for the development of autonomous citizens. When freedom is understood as autonomy, the proper contrast is not with determinism but with heteronomy—we fail to be free when we are governed by rules that are not our own (or, in the case of alienation, when they are in fact our own and yet we do not recognize them as such). Hegel writes of this state under the guise of the Unhappy Consciousness section of the *Phenomenology of Spirit*. There Hegel considers a religious practice in which a people's values are made universal but only on condition that they

his spirit is most prominent in the Gospel of John, though it appears elsewhere in the New Testament and would become a cornerstone of Christian theology.

submit themselves to the external authority supposed to be the immutable source of these values.

> §230 Hence, for consciousness, its will does indeed become universal and essential will, but consciousness itself does not take itself to be this essential will. The surrender of its own will, as a *particular* will, is not taken by it to be in principle the positive aspect of universal will. (138)

The bare recognition of a capacity to determine our individual and social identities does not yet give us any determinate content for such an identity. Instead, that determination results from our coming together and trying to get things done. By collectively sharing some determinate purpose, something we all recognize as valuable and strive to see realized, we are by the nature of that practice obliged to begin sorting out the incompatibilities that are brought with it, contingently and as a function of the kind of task we have set for ourselves. Thus even if at the outset of our collective endeavor we do not share much in common, the practical constraints elicited by the cooperative activity necessary to realize a shared purpose will, over time, draw us closer together and specify the relations obtaining among us.[37] In this sense a shared purpose stands to the members of a community as a universal subsuming different individuals—for purposes are properties that can be common across all of us. And constellations of purpose, embodied in sets of values or social practices, can also operate as genus-universals subsuming each of as species under this common identity, obliging us to sacrifice those particularities (whether kind-identity or property) that are incompatible with the realization of these values. In this way our shared purposive activity tends to make us into a kind of thing we otherwise would not have been. Seen by these lights, the process of working out a social telos is the process of both (1) determining for ourselves individually what kind of particular persons we wish to be within our society, and (2) finding a higher-order purpose that subsumes our various particular purposes (finding a universal purpose that is an essential property of each of us as the particular kind, the member of *this* society, we are). The two aspects of this process are further specifications of the two sorts of abductive inference discussed in sections 2 and 3. Because our purposes define our self-identities, and because we are, as selves, pure being-for-self, we can use our individual and collective purposive action

---

37. This all depends upon having selected a purpose that will admit of such unity, and a willingness on the part of individuals to sublimate their particularities to the realization of that purpose, of course.

to shape institutional development so as to allow for and become radically new kinds of persons.

Hegel finds in religion just such a shared purposive activity uniting a people as particular individuals under a common universal: "The principle by which God is defined for human beings is also the principle for how humanity defines itself inwardly, or humanity in its own spirit" (*Lectures on the Philosophy of Religion*, 2:515 [1827]). The Christian religion is the religion that would give birth to modernity precisely because the purposes expressed in Christian forms of worship are at bottom, Hegel thought, the purposes that animate modern institutions—a community of self-determined persons standing in reciprocal recognition with one another, aware that by these practices they are constituting the social and personal identities realized within them.

This general theory of conceptual content interpreted through the lens of the incarnation can now be leveraged to give us a determinate conception of human beings. It is because Hegel thinks of human beings as certain *kinds* of things—embodied, social, autonomy-craving creatures—that the universal he proposed to draw us under is one that gives us some understanding of the particularities we find actually realized among us and our cultures. Hegel believes that this struggle for autonomy and recognition is a driving motivation for purposive activity on the part of self-consciousness, and thus he believes that historical transitions can be understood in terms of this struggle. Hegel will eventually be led to say, as he famously does in the introduction to his *Lectures on the Philosophy of History*, that "the History of the world is none other than the progress of the consciousness of Freedom" (19).[38]

It was this philosophical interpretation of the Revealed Religion, and the correlate reading of history as the gradual working out of the content of this idea in a form suitable to interpenetrate a society and communicate it to its members in a specific set of practices, that allowed Hegel to develop his mature system. At the center of this system is his interpretation of historical development as the development of this idea, an idea that gives the read on the nature of persons, societies, God, and conceptual content itself. Because he believes the Christian story of the divine expresses a truth about our social practices of self-determination, because he thinks this theo-political point is characteristic of the "life of the concept" itself, and because he thinks this life is driven by self-consciousness's innate urge for freedom and recognition, Hegel is willing to read the history of such human endeavors as art, religion, statecraft, and philosophy as particular instances of the way in which this universal, this

---

38. Hegel, *Lectures on the Philosophy of History*, trans. J. Sibree (New York: Willey Book Co., 1944).

concept of God, the self, society, and conceptual content itself, is actualized over the course of historical development.

6. From Faith to Trust

Given Hegel's interpretation of modernity as autonomy, it is not surprising that the submission to the will of the Lord exhibited in Abraham's willingness to sacrifice his son would be interpreted as an exemplification of pre-modern conceptions of the individual's relation to her community.[39] But whatever right there may be to conceive modernity as the development of autonomous communities, or to think of pre-modern tradition as laying the conceptual groundwork on which this self-knowing and the practices that support it could emerge, anyone who would think critically about Hegel's sociohistorical storytelling must take into consideration facts about the development of religious and political institutions that Hegel was unaware of.[40] But I leave an

39. Whether Christianity is much better situated to underpin modernity is subject to debate, of course. After all, it is central to the Christian mythos that God sacrificed *his own* son, while Abraham at the last received a reprieve—the lamb that replaced Abraham's son was the son of God himself in the Christian version of this sacrifice. Even if Trinitarian doctrine would have it that the sacrifice was self-determined, it does well to bear in mind Jesus' plea and resignation in the garden of Gethsemane, and the stories in Matthew and Mark of Jesus on the cross crying out to God asking why he has been abandoned. One finds submission to the will of the Lord in Christianity as well. And while I have not discussed this at all, I do want to register that Hegel's own view, though it develops over the course of the decade in which he gives the lectures, remains embarrassingly parochial and rather slap-dash when it comes to discussing non-Western religious traditions. This is especially evident when considering Hegel's treatment of Islam, which is practically nonexistent, and in the Eurocentric readings he gives of Hinduism, Buddhism, and Taoism.

40. To take only one line of thought relevant to Hegel's own project, consider that we now understand the ancient Egyptian religion to be much older than Hegel supposed, occurring not contemporaneously with ancient Judaism but predating it by over a millennium. And with the translation of Egyptian hieroglyphics we found that the story of divine death and resurrection, and its role in sociohistorical mythmaking, occurs already in the Pyramid Texts of the Old Kingdom, remaining a staple of the ancient Egyptian religious life. In this tradition each pharaoh upon his death was thought to be reborn as Osiris, the lord of the afterlife, while the new pharaoh was crowned as his son Horus. In this way the ancient Egyptian religious mythos played an important role in securing continuity and order within the ancient Egyptian community, and the transitions out of the lawlessness and subjugation to external rulers characteristic of the two Intermediate Periods in ancient Egyptian history (into the Middle Kingdom and New Kingdom respectively) were associated with a concerted return to these Old Kingdom traditions. Over the course of ancient Egypt's two thousand year history, this mythopoeic story was gradually disseminated out from being the exclusive right of the pharoah into first the royal court and educated upper classes until, by the Alexandrian period, anyone could purchase papyrus copies of the Book of the Dead at market for their own use in religious ritual. Add to this the rise of modern biblical scholarship, beginning in Germany in the decades after Hegel's death, together with what we have come

engagement with Hegel over the particulars of his philosophical anthropology for another time. Instead, I will close out this paper by returning to the logical and metaphysical insights that animate these facets of Hegel's *Realphilosophie*, in the process tying together the main themes at work in this discussion.

Abductive inquiry into nature proceeds according to a kind of faith we have in the order and regularity of an independent reality, an operation of the "instinct of reason creating an anticipation that this or that characteristic . . . has its root in the inner nature or kind of an object, and arguing on faith of that anticipation" (*Encyclopedia Logic* 254). Here our thought is obliged to conform itself to the implication and incompatibility relations that obtain independent of our will. But the determination of our understanding of our personal identities is not bound by a regularity fixed independent of our own activity.[41] I characterized this difference by saying that the abductive determination of personal and social identity is an autonomous process, not a heteronomous one. The practices constitutive of our social lives afford persons two dimensions of autonomous self-determination, one by the increase of a kind-term's extension and the other by the increase of its comprehension. The kind-terms at issue are those for such social identities as professional colleague, friend, neighbor, educator, and citizen of a nation.

As we saw, the abduction of a kind on the basis of a property increases a concept's extension by drawing a new individual under it. Persons engage in this process by individually binding themselves to the kind-identities that are available within their communities, choosing to exhibit those properties that are essential to the identities they subsume themselves under, and sacrificing those properties that are incompatible with that identity. The abduction of a property on the basis of a kind, by contrast, allows persons to change the comprehension of a kind-identity by instituting new relations of entailment and incompatibility fixed by the abduced property supposed to be essential to that identity. The former activity is the process whereby *individuals* determine who they will be within a society; the latter activity is the process whereby *groups* of individuals collectively determine what sorts of kind-identities will be recognized within that community, and so on the whole what kind of community they will be—once again, "just as the former exhibits the power

to understand concerning the doctrines and influence of the mystery religions in the ancient Mediterranean, and one must come away with a view on the sociohistorical significance of the Christian mythos that is somewhat unlike Hegel's.

41. This is not to deny the possibility of an essence of persons *qua* persons; it is just to note that most of what we are actually interested in by way of personal identity is not what some metaphysicians have christened with "essence."

of Spirit over its actual existence, so does the other exhibit the power of Spirit over the specific Notion of itself" (*Phenomenology of Spirit* §669, 407). These two sides of spirit's capacity for self-determination afford human beings a power unlike anything found in the inanimate and organic natural world. It also puts us into relations with one another that are likewise unknown in the nonspiritual world. Even though someone is of a certain kind in our community, and so has a certain status here, their capacity for self-determination means that we cannot be deductively ensured that they will exhibit the properties implied by that kind membership. We must, in a sense, take it on faith that they will.

This is not the faith we have in an independent reality whose determinations are fixed by natural law, however; it is the faith of persons standing in a reciprocal relationship with one another, each recognizing the other as a source of self-determination bound by various relations of obligation and permission. To talk about this difference we need a way of marking off the structural features of a community of heteronomous individuality from those features characteristic of societies with autonomous individuals. Call the former a community of faith and the latter a community of trust.[42] The community of faith is a community whose members are bound together by relations of self-determination that they do not recognize as self-determined. As against the community bound together by faith, the community of trust is united by relations of self-determination and reciprocal recognition among individuals who are aware of their roles in this process. In this they live as self-conscious spirit, expressions of a new form of identity that, prior to their engaging in this relationship with one another, did not exist. No community, of course,

42. Though he does not take up Hegel's discussion of religion, this distinction is partly owed to Robert Brandom's *A Spirit of Trust*, the manuscript for his reading of Hegel's *Phenomenology of Spirit*. It might seem that talk of "trust" is not the right way to frame the distinction I am marking here. For in section 147 of the *Philosophy of Right*, Hegel writes: "The subject is thus directly linked to the ethical order by a relation that is more like identity than even the relation of faith or trust," *Hegel's Philosophy of Right*, trans. T. M. Knox (New York: Oxford University Press, 1967). But the discussion surrounding this passage makes clear that there is no tension here. Hegel thinks that the ethical life of an individual, by which he means the body of laws and customs that define his community, is one that, properly understood, is not a *relation* that the individual stands in as an independent thing over and against another independent existent thing. We can put this point by saying that Hegel denies that one's national identity, say, is a two-place relation one stands in to one's nation. Instead, he thinks that individuals are *constituted* by their social identity—we might say they are one-place relations or unary predicates (perhaps more properly, they are kind-restricted quantifiers). None of this need conflict with the observation that to so constitute one's identity in this regard one must stand in relations of trust with one's fellows, as those fellows genuinely *are* independently existing things. My thanks to Brandon Hogan for bringing this passage to my attention.

can extricate itself from fate entirely; self-determination is subject to the contingencies of nature, and every autonomous community will have its own historically conditioned telos, something that its individuals must struggle to come to understand and direct. But a people whose spirit comes about as the result of their engaging with their fellows in the process of self-consciously constituting a recognitive community, collectively and individually making various trade-offs so as to form a more perfect union with one another by determining what will count as the kinds and properties that define them, is a people bound by relations of trust. In the practice of this form of life, which one might want to allow was a sort of worship (or a successor concept to it), a people place their faith not with an independent other, an implacable natural order or a lawgiver in dominion over his subjects, but with one another, living as mature, self-aware individuals in a society of equals.[43] Such a community stands in relations of *trust* with that (i.e. one another) which determines the property/kind relations characteristic of their identities, not one of *faith* with a supposedly immutable independent power.

The image of Abraham with his son on Mt. Moriah is an image of the very faith that Hegel thinks anathema to modernity. It is an image of a people bound together under a heteronomous abductive inference. This is not to say that for we Hegelians faith has no role to play in modern society; still less is it to deny someone like Johannes de silentio his Abraham, or to make light of the struggle for faith Johannes discusses. In fact, in the *Lectures on the Philosophy of Religion* Hegel frequently speaks of the need for the "witness of Spirit" in the individual lives of a religious community if its concept is to be realized, and it is easy to read Hegel agreeing with the admonishment in the epilogue to *Fear and Trembling* that

> every generation begins primitively, has no different task from that of every previous generation. . . . No generation has learned from another to love, no generation begins at any other point than at the beginning, no generation has a shorter task assigned to it than had the preceding generation.(108)

Compare this with Hegel's characterization of history in the final paragraph of the *Phenomenology of Spirit* as the "slow-moving succession of Spirits" that each self must in turn "penetrate and digest," needing to "start afresh to bring itself to maturity as if, for it, all that preceded were lost and it had learned nothing

---

43. Richard Rorty's *Achieving our Country: Leftist Thought in Twentieth-Century America* (Cambridge: Harvard University Press, 1998) merits consultation here.

from the experience of the earlier Spirits" (492). But Hegel can also say that while every generation must take up this task, and though this may require the witness of spirit, every *modern* generation must also struggle to come to *trust* with one another.[44] And the autonomy of trust is a social purpose that cannot be sustained by a submission of self to heteronomous faith.[45]

44. This is not to rule out the developmentally progressive viability of a future generation's coming to religious faith in the manner of self-abnegation, and one might look to the way in which the notion of submission has been used at different periods within Islamic cultures for a suggestion as to how such a faith might proceed ("Islam" from a word meaning "submission"). The current point is simply that any such faith would have to accompany the self-conscious self-determination, and warranted trust in one's fellows, if it were to count as a properly *modern* faith.

45. I do not mean to be suggesting that Kierkegaard (or Johannes) thinks such a faith could play this social role. It is central to the line of thought developed in *Fear and Trembling* that the faith emblematic of Abraham is one that operates *outside* the conventions of an ethical community, involving a "teleological suspension" of the ethical. These remarks are meant to help clarify Hegel's view rather than pit Hegel against Kierkegaard.

6

KIERKEGAARD

*Resignation and the "Humble Courage of Faith" in
Kierkegaard's Fear and Trembling*

Andrew Tebbutt

Among the several depictions of faith in Søren Kierkegaard's *Fear and Trembling*, the "teleological suspension of the ethical," an event in which faith effects a striking tension between one's relation to God and one's ethical duty, arguably takes center stage.[1] In the context of Abraham's obedience to God in offering his son as a sacrifice, faith appears as the means by which one can maintain devotion to "the absolute," while trusting that, in spite of one's own incapacity, the end result will be ethically harmonious. While the dramatic intersection between faith and ethics in *Fear and Trembling* offers no shortage of material for consideration, this paper approaches the notion of faith from a slightly different angle, inquiring about the manifestation of faith prior to any explicit ethical crisis or conflict of duties. Specifically, I ask here what sort of faith serves as the precondition that allows someone such as Abraham to be able to endure the trial concerning Isaac. Drawing on Johannes de silentio's description of the "pre-Moriah" Abraham, as well as his description of the knight of infinite resignation, I argue that faith, in its "first movements," is for Kierkegaard a kind of humility in which, before being able to endure a specific ethical crisis, one trustingly submits one's entire future to God as "the absolute." I will approach this particular interpretation of faith by way of John J. Davenport's treatment of the encounter between faith and ethics in *Fear and Trembling*.[2]

---

1. I would like to thank Ric Brown and Leo Stan for their helpful comments on earlier versions of this essay

131

On Davenport's reading, we are able to interpret Kierkegaardian faith not as requiring an eschewal of ethical norms and duties, but rather as a trusting expectation of an ethically sound resolution or vindication, gained, however, by virtue of an agency unfathomable by human understanding. For Davenport, rethinking God along the lines of a divine *fulfiller* of ethical norms (rather than simply as the founder of ethical norms, and also, somehow, as the author of an unethical command) provides the means by which to preserve the integrity of Kierkegaard's "absolute relation to the absolute" (faith) *and* the possibility of ethical hope (responsibility). In attempting to complement this eschatological reading of faith, I will first discuss the relation between faith and ethics in *Fear and Trembling*, making use of Davenport's analysis. I will then show how the "eternal validity" found in infinite resignation marks a failure to reach the kind of relation to the eternal that Kierkegaard envisions for faith. Drawing on Kierkegaard's notion of "the expectancy of faith" from his 1843 discourse, I will show how resignation not only falls short of eschatological trust in God as "Omega hope-fulfiller," but is more primordially closed off to God as "Alpha hope-provider," the latter being the figure of God in whom Abraham places his trust prior to the sacrificial ordeal. In short, my reading of *Fear and Trembling* is meant to show that individuals can trust God eschatologically as the fulfiller of ethical hopes only insofar as they have first overcome the obstinacy of resignation and have humbly related to God as the original (Alpha) provider of meaning and religious hope.

In "Faith as Eschatological Trust in *Fear and Trembling*," Davenport demonstrates that the famous Kierkegaardian "teleological suspension of the ethical" should not be understood as a total abandonment of ethics. Instead, faith signifies a kind of trusting orientation in which the ethical and the absolute converge by virtue of the former being preserved by the latter. As Davenport writes, "the *telos* toward which the ethical is suspended in Kierkegaardian faith is the *promised eschatological outcome* in which the highest ethical norms will be

---

2. I am indebted to Davenport's "eschatological" reading of faith in *Fear and Trembling* for providing the original impetus for the present essay. Presented in his "Faith as Eschatological Trust in *Fear and Trembling*," in *Ethics, Love and Faith in Kierkegaard*, ed. Edward F. Mooney (Indianapolis: Indiana University Press, 2008), Davenport's reading effectively distances Kierkegaard's text from any endorsement of the religious violation of ethical obligation, while equally avoiding the conclusion that Kierkegaardian faith amounts to total unintelligibility. Faith as eschatological trust, while it relinquishes human effort and knowing in placing its confidence in an absolute agent, nevertheless continues to hope for the (promised) fulfillment of ethical ideals. The present paper attempts to add to the eschatological reading an interpretation of faith as a kind of humility in which trust in an absolute agent receives its initial germination, prior to any specific ordeal requiring eschatological-ethical hope.

fulfilled by an Absolute power that transcends human capacities."[3] In trusting God absolutely, Abraham does not abandon his ethical hope that the sacrifice will not make him a murderer, but rather he abandons the possibility that *he himself* will be able to guarantee an ethical result *on his own strength or devising*. Davenport's basic conclusion is that Kierkegaard's God in *Fear and Trembling* must be understood as "Omega," that is, as the fulfiller of ethical hopes in whom the faithful, ethically minded person places her eschatological trust.

At the end of the "Preamble from the Heart" section of *Fear and Trembling*, de silentio reveals his intention to engage in a dialectical treatment of the paradox of faith, "in order to see how monstrous a paradox faith is . . . which no thought can grasp because faith begins precisely where thinking leaves off" (82).[4] In three philosophical *problemata*, de silentio addresses three questions regarding Abraham's sacrifice, and his faith that he would nevertheless continue to love Isaac in earthly life. First, is there some higher duty for the sake of which Abraham's ethical duty to love and protect Isaac is displaced as the highest human telos? Second, are human beings obligated absolutely to obey God's commands, as they appear and without hesitation or deliberation? Third, was Abraham's silence regarding the command privately given to him a selfish withdrawal, or is it somehow defensible within the scope of public ethical conduct? A crude account of de silentio's conclusions to these questions could take the following form: the ethical is not the highest telos for the human person, and hence can be suspended in cases in which it appears to be at odds with a person's absolute duty to God. Further, to the extent that one's duty to God addresses the individual in her private "concealment" (109), the suspension of the ethical entails the suspension of the universal, publicly accessible arena of meaning, in which case someone in Abraham's position cannot communicate his faith or God-relation to others. Among these points is contained the most basic teaching of the three *problemata*: while, on the one hand, de silentio instructs that the universal ought not to be conflated with the absolute, on the other hand he shows, in describing faith, that the universal (one's ethical obligations) and the absolute (one's duty to God) are in fact not at odds.

The encounter between faith and ethics depicted in the text, in which Isaac is somehow not ultimately murdered and Abraham's obedience remains ethically defensible, serves Kierkegaard's purpose of making a specific point about the nature of God. Put simply, Kierkegaard, in the latter half of *Fear and*

---

3. Davenport, "Faith as Eschatological Trust," 199.

4. Søren Kierkegaard, *Fear and Trembling*, trans. Alastair Hannay (London: Penguin Books, 1985). All parenthesized citations refer to *Fear and Trembling*.

Trembling, wants to show that a person's relation to God cannot be interchanged or substituted for a relation to the universal (here the ethical). Seen as early as halfway into *problema* 1, the result of the possibility of a teleological suspension of the ethical is that

> we see the need for a new category for understanding Abraham. Such a relationship to the divine is unknown to paganism. The tragic hero enters into no private relationship with God, but the ethical is the divine and therefore the paradox in the divine can be mediated in the universal. (88–89)

This "new category" assigned to Abraham implies a relationship to God, the "divine," that is beyond that occupied by "paganism" or the tragic, ethical hero. Following the emergence of this "new category," *problema* 2 makes a distinction between the will of God as absolute and all universal, ethical categories. However, in separating the figure of the divine from all universal mediation, de silentio does not intend to dispense with ethics. Once he has unveiled the absolute as the truly highest human telos, de silentio suggests the following:

> When people now say that it is a duty to love God, it is in a sense quite different from [that in which God is equated with a universal ethical principle]; for if this duty is absolute the ethical is reduced to the relative. It doesn't follow, nevertheless, that [the ethical] is to be done away with. Only that it gets a quite different expression, so that, e.g., love of God can cause the knight of faith to give his love of his neighbour the opposite expression to that which is his duty ethically speaking. (98)

On Davenport's reading, this modified expression of the universal is made possible in a situation in which an ethical obstacle is withstood by virtue of a more primary relationship to the divine absolute. The ethical is not "invalidated," but it is handled altogether differently to the extent that Abraham's love for Isaac is suspended *eschatologically*: Abraham's will to fulfill his ethical duty now relies on an objectively uncertain possibility in which he can only have faith.[5] To adjust the equation that begins the first *problema*, it is the absolute person (God) who "applies at every moment" on which depends my ethical duty, which "applies to everyone" (83). It is by entering into an absolute,

---

5. Davenport, "Faith as Eschatological Trust," 220.

exception-less relation to God that Abraham renders tempting any duty that is *strictly* ethical, that is, any duty that tempts him either to "absolutize" the universal or "universalize"—and thereby cheapen—the absolute, collapsing the divine figure into the universal in the form of an abstract principle or concept.

But what would inspire an ethically minded individual to enter into such an absolute relation? For Davenport, the answer is this: nothing short of a precisely *ethical* resolution. His point is that Abraham's faith, which does not amount simply to a higher ethic than the one suspended, but rather suspends duties to *all* universal norms, is directed toward the ultimate restoration even of ethical norms.[6] As he writes:

> Faith cannot consist in our being willing to violate our duties to love other persons in order to do something inspired by trust in an eschatological promise: *for . . . the content of such a promise is precisely the fulfillment of agapic ideals.* In fact, faith in such a fulfillment cannot require us to *do* anything beyond continuing to strive for ethical perfection: what it adds is a reason to trust, against all odds or apparent evidence, that our ethical wish can come true.[7]

On this reading, faith signifies the recognition of a failure to realize ethical hopes on the strength of individual human effort and the consequent eschatological trust that, nevertheless, such hopes can indeed be realized on the strength of a different or "higher" power. Thus, Abraham's trusting obedience to God does not mean that he abandons his love for or ethical duty toward his son. Rather, as de silentio writes, "Abraham must if possible love [Isaac] even more," when the demand falls on his ears; "only then can he *sacrifice* him" (101). In this way, central to Kierkegaard's text is the notion that existential faith, which is structured as an absolute devotion to that which transcends one's universal duty, possesses an eschatological content characterized by nothing other than ethical perfection.

Faith in God calls the individual to a duty that is *higher* than ethics, yet one that is not *opposed to* ethics. Davenport suggests that understanding the relation to the universal as "the agent's volitional response to moral ideals (such as loving those entrusted to her care)," and the relation to the absolute as "established by an eschatological promise reciprocated in trust" explains "how the first relation can be supported by the second."[8]

6. Ibid., 214.
7. Ibid., 218. Emphasis mine.
8. Ibid., 218.

That one's absolute relation to God is absolutely distinct from one's relation to the ethical does not prevent the first relation from being undertaken for the express purpose of sustaining the second. The crucial upshot of this ethical assurance is that it avoids reducing God to the universal, that is, reducing God to "an invisible, vanishing point, an impotent thought [whose] power is to be found only in the ethical, which fills all existence" (96). As de silentio says, if "the ethical is the divine and . . . the paradox in the divine can be mediated in the universal," then "no private relationship with God" is possible (89). Further, in faith the singularity of the individual believer is similarly rescued from such mediation. In the "private relationship" of faith, both God and the believer are individual "persons," and the particularity of each, while by no means unrelated or antipathetic to universals, is sustained against universalization, dissipation, or mediation. The God who promises ethical fulfillment is hence much more than a source of divine commands. As Davenport writes, "when faith is defined *existentially* as absolute trust in God's eschatological promise to us as unique individuals, then our duty to love God must in turn mean *more* than simply obeying God as the metaethical Alpha or source of moral norms; it also means trusting in God as Omega, the actualizer of revealed eschatological possibilities."[9]

Two basic conclusions can be drawn from the above. First, remaining devoted to the ethical requires having faith in God as absolute fulfiller when human efforts and calculations fall short. Our absolute duty to God is therefore to have faith in him. Second, the nature of this faith–relation reaches much deeper into one's personhood than would mere ethical duty. While in faith I can operate ethically—that is, according to the universal—I nevertheless locate my ultimate telos, and hence my own particular individuality, in the absolute that grounds the universal itself. In faith, as de silentio says, there is a "wonderful glory . . . in becoming God's confidant, the Lord's friend," related as person to person "in addressing God in heaven as 'Thou'" (105). In calling God "friend," I depend on him for the fulfillment of an ethical hope—the precisely *ethical* resolution in which we are *both* mutually interested.

Despite the terrifying transgression of ethics commanded by God, God is not Abraham's enemy. However, there is more than one way to call upon God as "friend." While the possibility of a relation to God as personal fulfiller has provided a necessary advancement on the severely limited concept of God as an ethical principle, there remains the question of the relation to God undertaken in infinite resignation. Infinite resignation is an art of spiritual transformation

---

9. Ibid., 216. Emphasis original.

in which, as de silentio reports, one's "love of God" is derived from one's "eternal consciousness" (77). In infinite resignation the individual lays claim to an "eternal validity" such that impossibilities discovered in the finite, temporal world can be renounced and spiritualized into possibilities "in an infinite sense" (75). Whereas in faith Abraham expects fulfillment of what he is promised in earthly life, in resignation one relocates one's hope in the eternal realm. This act employs the concept of the divine in a functional way, as that from which one derives one's eternal hope. While God is in this case certainly more than simply an ethical concept, a faith that is oriented toward finite, temporal existence engages with a figure of the divine beyond even that of infinite resignation.

In order to portray the posture of infinite resignation, de silentio uses the example of a young "lad" whose love for a particular princess is denied all possibility of being expressed and fulfilled in earthly life:

> [The lad's] love for the princess would take on for him the expression of an eternal love, would acquire a religious character, be transfigured into a love for the eternal being which, although it denied fulfillment, still reconciled him once more in the eternal consciousness of his love's validity in an eternal form that no reality can take from him. (72)

Recognizing the impossibility of the fulfillment of his beloved ideal, the lad recalibrates his love and directs it toward eternity. The eternal "validity" and love of "the eternal being" gained in resignation are the compensations for him whose love could not be realized in time. If there is love to speak of in infinite resignation, it is the "transfigured" love directed toward God in response to a finite impossibility. God replaces the beloved object, and where all earthly hope is disappointed, the achievement of an "eternal consciousness" is taken to be equivalent to a love of God (77). While this God, in whom one "reconciles" oneself, is more than a concept or signifier, the "eternal being" found in resignation functions as the "Omega" or divine fulfiller only in a limited sense, that is, as compensation for the loss of something *else*. Hardly the personal God who assures ethical vindication, the God of infinite resignation is nothing other than the spiritualized or eternalized form of all of one's earthly hopes.

With regard to the reference to "the eternal" in the context of resignation, I now turn to one of Kierkegaard's non-pseudonymous discourses entitled "The Expectancy of Faith," in which he states summarily that what faith expects is "victory—or, as Scripture so earnestly and so movingly teaches us, that all things must serve for good those who love God. But an expectancy of the future that expects victory—this has indeed conquered the future."[10] Davenport writes that this expectancy of faith "employ[s] our innate capacity to find meaning in the future," and he locates the specific expectancy of ethical fulfillment or vindication within the broader scheme of expectancy of victory and a conquered future.[11] In faith, one trusts God to fulfill what human effort and calculation cannot: in this sense, the future, as manifold open possibilities, is "conquered."[12] Thus, Abraham would count as one who possessed a hope among the manifold set of possibilities, his (ethical) future having been conquered by God's provision. Clarifying further, Kierkegaard explains that faith does not "speak of many victories," since "faith expects only one, or, more correctly, it expects victory."[13] Faith does not expect victory in matters taken individually; it does not even expect that *all* individual matters will be conquered or resolved. Faith expects nothing other than victory, that is, literally, no-*thing* other than that the future as a whole will become meaningful and will be conquered on the strength of the eternal. Faith demands, therefore, that one develops an expectancy "without a specified time and place," since having faithful expectancy in God means—originally—to open myself to *God's* future, not knowing what that could be.[14]

Kierkegaard adds that "by the *eternal*, one can conquer the future, because the eternal is the ground of the future, and therefore through it the future can be fathomed."[15] This reference to the eternal recalls the "eternal validity" boasted by the knight of infinite resignation; yet, as I have suggested, the relation to the eternal in infinite resignation falls short of that of faith. A question thus arises: is "the eternal" meant to signify that which grounds one's expectation of a conquered future, or the "eternal being" in which the resigned lover places his disappointed temporal hopes? Both faith and infinite resignation make appeals to the eternal as an essential precondition, so how can the difference between these two existential modes be accounted for?

I want to suggest that faith and resignation differ according to the way in which each mode treats God as "the eternal." Resignation appeals to the eternal as that which is diametrically opposed to temporality. Resignation achieves its

---

10. Søren Kierkegaard, *Eighteen Upbuilding Discourses*, trans. Howard V. Hong and Edna H. Hong (Princeton: Princeton University Press, 1990), 19.

11. Davenport, "Faith as Eschatological Trust," 199.

12. Ibid., 199.

13. Kierkegaard, *Eighteen Upbuilding Discourses*, 21.

14. Ibid., 23.

15. Ibid., 19, Emphasis mine.

"love of God" in expecting fulfillment of its hopes in "eternity," as it were. A resigned eschatology is directed away from the space of finite, actualizable possibilities, such that "no reality," as de silentio says, can render its eternal love invalid. By contrast, the "eternal" of Kierkegaard's upbuilding discourse is the ground of the future at "every moment," that is, *in time*. In faith, the whole of time, even present temporality, is conquered, in such a way that, as shown above, Abraham can have faith that Isaac will be returned in this temporal life. Thus, whereas infinite resignation appeals to an eternal God in an attempt to take leave of temporality, the knight of faith looks to the eternal as a reason to trust that all of time—one's future—is conquered.

In view of this contrast between faith and resignation, it is possible to demonstrate that resignation is ultimately self-deceived in its approach to God and to the world. I want to suggest that a clear understanding of the logic of resignation will aid in preventing the faithful relation to God—one in which the individual trusts God as fulfiller of ethical hopes and conqueror of the future—from collapsing into a resigned "love of God" that amounts to nothing more than a "transfigured" fixation. That is, while eschatological trust in ethical fulfillment is not necessarily tied to any one particular hope, it is possible for what may look like faith in God as the guarantor of final vindication or goodness to be simply a guise for an obstinate resignation. As is clear in the case of de silentio's lad, the resigned "love" of the eternal is the result of a rigid fixation on a particular worldly object. From this angle, the tension between resignation and faith is one between an expectation of something in particular and the expectation of nothing, that is, *nothing but victory*. But to expect nothing but victory is to trust that God is more than just a fulfiller of hopes, but that God is also the original *author* of the future as well. God must be, as it were, both Omega *and* Alpha.

Johannes de silentio introduces "the stage of infinite resignation" as the last stage through which Abraham passes on his way to faith, a stage that "disdains" the insouciance that it perceives in faith (66). Such an attitude, in placing value in the individual's ability to manipulate or have knowledge of his or her fate, reveals that resignation fails to recognize the true nature of the trusting expectancy of faith in which the unknown outcome of life is interpreted as "conquered" by God. De silentio, whose self-conscious resignation allows him to recognize the shortcomings of his own position, warns that "if one imagines one can be moved to faith by considering the outcome of this story, one deceives oneself, and is out to cheat God of faith's first movement, one is out to suck the life-wisdom out of the paradox" (66). What does de silentio's confession tell us about how infinite resignation, in its attempt to grapple with "outcomes," "sucks the life-wisdom" out of faith's "first movement"?

Answering this question requires turning to the "Speech in Praise of Abraham" in order to witness the "first movements" of Abraham's faith. There, de silentio makes three claims about greatness, which culminate in the statement that the "greatest of all" was great insofar as he loved God, expected the impossible, and strove (or struggled) with God. Assuming that Abraham satisfies each of these three criteria, this schema corresponds, albeit loosely, to the three acts of faith described in the "Speech." Abraham's ordeal concerning the sacrifice—the ostensible focus of the whole of the rest of the text—is thus the *third* act of faith he performs, as far as de silentio's eulogy is concerned. Not only did God "tempt" Abraham and ask for his beloved son as a burnt offering, but Abraham also "[left] the land of his fathers to become a stranger in the land of promise," and "accept[ed] the promise that all nations of the earth should be blessed in his seed" (52, 50, 51). Each of these acts is said to have been done by faith, and the presence of the first two movements works to support Alastair Hannay's reading that Abraham, in responding to the command, is attempting to "show God his faith" and "put the possibility of his continuing to exercise his [fatherly] concern into God's hands" (26). On Hannay's reading, Abraham must have, in some sense, possessed faith in God prior to the Akedah.

But in what sense, exactly, is it an already faithful Abraham that receives the terrifying command? De silentio notes—before any mention of the journey to Moriah—that Abraham "sacrificed everything" (50). I want to suggest that this "everything," while it certainly includes the final sacrifice for which Abraham is famous, is not limited to the ordeal with Isaac. Rather, a far more indeterminate, though by no means unchallenging, sacrifice preceded the dramatic ordeal:

> It was by faith that Abraham could leave the land of his fathers to become a stranger in the land of promise. He left one thing behind, took another with him. He left behind his worldly understanding and took with him his faith. Otherwise he would surely not have gone; certainly it would have been senseless to do so. It was by his faith that he could be a stranger in the promised land; there was nothing to remind him of what was dear, but the novelty of everything tempted his soul to sad longing. (50–1)

Here, there is a noticeable lack of any ethical crisis in need of eschatological faith: no human ethical striving is shown to come up short, nor is there any sign of hope for ethical resolution on the strength of the absurd. And yet, says de silentio, this act was undergone "by faith." The precise mode of faith depicted here recalls the posture of expectancy that Kierkegaard describes in "The Expectancy of Faith." There, it is said, one approaches the open manifold of the future by means of the eternal, that power, namely, that transcends the present such that the person of faith can return to a present that is wholly "conquered." Kierkegaard writes that the most uplifting and "ennobling" struggle, the "struggle with the future," is one carried out against the impulse to "change [the future] into something present, something particular; but the future is not a particular, but the whole."[16]To address the future in faith is to address it as a whole, that is, to entrust the whole of the future to the power of the eternal in such a way that, as was the case for Abraham, "everything" is conquered. In Abraham's willingness to become a "stranger in the land of promise," he surrendered all that was familiar to the author of the promise, resisting continually the temptation to retreat back into familiarity. Thus, prior to any eschatological expectation of a *particular* ethical vindication in the case of Isaac, Abraham's "first movement" of faith is characterized by the relinquishment of all particularity for the sake of an expectation that expects the "whole" future to be conquered. Similar to the way in which the knight of faith can declare "I nevertheless believe that I shall get her," Abraham thus believes that his future can be conquered, that he can be reassured in his longing, and that all the things he left behind would surely be returned on the strength of the eternal ground of the future.

We are now in a position to see how faith, the "first movement" of which is a submission of all worldly particularity by means of a trusting expectation of a conquered future, can achieve a relation to the eternal God beyond that of resignation. Characteristic of resignation is the self-deception by which one's inability to relinquish the object of one's love is cloaked by the pretense that one loves God. Yet it is only in faith that one's alignment with God, the eternal ground of the future, is genuine, since no sublimated attachment to a beloved worldly object interferes with the God-relation. In faith, one can say, "I am not deceived, since I did not believe that the world would keep the promise it seemed to be making to me; my expectancy was not in the world but in God."[17] Faith, as Kierkegaard writes, is not simply a human power directed *toward* the eternal in her attempt to escape the world, but is rather the "eternal power *in* a human being" that sustains her very engagement in worldly affairs.[18] Such

16. Ibid., 19.
17. Ibid., 23–24.
18. Ibid., 19.

unity with God through an original entrustment of one's future to an eternally assured victory is thus the counterpart to the unity with God that, through the convergence of ethical hope and absolute duty, prepares the way for particular tests of faith—tests that therefore take place in a world already conquered. The ability to shares a *telos* with the absolute (for Davenport, a specifically ethical one) is the result of one's willingness to dispense with one's own particular desires and adopt those of the absolute, eternal ground of all temporality. This is the sense in which one loves God, and why, as in *Works of Love*, Kierkegaard can say that love "connects the temporal and eternity."[19] In loving God one humbly surrenders one's whole world, future, familiarity, and particularity and invites God as eternal to be the ground of each. Prior to any ordeal concerning a particular object, therefore, the person of faith has withstood the victory of a "giving-up, getting-back" exchange that concerns particularity in general, absolutely.

The precise manner of loving God given in faith is reflected in terms of selfhood as a "second immediacy," which, as Robert L. Perkins writes, "has God as its center and source rather than the self." For Perkins, "the second immediacy, being grounded in the power that constituted it, is more primitive, that is, more basic to the self than an immediacy developed in the experience and history of the self."[20] In being rooted in the very power that gives rise to it, this immediacy allows for a genuine relation to God, the world and oneself, free from the sublimated hopelessness of resignation. Assured against self-deception, the self of the second immediacy relates to God as "Alpha," that is, as absolute ground and originator of its hopes and ends. As a "first movement" of expectancy that prepares for the individual's very entrance into the world, there is no "going further" than faith. Faith implies rather a perpetual humility before Alpha God—who amounts to far more than simply "the metaethical Alpha or source of moral norms"—in such a way that one is afforded a continually refreshed and renewed future, in that one can always expect and trust in God's victory.[21] Such a relation to the absolute makes faith's perpetual renewal enough for a human lifetime.

In characterizing faith as the expectation of nothing but victory, as trust in a conquered future, and as a self centered on God, we are in a position to

19. Søren Kierkegaard, *Works of Love*, ed. Howard V. Hong and Edna H. Hong (Princeton: Princeton University Press, 1998), 6.

20. Robert L. Perkins, "Abraham's Silence Aesthetically Considered," in *International Kierkegaard Commentary:* Fear and Trembling *and* Repetition, ed. Robert L. Perkins (Georgia: Mercer University Press, 1993), 167.

21. Ibid.

assess the precise pathology of resignation, which longs for a particular object, treats the future as altogether lost, and is ultimately self-centered. De silentio's portrait of resignation shows how, in falling short of faith, it lays claim to a certain "peace" at the hands of pride and self-effort. De silentio says that "in infinite resignation there is peace and repose; anyone who wants it, who has not debased himself by—what is still worse than being too proud—belittling himself, can discipline himself into making the movement" (74). The basic picture that emerges in the "Preamble from the Heart" is one in which resignation, recoiling into the "repose" of self-reliance in the face of disappointment, scorns any act of giving up of the beloved object as a sign of weakness or disintegration of the soul. Faced with temporal failure, the resigned individual can still take pride in her ability to quiet her soul and relocate her love in the eternal. Despite her boast that "it is only lower natures that imagine they are deceived," the resigned does not relate to the future or the eternal in the way that she imagines, since her love of God is simply self-love, for what reigns as absolute in the life of the resigned is the love-object that she has determined for herself (74).

The "first movement" of relinquishing the familiar and the particular exemplified by Abraham is viewed, from the perspective of resignation, as an act of forgetting, which, for one whose fixation on a beloved object is definitive of her existence, is an act to be avoided at all costs. Indeed, holding on to one's desire despite the temporal impossibility of its fulfillment is taken to be the precise virtue of resignation. As de silentio writes:

> The desire which would convey [the knight] out into reality . . . now bends inwards but is not lost thereby nor forgotten. At times it is the unconscious workings of the desire in him which awaken the memory, at others it is he himself that awakens it, for he is too proud to want to let the whole content of his life seem to have been but a fleeting affair of the moment. (73)

As this quotation makes clear, essential to the structure of resignation is the *refusal* to let go, surrender, or forget the love-object. Resignation depends on "the strength to concentrate the whole of [one's] life's content and the meaning of reality in a single wish" (72). The pride found in one's ability to maintain a virtuous commitment to this wish makes faith appear to the resigned as a weak fault of "lower natures" which one must actively resist:

> So the knight makes the movement, but what movement? Does he want to forget the whole thing? Because in that too there is a kind of concentration. No! for the knight does not contradict himself,

> and it is a contradiction to forget the whole of one's life's content
> and still be the same. He has no inclination to become another,
> seeing nothing at all great in that prospect. Only lower natures forget
> themselves and become something new. (72)

I want to suggest that if Abraham did indeed pass through the stage of infinite resignation as de silentio suggests, the precise point at which this would have taken place would be the threshold of the first movement of faith. If overcoming resignation requires "forgetting" oneself and one's particularized "life's content," then it is clear that the willingness to step into the empty and the unfamiliar and thus re-create one's particularity (to become something new) on the power of the absolute is the remedy. But resignation is proud of not being a "lower nature" and would not have the individual belittle himself in this way. To waver—and anything but an adamant fixation on the love-object would be considered wavering by the resigned lover—"is not the manner of the knight of infinite resignation, he does not renounce the love, not for all the glory in the world" (71). The resigned lover is content to remain within the wholly familiar, having already determined the content of his victory, and thus precluding any possibility in which victory could be won in the temporal.

Resignation abides by the further maxim that "it is only lower natures who have the law for their actions in someone else, the premises for their actions outside themselves" (73). Rather than relinquish his own particularity and relocate his expectancy in the empty, unspecified victory of God's future, the resigned is content to find meaning, assurance, and confidence in his own ability to remain steadfastly connected to the eternal, through his own proud act of compensation in the face of failure. The strategy of resignation in being "sufficient unto oneself" is certainly possible, if the goal is nothing other than an "eternalized" fixation on a beloved object (73). Faith, on the other hand, promises diversity—indeed the whole world becomes an occasion for victory, as suggested by the dynamic existence of the polymorphous figure imagined by de silentio, who "delights in everything he sees" (69). The irony of de silentio's confession is that while resignation refers pejoratively to those "lower natures" whose faith resembles weakness, it is precisely by becoming "lower," that is, by becoming humble, that one approaches the Abrahamic relation to God as Alpha provider. In fact, when de silentio talks specifically about himself, it is not with the condescending tone of the proudly resigned, but it is as one who has understood that his "courage is not that of faith" (63). De silentio's is a confession that the path out of resignation is slow, arduous, and lined with failures, and he cautions his reader against the desire to immediately expect the reception of her beloved object. "I cannot close my eyes and hurl myself trustingly into the absurd," admits de silentio; "for me it is impossible, but I do not praise myself on that account" (63). Indeed, our author is not proud, yet there is something that he too loves more dearly than the absolute, confining him to his own inward-turned desires, such that his relation to God is, unlike Abraham, "incommensurable with the whole of reality" (63).

Johannes de silentio is an observer who has allowed Abraham's life of faith to shed light on his own shortcomings. His response is to nudge the reader toward the commensurability with the absolute that he himself lacks. But this does not require that anyone who would have faith must endure the sort of trial that Abraham faced at Moriah. Rather, among the most applicable teachings of *Fear and Trembling* is the one exemplified in the first movements of Abraham's faith, namely that a humble submission of one's particular desires in view of the conquered future provided by God is the first weapon to be wielded in the struggle against the future. And such a struggle consists of cultivating the *capacity* to endure ordeals, that is, the capacity to trust God eschatologically. In paying special attention to the nature of infinite resignation, we are thus given a glimpse into the proud self-devotion and self-deceiving exploitation of the eternal that the first movements of faith are meant to overcome. Faith makes possible an alignment of oneself and one's hope with God in two senses: first, as one places in suspension all of one's particular hopes on the strength of a divinely conquered future, and second, as one trusts that one's ethical hopes are shared, and ultimately fulfilled, by God. And while the terrifying aspect of the binding of Isaac takes center stage in *Fear and Trembling*, it is possible that the original cultivation of faith in which one learns to practice the humility of hoping for nothing but God's victory, though comparatively subtle, offers an equally challenging set of obstacles. To borrow de silentio's warning, those intimidated by the task of relinquishing their own preferences and self-effort "must be honest and not pass off this lack of courage as humility, since on the contrary it is pride, while the courage of faith is the only humble courage" (101).

PART III

Post-Traditional Readings

7

———————

KAFKA

A Tale of Two Abrahams

Matthew T. Powell

> *I have vigorously absorbed the negative element of the age in which I live, an age that is, of course, very close to me, which I have no right ever to fight against, but as it were a right to represent. . . . I have not been guided into life by the hand of Christianity——admittedly now slack and failing——as Kierkegaard was, and have not caught the hem of the Jewish prayer shawl——now flying away from us——as the Zionists have. I am an end or a beginning. (February 25, 1918)*

Five months after being diagnosed with an acute case of tuberculosis that would eventually take his life, Franz Kafka found himself (and the world) at a crossroads. A man already prone to introspection and existential angst, now faced with the prospect of a premature death, Kafka felt himself on the edge of existence more keenly than ever. For Kafka, the modern world and he with it had finally come to rest at the very edge of the immeasurable expanse that separates humanity from God. In his biography of Kafka, Max Brod would say of his close friend that "no one was so burningly conscious of the 'distance from God' as he was."[1] In the post-Enlightenment, post-Romantic, postmodern world the individual had been freed from the bonds of religion, and like a lost child had wandered dangerously close to the edge of an abyss, giving rise to the existential. There, on that edge, Kafka (and the world) would be forced to find their way across the expanse or to abandon the prospect altogether.

In the five months following his diagnosis, Kafka ended his second (and final) engagement to Felice Bauer and broke free from their five-year relationship. He took an extended leave from his duties at the Worker's Accident Insurance Institute for the Kingdom of Bohemia. He quit his diaries, choosing only to document some narrative fragments and aphorisms in a series of notebooks.[2] And he renewed his interest in the writings of the nineteenth-century Danish philosopher, Søren Kierkegaard, whom he had turned to years earlier in his first attempts to remove himself from his relationship with Felice. Kafka's first written reference to Kierkegaard some five years prior claimed quite earnestly, "He bears me out like a friend."[3]

In 1918, however, years after the birth of this "friendship," Kafka's interest in Kierkegaard was directed more toward the philosophical and less toward the personal. It was Kierkegaard's discussion of Abraham, and most especially his portrayal of faith through an elaborate exposition of the Akedah story, that interested Kafka at this time. What Kafka found in Kierkegaard was a scholar not afraid to accept that the individual is fundamentally alone in the universe. As a result, what had begun for Kafka as a search for justification of his personal actions had turned into an existential kinship that crossed time and culture. For it was Kierkegaard who approached the gap between God and humanity not with awe and wonder but with a firm resolve that humanity could go no further until it had come face-to-face with the abyss and accepted the absolute fracture between the transcendent and the mundane. Humanity must come to accept that it is defined not by its proximity to the divine Other, but by the overwhelming distance that defines the relationship. In a series of diary entries, journal reflections, and letters to friends that span a ten-year period, we can witness Kafka attempting to engage Kierkegaard in his depiction of faith as that which bridges the gap between human and divine. At the center of this discourse is the figure of Abraham, sent by God to the mountain of Moriah

1. Max Brod, *Franz Kafka: A Biography* (New York: Da Capa Press, 1960), 180.

2. Shortly after his diagnosis, Kafka stopped writing in his diary and switched to what are now referred to as the "Blue Octavo Notebooks." Max Brod describe these tiny one-eighthsized notebooks as the "kind we used to call 'vocabulary notebooks' at school." This material is far less personal and more apt to be called a journal than a diary. Kafka would return to writing in his diary in June of 1919.

3. Franz Kafka, *The Diaries: 1910–1923*, ed. Max Brod, trans. Joseph Kresh and Martin Greenberg (New York: Schocken Books, 1976), 230.

to sacrifice his long-awaited son. This apparently random series of comments and reflections, written by Kafka some seventy years after Kierkegaard's *Fear and Trembling*, amounts to a unique conversation concerning the nature and function of faith in the modern world.

In November of 1917, Kafka would write to his close friend Oskar Baum, "I know only *Fear and Trembling*."[4] In the years that followed, Kafka would also read (and re-read) *Either/Or* and *Repetition*. These three texts, along with a published edition of Kierkegaard's late diaries and two popular biographical works on Kierkegaard published in Kafka's lifetime, formed the likely extent of Kafka's knowledge of the Danish philosopher.[5] And yet, Kafka's remarks in regard to Kierkegaard indicate a unique insight into Kierkegaard's depiction of the human condition, the struggle of faith, and the fundamental nature of the absurd. Indeed, it is in *Fear and Trembling* that Kierkegaard posed his most piercing question about the human existential condition that Kafka would, almost a century later, feel compelled to answer: "What if the lonely man who climbs the mountain in Moriah . . . who treads surefootedly over the abyss . . . should be distracted, what if he has made a mistake?"[6]

THE DEMANDS OF THE MODERN EXISTENTIAL CONDITION

For Kafka and Kierkegaard, it is the gap between the finite and the infinite that defines the human condition and places the individual firmly on the edge of existence. It is this existential dialectic that dominates the work of both men. The conviction of the self as fundamentally alone is the starting point of existential thought. It defines the individual as both isolated in and estranged from the universe. The recognition of this fact leads the individual to fear and despair, and compels a search for a solution to this estrangement. In existential thought, the individual is most fully aware that he or she is both alone and finite. And yet, the individual is also capable of conceiving both communion with that which is other than the self and the infinite. In other words, the individual in accepting (defining) his or her reality as temporal and particular does so over against what is dialectically opposite. In defining the self as particular, the individual affirms the universal. In defining the self as finite, the individual

4. Kafka, *Letters to Family, Friends, and Editors*, trans. Richard and Clara Winston (New York: Schocken Books, 1977), 162.

5. *Das Buch des Richters*, published in 1909, was the first text by Kierkegaard to be read by Kafka in August 1913. He would later also read *Sören Kierkegaard. Sein Leben Und Seine Werke* by O. P. Monrad (1909), and *Sören Kierkegaard und sein Verhaltnis zu ihr* by Raphael Meyer (1905).

6. Søren Kierkegaard, *Fear and Trembling* (New York: Penguin Books, 1985), 90.

affirms the infinite. And in defining the self as qualified, the individual affirms the absolute. The result is the revelation of a wide gulf that stretches between this life and what exists outside of this life and defines it. The existential realization rips open a gaping chasm between this world and that which exists outside of this world and defines it. As a result every individual is trapped between the self as limited and particular and the divine Other as limitless and universal.

Somewhere within this tension between the self as finite and the Divine as infinite there exists the necessity of choice. The very fact that we are aware of our condition, but also simultaneously aware of the possibility of the self, forces the self to choose between the finite and the infinite—to choose between isolation and communion. For Kierkegaard, this choice is necessary in order to become truly human. "If a person could continually keep himself on the spear tip of the moment of choice," he or she "could stop being human."[7] But once we have realized the abyss between human and God, once we have defined ourselves in terms of the possibility of ourselves, we must decide our relationship to the universal, the absolute, the infinite. We must decide our relationship to the Divine. And this "original choice is forever present in every succeeding choice."[8] The existential dialectic compels a synthesis. It compels a choice that is continuously present. For Kafka, this choice requires the acknowledgement of the Divine, but does not hold the possibility of synthesis. There is no unequivocal solution to the existential dilemma, only compromise. Embracing the finite and ignoring the possibility of the infinite is our only solution to the existential dilemma. It is our only hope to escape suffering, and our only hope for happiness. "Theoretically there is a perfect possibility of happiness: believing in the indestructible element in oneself and not striving towards it."[9] This is the crossroads where Kafka found himself and his world at the beginning of the twentieth century, a crossroads defined by Kierkegaard in the middle of the nineteenth century.

Having chosen to define the human condition in terms of the existential dialectic, which in turn produces the space between God and humanity, both Kierkegaard and Kafka also shared a distinct understanding of what defined that space: the absurd. It is the absurd that most accurately exposes and explains the gap between the finite and the infinite. In using the Abraham story to explore

7. Kierkegaard, *The Essential Kierkegaard*, ed. Howard V. Hong and Edna H. Hong (Princeton, NJ: Princeton University Press, 2000), 72. From *Either/Or, A Fragment of Life*.

8. Ibid., 80.

9. Kafka, *The Blue Octavo Notebooks*, ed. Max Brod, trans. Ernst Kaiser and Eithne Wilkins (Cambridge, MA: Exact Change, 1991), 52

the possibility of faith, Kierkegaard chose a literal interpretation of the exchange between God and humanity transforming it into a metaphor for the absurd—and for faith. This exchange can be understood in no other terms than the absurd. Anything less would limit the Divine or elevate the human in a way that fails to accept the existence (or extent) of the gulf that rests between them. In describing Abraham's response to the Divine, Kierkegaard frames the discourse in terms of the exchange between finitude and infinitude.

> He resigned everything infinitely, and then took everything back on the strength of the absurd. He is continually making the movement of infinity, but he makes it with such accuracy and poise that he is continually getting finitude out of it, and not for a second would one suspect anything else.[10]

The movement between the finite and the infinite, between human and Divine can only be characterized as absurd. To reclaim the self once it has been abandoned to the abyss the individual must possess faith, and that faith is grounded in (and defined by) the absurd.

Inevitably, what distinguishes Kierkegaard from Kafka (and vice versa) is their respective understanding of the capacity of faith. The gap between God and human produced by the existential dialectic and defined by the absurd forces the individual to search for a solution to the estrangement between the self and God. For Kierkegaard, faith is the solution to the alienation that is fundamental to the human condition. Faith allows the individual to bridge this gap between God and human. For Kafka, faith is not defined by the absurd. It is merely a mask for the absurd. It is the veil that covers over the gap between God and humanity. Faith is simply that which sustains existence in the finite by covering the immediate presence of the absurd (and the gap) for the individual. For Kierkegaard, faith defines what is possible. It does not close the gap between God and human, but it does allow the individual to traverse the gap and radically alter his or her existence. In this way, Kierkegaard defines faith as transformative, as fundamentally altering the existential human condition. For Kafka, faith does not close the gap between God and human, nor does it afford the individual the opportunity to cross the expanse. Instead, faith is the sole requirement for existence on this side of the abyss. Its only ability is to sustain the individual in this world. The "mad strength of faith" is necessary merely to suffer through this world.[11] It emboldens us to accept the finite in the

---

10. Kierkegaard, *Fear and Trembling*, 70.
11. Kafka, *Blue Octavo Notebooks*, 54.

face of the infinite. Without faith, life itself is unbearable. For Kafka, Abraham is not the model of faith because he is able to transcend this world and connect to the Divine in an intimate, personal, and transformative way. Abraham is the model of faith because he is able to blindly accept the absurd nature of a personal devotion to (and conviction of) an invisible absolute. Abraham's faith rests on his ignorance. It rests on his absolute trust in the distinction between his finiteness and God's infiniteness.

KIERKEGAARD'S ABRAHAM

> O, once I am dead, *Fear and Trembling* alone will be enough for an imperishable name as an author. Then it will be read, translated into foreign tongues as well. The reader will almost shrink from the frightful pathos in the book.[12]

Fear and Trembling is a comprehensive account of Abraham as the "Father of Faith" and as the model for the individual confronted by God. For Kierkegaard, faith is both the work of a lifetime and the lifetime effort of the individual to respond to the Divine. And in *Fear and Trembling*, Kierkegaard (via Johannes de silentio) constructs a multi-dimensional view of faith as the unique exchange between the individual and the Divine that produces an inexplicable transformation. Kierkegaard presents the story of Abraham as the story of every person. We are all called by God to respond as completely distinct and autonomous beings in utter freedom to the divine offer to enter into a relationship that places us above the universal and in a complete and direct relationship with the absolute.

Kierkegaard's Abraham is a man fundamentally alone and thoroughly challenged by God. As such, he is for Kierkegaard a true existential hero. When confronted by God, Abraham has the choice to respond to God or to ignore God. To respond to God and completely resign the self to the Divine is to understand faith as "that power whose strength is powerlessness."[13] It is to seek "wisdom whose secret is folly."[14] It is to have "hope whose outward form is insanity."[15]

12. Kierkegaard, *Journals and Papers*, electronic source (Charlottesville, VA: InteLex Corporation, 1995), 6.221 (X.2 A 15).

13. Kierkegaard, *Fear and Trembling*, 50.

14. Ibid.

15. Ibid.

It is the choice of faith. The choice of faith is one made in "cosmic isolation"[16] where no other individual can know the "terrible responsibility of solitude,"[17] where only "God sees in secret and knows the distress and counts the tears and forgets nothing."[18] Abraham's response to God at this particular point in time is a singular example of an infinite number of choices faced over a lifetime. In responding to God's command to sacrifice Isaac, Abraham faces the same choice every individual faces every day, and all day. Every individual is constantly confronted by God and challenged to respond to the call of faith. And to respond to the call of faith is to exclaim, "Here I am!"

The choice faced by the individual confronted by the divine in isolation is the demarcation between the ethical and the religious stage of existence. It is the line that separates our responsibility to this world from our responsibility to what defines this world. It is the entrance to the bridge that joins the finite to the infinite. Kierkegaard's Abraham is no ethical hero. He is an existential hero. He is a hero of faith. As such, it is the movement of Abraham from the ethical stage to the religious stage that marks him (and this story) as a true exemplar. Abraham at Moriah is a metaphor for the personal encounter between God and human that occurs to all humans at all times. In this way, the opportunity presented to Abraham at Moriah is the same opportunity presented to all individuals all the time.

The difference between the ethical and religious stage of existence is that the ethical stage is universally applicable, while the religious stage is uniquely particular. The ethical stage applies to all individuals at all times. The religious stage applies only to the specific individual and only at a particular moment (and consequently at every particular moment). The religious stage transcends the ethical stage because the ethical stage is simply the relationship of the individual to the world (the finite), while the religious stage is the relationship of the individual to God (the infinite).

> Faith is just this paradox, that the single individual as the particular is higher than the universal, is justified before the latter, not as subordinate but superior, though is such a way be it noted, that it is the single individual who, having been subordinate to the universal as the particular, now by means of the universal becomes that individual who, as the particular, stands in absolute relation to the absolute.[19]

16. Ibid., 107.
17. Ibid., 138.
18. Ibid., 144.

Before the events at Moriah, Abraham is a champion of the ethical. He is a knight of resignation who has gained access to the universal by continually seeking the greater good. After Moriah, Abraham is the champion of faith. He is a knight of faith who has transcended both the ethical and the universal by subordinating the universal to the self and subordinating the self to God. As a result, Kierkegaard's Abraham makes God absolute rather than universal. His duty in faith is to the absolute, not the universal. "The single individual as the particular is higher than the universal and as the particular stands in absolute relation to the absolute."[20]

And yet, the faith of Kierkegaard's Abraham does not simply connect him to the Divine. Abraham's faith is a faith for this world. "Abraham had faith, and he had faith for this life."[21] The bridge of faith that Kierkegaard proposes does not simply transport the individual from the finite to the infinite, it connects the finite to the infinite. Kierkegaard's bridge of faith runs both ways. "His faith was not that he should be happy sometime in the hereafter, but that he should find blessed happiness here in this world."[22] As Abraham transcends this world and the ethical in order to connect to the Divine, he does not abandon this world. In fact, the double movement of faith proposed by Kierkegaard claims that in transcending this world by subordinating it to the self, the individual regains this world more fully than before. The double movement of faith enables the individual to gain access to the infinite while in turn gaining greater understanding of the finite. As such, Abraham's faith does not lead him to resign himself to the loss of Isaac. In fact, his faith produces quite the opposite. Abraham's faith allows him to realize that in sacrificing Isaac he will regain Isaac. "Through faith Abraham did not renounce his claim on Isaac, through his faith he received Isaac."[23] This fact is fundamental to understanding Kierkegaard's conception of the double movement of faith. God could take Isaac by Abraham's hand if God wanted to, but God could also "give him a new Isaac, bring the sacrificial offer back to life."[24] This is the absurd upon which the whole of Abraham's faith must rest. It is the absurd upon which all of faith rests.

Kierkegaard chose the Akedah story as the supreme example of faith not because Abraham was called upon by God to sacrifice his son, but because Abraham was called upon by God to sacrifice Isaac after having been told by

19. Ibid., 84–85.
20. Ibid., 108.
21. Ibid., 53.
22. Ibid., 65.
23. Ibid., 77.
24. Ibid., 65.

God that through Isaac his descendants would equal the number of stars in the heavens. As a result, Abraham was not simply called upon to sacrifice his only child. He was commanded to sacrifice Isaac and still believe that through Isaac a multitude of descendants would arise. Such a proposition is not hard to believe; it is truly absurd. Faith is not believing in the possible, it is holding firm that the impossible is true, that the impossible is the only possible outcome. In the absurd faith becomes possible. This was the revolution of Kierkegaard's thought, that faith while dependent on historical events was not dependent on reason. Instead, faith must be understood in terms separate from reason. Abraham "believed on the strength of the absurd, for all human calculation had long since been suspended."[25] To have faith in God, Abraham must necessarily believe that Isaac will not be lost.

The reward of faith for Kierkegaard is the transformation of the self. Faith bridges the gap between God and human, connecting the infinite to the finite and granting an "eternal consciousness." In faith the possibility of the self is realized in full. The transformation granted in faith is the realization of the possibility of the self in full communion with the divine Other. Faith grants the individual an absolute connection with the absolute. It enables free and complete access to the infinite, and therein to the finite. The individual, once in isolation, is now in complete communion. The individual, once estranged, is now fully reconciled——with the self and with that which defines the self.

> This movement is one that I make by myself, so what I win is myself in eternal consciousness, in a blessed compliance with my love for the eternal being. Through faith I don't renounce anything, on the contrary in faith I receive everything, exactly in the way it is said that one whose faith is like a mustard seed can move mountains.[26]

The radical transformation of faith is that it completely removes our limits. In our existential isolation, we are limited to the finite. In faith we are granted access to the finite and to that which exists outside the finite and defines the finite. Faith is the ability to realize the self in and through the Divine. Kierkegaard's Abraham represents the human ability to completely abandon the self in the effort to fully realize the self. The story of Abraham and Isaac at Moriah, as told by Kierkegaard, is the story of a man who through God was able to transcend his limited isolation, to commune with the Divine, and to realize the absolute possibility of the self.

25. Ibid.
26. Ibid., 77

KAFKA AND KIERKEGAARD

18 December. All this time in bed. Yesterday *Either/Or.*[27]

Right up to the end of his life Kafka was reading Kierkegaard. This penultimate entry into his diaries from late in 1922 indicates that Kierkegaard was still very much on the mind of Kafka as he struggled toward death. Nearly completely bedridden at this point, he would write only one more time in his diary in June of 1923——a caustic note about the pain and monotony of dying and the hopelessness of his vocation as a writer——and would be dead a year later. The wealth of material we possess by Kafka concerning Kierkegaard stretches from August of 1913 right up to some of the last words he would put on paper. This material spanning nearly ten years does not display a single cohesive attitude or approach to the religious philosophy of Kierkegaard. Instead, what we see is an evolution of thought on both the person and ideas of Kierkegaard.

Kafka began his relationship with Kierkegaard in 1913 by reading a selection of Kierkegaard's journals published in 1909 under the title *Das Buch des Richters*. Coming a year after meeting Felice and a year before their first engagement, Kafka turned to Kierkegaard's journals to locate an individual who "despite essential differences" shared a "case very similar to my own."[28] Much like Kierkegaard, Kafka struggled greatly with the tension between his vocation as a writer and the social responsibility he felt to marry and start a family. Brod notes Kafka's reading of Kierkegaard's journals, telling us that from these texts "the similarity between Kierkegaard's fate and his own [became] clear to him [Kafka]."[29] Kierkegaard quickly became for Kafka a model by which to measure himself. In a diary entry from 1916, Kafka would claim that Kierkegaard "knew very clearly how matters stood" and was not afraid to make a decision.[30] The decisiveness Kafka admired in Kierkegaard centered clearly on his ability to walk away from his relationship with Regine in order to pursue his true vocation as a writer. Kafka faced the same decision in the spring of 1914.

In April of 1914, Kafka became officially engaged to Felice for the first time. In March of that same year we find an exhaustive entry in his diary where Kafka debates the decision to marry and lead a "normal" life or to pursue the "unique aspiration and sole vocation" he knew was his only means of survival.[31]

27. Kafka, *The Diaries*, 423.

28. Ibid., 230.

29. Brod, *Franz Kafka*, 144.

30. Kafka, *The Diaries*, 370.

This struggle between pursuing a normal life and his vocation as writer would define Kafka for the rest of his life.

> An official's life could benefit me if I were married. It would in every way be a support to me against society, against my wife, against writing, without demanding too many sacrifices, and without on the other hand degenerating into indolence and dependence, for as a married man I should not have to fear that. But I cannot live out such a life as a bachelor. . . . I couldn't marry then; everything in me revolted against it, much as I always loved F. It was chiefly concern over my literary work that prevented me, for I thought marriage would jeopardize it. I may have been right, but in any case it is destroyed by my present bachelor's life. I have written nothing for a year, nor shall I be able to write anything in the future.[32]

By July the engagement would be broken, only to be renewed again a few years later. The diary entries in between the start of the engagement and its end indicate a man overcome by indecision and desperate to free himself from the call to normalcy that had entrapped him. At the end of July 1914, Kafka was desperate to re-commit himself to his writing. "I am more and more unable to think, to observe, to determine the truth of things, to remember, to speak, to share an experience; I am turning to stone, this is the truth. . . . If I can't take refuge in some work, I am lost."[33] And three days later:

> Now I receive the reward of living alone. But it is hardly a reward; living alone ends only with punishment. Still, as a consequence, I am little affected by all the misery and am firmer in my resolve than ever. . . . I will write in spite of everything, absolutely; it is my struggle for self-preservation.[34]

When we find Kafka again focused on Kierkegaard, some four years later, he is singularly interested in the theology of the man, having finally decided that "the 'physical' similarity to him that I imagined I had after reading that little

31. Maurice Blanchot, in his essay "Kafka and the Work's Demand," does well to explain Kafka's overwhelming compulsion to write. According to Blanchot, Kafka's commitment to his writing was more than a choice, it was a necessity. See Blanchot, *The Space of Literature*, trans. Ann Smock (Lincoln, NE: University of Nebraska Press, 1982), 57–83.

32. Kafka, *The Diaries*, 262.

33. Ibid., 295.

34. Ibid., 300.

book . . . has by now entirely evaporated."[35] Max Brod, in referencing his letters with Kafka from this time, states, "They throw light on Kafka's studies of Kierkegaard, which grew deeper and deeper, and on his religious and ethical development."[36]

Early in his relationship with Kierkegaard, Kafka looked to Kierkegaard as a mentor and as a figure whose vocational call could serve as a model for his own desire to forgo social expectations and pursue the solitude necessary to write. In his personal writings following the diagnosis, however, Kafka's interest in Kierkegaard transformed into an examination of the philosophical kinship shared by the two men. During his remaining years, Kafka was fascinated by two texts in particular, *Fear and Trembling* and *Either/Or*.[37] Of these two texts *Fear and Trembling*, and especially its depiction of Abraham, would promote the greatest response from Kafka. It was this text that Kafka would request that Max Brod read, sparking a debate that would provoke Kafka's most extensive output concerning Kierkegaard.[38]

Kafka's most explicit material regarding *Fear and Trembling* comes from two distinct points in his later life. The first extensive discussion of Abraham comes from the period shortly after his diagnosis. During this time we find a series of letters from Kafka to Brod where the topic of Kierkegaard's theology has become central to their correspondence. In conjunction with these letters we also find a series of journal entries, written at the same time, that reference many of the concerns being addressed in his letters to Brod.[39] The second overt reference to *Fear and Trembling* comes from a letter to Robert Klopstock three years later in 1921. Klopstock was a doctor and fellow patient whom Kafka met during his diagnosis. He became one of Kafka's closest friends through the last years of his life, eventually serving as Kafka's primary caregiver in his final days. The impetus behind this letter, which stands out as much for its lack of context as its content, is unknown. No other decidedly Kierkegaard-related material from this period is available, but one can plausibly assume that Kafka had begun a similar discussion with Klopstock concerning Kierkegaard as he

---

35. Kafka, *Letters to Friends, Family, and Editors*, 199. The "little book" referred to here is *Kierkegaard's Relationship to "Her" (Sören Kierkegaard und sein Verhaltnis zu ihr)*. See n5.

36. Brod, *Franz Kafka*, 164.

37. Kafka's feelings about *Either/Or* appear to be mixed. Of the multiple references made to this text throughout his *Nachlass*, some speak of the text as illuminating while others decry its "hatefulness" and "repugnance." And yet, this was the text Kafka came back to in his final years.

38. See letter to Max Brod, February of 1918. Kafka, *Letters to Friends, Family, and Editors*, 200.

39. The fourth of the *Blue Octavo Notebooks* are dated to February, 1918. These journal entries therefore coincide with the letters between Brod and Kafka from the same time.

had with Brod three years earlier. By means of this overt material concerning Kierkegaard and Abraham as well as the distinctly personal reflections from Kafka's diary and notebooks that describe his perspective on faith and the human condition, it is possible to construct both Kafka's understanding of faith in relation to the existential dialectic as well as a model of Kafka's Abraham that stands as a direct response to Kierkegaard's Abraham.

Kafka's Abraham

It would be far too simple to claim that Kafka rejects the concept of faith. Kafka does not reject faith. The existential choice for Kafka is the choice of faith just as it was for Kierkegaard. What is different for Kafka, however, is that the choice of faith merely enables the individual to accept the reality of this world as distinct and separate from God. It does not forge a connection between the finite and the infinite. Instead, it provides what is necessary to accept the finite——and the infinite. "Man cannot live without a permanent trust in something indestructible in himself, though both the indestructible element and the trust may remain permanently hidden from him. One of the ways in which this hiddenness can express itself is through faith in a personal god."[40] Faith is the ability to accept the fundamental human condition. It is the ability to accept the isolation and estrangement of the individual in the face of the infinite. For Kafka, faith is a requirement to survive in this world. Faith does not enable transformation, it merely sustains.

In the space between God and humanity lies an insurmountable chasm that is impossible to explain or express. As such, our only true indicator of the space between the finite and the infinite is the absurd. The absurd is that which cannot be adequately explained or expressed; it simply exists outside of understanding. The absurd is the only means of explaining the inexplicable. The absurd for Kafka, therefore, becomes not only the means of explaining the gulf between God and human, but also the means by which faith is possible. The absurd enables the individual to define the limits of finitude by explaining that which lies beyond. The absurd, then, is not only an explanation for the space between God and human, it is also camouflage for it. The absurd is the blanket thrown over the elephant in the living room. And yet, it is the only way to understand the figure of Abraham.

Unlike Kierkegaard, Kafka's Abraham is willfully ignorant of the abyss that separates him from God. Kafka's Abraham knows he is finite and that God is infinite, but this is the extent of his speculation concerning the Divine. This

---

40. Kafka, *Blue Octavo Notebooks*, 91.

is the extent of his relationship with the Divine. The gulf that lies between God and Kafka's Abraham is an unknown, distant land. It is the province of the absurd, concealed by faith. It does not——as it does for Kierkegaard's Abraham——represent possibility. It does not represent hope. One of the most obvious distinctions between Kafka and Kierkegaard on the subject of faith is the presence of hope. For Kierkegaard, faith and hope are intimately connected. The possibility of the self in communion with the Divine found in faith is the ultimate expression of hope. For Kafka, faith is not defined by possibility. Therefore, faith is not necessarily connected to hope. In his biography of Kafka, Brod cites a conversation between the two men of February 28, 1920.

> He: "We are nihilistic thoughts that came into God's head." I quoted in support the doctrine of the Gnostics concerning the Demiurge, the evil creator of the world, the doctrine of the world as a sin of God's. "No," said Kafka, "I believe we are not such a radical relapse of God's, only one of his bad moods. He had a bad day." "So there would be hope outside our world?" He smiled, "Plenty of hope——for God——no end of hope——only not for us."[41]

Hope is more than we can hope for. Hope is that which extends the individual's vision beyond the edge of existence. It is that capacity which both acknowledges and desires something beyond the limits of our finitude. This capacity is not present in Kafka's Abraham. He is bereft of hope. In the absence of hope, Kafka's Abraham is incapable of standing at the edge of existence and peering into the abyss. He therefore is incapable of conceiving a way across. The faith displayed by Kafka's Abraham leaves him firmly entrenched in the finite world and completely incapable of transcending himself in order to connect with the Divine. As such, Kafka's Abraham is a failure. Kafka's Abraham, in distinct contrast to Kierkegaard's Abraham, is "incapable of greatness."[42]

For Kafka, such hope-based faith is possible only by means of a radical misconception of the relationship between God and humanity. In order to accept the possibility of transcending the finite——the possibility of entering into an absolute relationship with the absolute——the individual must be willing to ignore the reality of the human condition and the inescapable limits of our finite natures. And the individual must create a God who is willing to enter into a personal and intimate relationship with humanity. For Kafka, no such

41. Brod, *Franz Kafka*, 75.

42. Kafka, *Letters to Friends, Family, and Editors*, 285.

God exists. In order to construct such a God, the individual must reject the world outside of the self and focus exclusively on the subjective. By focusing exclusively on a subjective perception of the world, the individual is more readily able to reject the limits of this world in favor of the apparent limitlessness of imagination. It is the self-deception of Kierkegaard's Abraham that allows him to escape the bonds of his finitude. Abraham's intellectual dishonesty makes it easier for him to reject the reality of his world and to become enthralled with the possibility of another. It allows for such intense concentration on the self that the world outside of the self is lost. And the ability to see beyond the self is also lost. It is only by means of such solipsism that the absurd is able to be overcome. Kierkegaard's Abraham passes over the abyss as if it were not there. His immeasurable leap to transcendence is what Kierkegaard so often refers to as the paradox of Abraham's faith. It is this paradox of Kierkegaard's faith, which cannot be expressed, that provides Kafka with his most pointed critique of Kierkegaard's Abraham.

Kafka's most detailed discussion of the Akedah story comes from his letter to Klopstock written over two days. In this lengthy analysis of Genesis 22, three versions of Abraham are presented that when taken together illustrate the existential confrontation between the individual and God. As such, each of the sketches in the letter presents us with a unique perspective on the awful struggle of faith as portrayed by the decision of Abraham to respond to God's call to sacrifice his son.

The first Abraham presented in Kafka's letter is a man so consumed by this world that he is incapable of answering the call of the Lord. Instead of responding, "Here I am," Kafka's first Abraham busies himself with his worldly responsibilities to purposefully disregard his sacrificial duties. This Abraham is perfectly capable and willing to sacrifice his son, "to carry out the order for the sacrifice as a waiter would be ready to carry out his orders, but he would still never manage to perform the sacrifice because he cannot get away from home."[43] We do not know for sure if this Abraham has actually heard the command from God. All we know is that this Abraham is an "indispensable" figure, unable to remove himself from his duties to his farm and home long enough to possibly acknowledge that God has singled him out. He cannot get away from his world, and he does not want to. All we can assume about this Abraham, and all the Abrahams who fail to heed God's call, are that they "are deliberately not finishing their houses . . . so as not to have to lift their eyes and see the mountain that stands in the distance."[44]

43. Ibid.
44. Ibid.

Kafka's second Abraham, the "real Abraham," is the least discussed of the three, but it is the absence of discussion concerning this Abraham that proves most enlightening. According to Kafka, the "real Abraham" is "no longer worth discussing."[45] This Abraham had everything from the start, and in order "to be led even higher, then something must have been taken away from him."[46] Whether this something was taken away, whether this Abraham traveled with Isaac to Moriah, Kafka does not say. The real Abraham is no longer relevant for Kafka. Whether he completed the task set before him by God is not important. What actually might have occurred on Mt. Moriah is not important. What Kafka finds most interesting in the Akedah narrative is how Abraham originally responds to the God's call. For this reason Kafka wants to speculate about an Abraham who cannot even get far enough to contemplate his commission because he is too busy trying to decide his relationship to the Divine. Kafka's Abraham is standing at the edge of the abyss, reacting to a God who may or may not be attempting to contact him. Kafka's Abraham is fully aware of the gulf between him and the Divine. This is why Kafka chooses to quickly move past the "real Abraham." He has no relevance in the modern world. The real Abraham would easily accept a command from God, but not a modern Abraham. A modern Abraham would be too overcome by his distance from God.

It is Kafka's third Abraham that most decidedly emphasizes this sense of alienation. This Abraham is ready and eager to perform the sacrifice, but he is completely incapable of believing that God has singled him out to do so. "He does not lack the true faith, for he has this faith; he wants to sacrifice in the proper manner, if he could only believe he was the one meant."[47] This Abraham is fully aware of the absurdity of the situation. Not the absurdity that God might want Isaac to be sacrificed, but the absurdity of God's choosing him. This Abraham cannot stop himself from asking if he is misguided or wrong. How could he possibly be worthy of being summoned by God? What kind of fool believes he has been commanded by God? And what if he is wrong? "An Abraham who comes unsummoned!"[48] This would be the most preposterous thing of all. Kafka's third Abraham is not all that different from the first. Both are tragically aware of the distance from God, and both are thoroughly

45. Ibid.

46. Ibid.

47. Ibid.

48. Ibid., 286. Kafka emphasizes this dilemma by offering an illustrative story in which the worst student sitting in the back of a classroom wrongly hears his name called and rushes up to the front of the room to accept the award for the best student in the class.

overwhelmed by the proposition of an encounter with the divine Other. The first Abraham chooses to ignore the possibility of the situation. The third Abraham cannot stop obsessing over the possibility of the situation. Neither Abraham can (or will) respond. Both are held captive by the abyss. Both are held captive by the overwhelming possibility of difference, and as such are rendered impotent. Kafka's Abrahams represent a radical disbelief in the possibility of a God who would respond to humanity on such a personal level. His Abrahams cannot accept the possibility of a personal relationship with the Divine as a reality, because they cannot accept the concept of true communion with that which exists outside the self and defines the self.

Kafka's reading of the Abraham on Moriah does not focus on the events as they were but on those events as they might be. Instead of focusing on Abraham's decision whether or not to kill Isaac as directed by God, Kafka short-circuits the story by examining whether and why Abraham would respond to God in the first place. The action of taking Isaac's life when commanded by the Divine is inconsequential to Kafka, because how could one not do God's bidding if one truly knew it was God doing the bidding? What Abraham did on Mt. Moriah is unimportant, but what Abraham did in his home three days prior is of monumental importance.

The events on Mt. Moriah are of little consequence to Kafka except for how the choices that produced these events inform his present situation. In his reading of Gen. 22:1-18 the ultimate question of faith is weighed by Kafka, not for Abraham but for himself. To act on God's command is a given, but to respond to God's call is a continuous dilemma. How do we respond to a God who is defined first and foremost by his distance from us? How can we act on a divine command if we cannot even be sure the command was meant for us?

Both Kafka and Kierkegaard portray Abraham as a man alone in the universe and confronted by the divine Other. But where Kierkegaard sees the possibility in such an encounter, Kafka sees only the terror. Where Kierkegaard begins Abraham's encounter with the Divine from the perspective of hope, Kafka begins his encounter from the perspective of alienation. Kierkegaard's Abraham is positioned for triumph and transcendence. Kafka's Abraham is positioned for fear and despair. Kierkegaard's Abraham sees only God before him in this confrontation. Kafka's Abraham sees only the abyss. If Kierkegaard's Abraham rejects this world in favor of a delusion generated by hope, then Kafka's Abraham rejects everything outside of this world and establishes his faith firmly as a willful ignorance that conceals the very edge of existence.

Canaan vs. the Desert

In January 1922, two years before his death, Kafka suffered what he described as a "breakdown" in which it was "impossible to sleep, impossible to stay awake, impossible to endure life, or, more exactly, the course of life."[49] In his diary Kafka strained to define this experience, which he understood as the fracture between his internal and external worlds. "The clocks are not in unison; the inner one runs crazily on at a devilish or demonic or in any case inhuman pace, the outer one limps along at its usual speed."[50] This fracture was the result of an endless introspection which Kafka felt was spiraling out of control. Becoming lost deeper and deeper inside of himself, a prisoner to his own thoughts, Kafka knew only that he must find, or at least determine, the terminus of this introspection. And while he feared the inevitable result to be madness, Kafka also clung to the possibility that this path was the natural pursuit of every human: that faced with the absolute or even the possibility of the absolute, we are all capable of falling into the imposing chasm that separates our finite worlds from the all too easily imagined infinite.

> The solitude that for the most part has been forced on me, in part voluntarily sought by me——but what was this if not compulsion too?——is now losing all of its ambiguity and approaches it denouement. Where is it leading? The strongest likelihood is, that it may lead to madness; there is nothing more to say, the pursuit goes right through me and renders me asunder.[51]

Kafka's (perceived) breakdown illustrates the full force of the existential realization. For Kafka, the revelation of the existential dialectic traps the individual in an extremely dangerous place. The realization that we are alone and estranged from that by which we are defined can lead to madness. If unchecked the existential realization becomes a yawning abyss into which the individual falls, never to land. The pursuit to expose and explain the space between God and humanity forces the writer to attempt to define the indefinable. It becomes the attempt to express the infinite in the finite. It is the quest to render the absurd.

For Kafka, the choice produced by the existential realization is to remain in isolation in order to investigate the limits of our finiteness, or it is to abandon that speculation altogether and to lead a normal life. Kafka's struggle

49. Kafka, *The Diaries*, 398.
50. Ibid.
51. Ibid., 399.

to pursue either a normal life or the life of a writer was far more than a career choice. Kafka understood very well that his vocation as writer was not only a call to identify the existential human condition but also to examine the space between human existence and that which defines it. Kafka's attraction to Kierkegaard was that he knew him as a kindred spirit. Kierkegaard chose to spend his life at the very edge of existence, chronicling, defining, and mapping the space between the finite and the infinite. Kafka knew he was called to do the same, and he turned to Kierkegaard time and again for support—both personal and intellectual. What connected Kafka and Kierkegaard right from the start was the struggle each found between solitude and community. A life of solitude meant a life devoted to examination of the existential dialectic. A life in community meant to abandon that task and to settle for the social constructs that shield us from the existential realization.

In another diary entry from January 1922, a mere week after his "breakdown," Kafka attempted to explain the continual struggle of his life. For Kafka, the world was divided between solitude and community. In solitude, Kafka was truly connected to his purpose and his calling in life but he was also excluded from the ordinary world of community. In community, Kafka was shielded from the trials of the existential dilemma, but he was always aware of abandoning his vocation.

> Though indeed I should not judge the matter so precisely, for I am now a citizen of this other world, whose relationship to the ordinary one is the relationship of the wilderness to cultivated land (I have been forty years wandering from Canaan); I look back at it like a foreigner.[52]

Using a most revealing biblical metaphor, Kafka framed the existential choice in religious terms. Life for Kafka had been since his youth the choice between living in Canaan or in the desert. In Canaan he could live the normal life, the life his community expected from him. In the desert, he would live in isolation as a composer of the void. This ordinary world of community was a constant attraction for Kafka, but every time he committed to the world of Canaan he invariably felt as if he had abandoned what he had been born to do:

> It is indeed a kind of Wandering in the Wilderness in reverse that I am undergoing: I think that I am continually skirting the wilderness and am full of childish hopes (particularly in regards to women)

_____

52. Ibid., 407.

that "perhaps I shall keep Canaan after all"—when all the while I have been decades in the wilderness and these hopes are merely mirages born of despair, especially at those times when I am the wretchedest of creatures in the desert too, and Canaan is perforce my only Promised Land, for no third place exists for mankind.[53]

Kafka had repeatedly flirted with the notion of a "normal" life. He had by 1922 been engaged twice to Felice Bauer and a third time (even more briefly) to a woman named Julie Wohryzek. But despite these many failed attempts to abandon the desert for Canaan, Kafka always found his way back to his true calling. In the last years of his life, Kafka time and again found himself alone in the desert, thoroughly devoted to exploring the limits of the existential condition. As a result, he was continually in danger, continually on the cusp of falling headlong into the void, and continually frightened by the prospect of madness.

The fundamental choice that springs forth from the existential dialectic for Kafka is the decision to examine the expanse that separates God from humanity, or simply to abandon the endeavor altogether. To abandon the endeavor and to live firmly in this world means not only to abandon the investigation of the space between, but also to reject it. To live in Canaan is not to abandon the desert. It is to reject the desert. Those who live in the desert will always be attracted by the comforts of Canaan, but those who have committed to live in Canaan have surely rejected the desert. "But I live elsewhere; it is only that the attraction of the world of men is immense. In an instant it can make you forget everything. But great also is the attraction of my world: those who love me love me because I am 'forsaken.'"[54] To reject the desert and embrace Canaan is for Kafka to embrace the social constructs that shield us from the edge of existence that lies precariously close. The division between the desert and Canaan is the division between a frightful reality and a blissful naïveté. To embrace the life in Canaan is to remain willfully ignorant. It is to accept that our limited and finite capacity is the true extent of our possibility. And because there is no third option, "no third place exists for mankind," our sole choice is between solitude and community.

53. Ibid., 407–8.
54. Ibid., 409.

8

LEVINAS

Unbinding the Other: Levinas, the Akedah, and Going beyond the Subject

Laurence Bove

In the long dialogue concerning the Akedah, Soren Kierkegaard brought the story into the mainstream of Western philosophy.[1] Long a subject of preaching and prayer for Jews, Christians, and Muslims, Kierkegaard made the story of Abraham and the binding of Isaac, the Akedah, a topic of nineteenth- and twentieth-century philosophical judgment and reflection. As part of the fabric of Western philosophy, the story of Abraham raised questions that combined philosophical anthropology, ethics, and religion. As a philosophical trope, comment on the story flows from Kierkegaard to Rosenzwieg, to Buber, to Levinas and beyond.

The warp and woof of Abrahamic philosophical dialogue explores the subjective, the phenomenological, and most importantly the intersection of ethics, religion, and secularity. Kierkegaard's notions of Abraham as the "'knight of faith," and his "truth is subjectivity" and "indirect method" became a legacy that still spurs insight and opposition. Declaring the "individual" and the "leap of faith" as a constitutive part of human existence, Kierkegaard at once became a foe of the growing Hegelian materialism that became Marxism and the overly stilted declarations of a Christian Church that did not live up to its central tenets. Kierkegaard regarded himself as a corrective to the growing tendencies emerging in modern societies that treated the person as an object

---

1. Soren Kierkegaard, *Fear and Trembling and The Sickness unto Death*, trans. Walter Lowrie (New York: Doubleday, 1954).

and the group as determinant of the person. He is prescient and prefigures Buber's and Marcel's analysis of the detrimental effects of treating persons as part of a "mass man," reduced to objective traits that oppress and manipulate. Likewise, Kierkegaard provided counterpoint to the growth of Marxism with its reliance on the structures of the state and notion that persons are derivatives of social and economic structures.

Emmanuel Levinas is heir to the story of Abraham and the binding of Isaac in a number of ways, as a philosopher in the continental tradition, and as a Judaic scholar. He functioned in each of these capacities, and developed a complementarity wherein each informed the other. But this does not mean that he did both at the same time. The mutuality of each perspective affects him; but his philosophical analysis stands on its relevance to the philosophical questions addressed. After Kierkegaard's analysis, various themes of twentieth-century philosophy build upon Kierkegaard's quest to go beyond the object to the subject. Levinas concludes that we must go beyond the subject to the other.[2] In this essay we follow Levinas as to how and why he transcends Kierkegaard's notion of Abraham as the "knight of faith" and develops his own distinctly relational nonviolent view.

Levinas took Kierkegaard's philosophical turn and built his ideas on those of Rosenzweig and Buber to articulate and animate the contribution of Jewish thinking to contemporary thought. Levinas, looking through the lens of Rosenzweig and Buber, was able to articulate Kierkegaard's achievements and limitations and, most importantly, to articulate ways to go beyond Kierkegaard's limitations. Levinas's analysis joins Rosenzweig's *Star of Redemption*[3] and Martin Buber's *I-Thou*[4] as a distinct line of thought that seeks to escape Kierkegaard's excessive, encapsulated, and violent subject. Levinas's analysis of why Kierkegaard did not go far enough to escape the isolation and violence of an encapsulated Abraham was informed by his own unique philosophical approach to an ethics beyond being that was centered on the other. Levinas further develops his thoughts on the notion of relations to the other as it oscillates between ethics and religion. He develops a triadic notion of the other that is distinct from Buber's dyadic approach. Levinas's interpretation emphasizes the key feature of the Akedah as the ability of Abraham to listen to the second voice of the angel, drop the knife, and unbind Isaac. This choice of nonviolence was, in Levinasian terms, a return to the ethical. Levinas's

2. Emmanuel Levinas, *Proper Names*, trans. Michael B. Smith (London: Athelone, 1996).

3. Franz Rosenzweig, *The Star of Redemption*, trans. Barbara E. Galli (Madison, WI: The University of Wisconson Press, 2005).

4. Martin Buber, *I and Thou*, trans. Ronald Gregor Smith (New York: Scribner, 2000).

account of interiority and intersubjectivity and its "foundational" role in ethics, social philosophy, and theology plays an important part in understanding why Levinas thought that the high point of Abraham's story was a return to ethics, not abandonment, as Kierkegaard infers.

After we conclude the direct analysis of Levinas's understanding of the Akedah, we can reflect upon whether Levinas achieves his goals of escaping the limitations that plagued Kierkegaard. Is it necessary to go beyond the subject to the other? And, is it a basis of nonviolence? Does this "great Jewish story" that is the possession of so many in the Jewish, Christian, Muslim, and secular worlds have the potential to provide a cultural common ground for inter-religious dialogue and nonviolent conflict resolution? As the human family seeks to find peaceful paths of human flourishing, the story of the binding of Isaac provides a rich legacy and holds great potential.

In short, Levinas says Kierkegaard did not go far enough in the story. Ironically, the iconic portrayal of Abraham by Kierkegaard leads to a question. Perhaps the suspension of the ethical was misnamed? Even though Levinas challenges Kierkegaard's philosophical analysis, one can give to Kierkegaard the credit for walking a long way on the journey: the indirect method, the truth of subjectivity, all these are durable achievements, but a major thrust concerning the suspension of, or affirmation of, the ethical foreshadows the meaning of ethics as adherence to universal rules and the adherence to general norms. Going further in the story illumines the nature, role, and harmony of the ethical and the religious. Kierkegaard's fear and trembling and leap of faith gave way to Levinas's affirmation of the other and a choice to care. But what is the route that Levinas followed to come to these conclusions—the road that led to what Levinas calls the "asymmetric" relationship of choosing the other?

That there are philosophers who are Jewish is a truism, but to articulate the contributions of Jewish thought is another matter. Levinas is in a long tradition of Jewish intellectuals who sought to be free of Greek and later Hegelian categories that pervade most philosophical discourse, including Kierkegaard's. Buber's distinction of I-It and I-Thou sets the stage for Levinas's ability to break beyond Kierkegaard's limitations and assert more about the asymmetric relationships at the heart of the ethical and the theological. Kierkegaard achieved a first—a philosophy that pitted the unique individual against the backdrop of the Hegelian hegemony of the universal. Against the preeminence of the philosophical and rational, Kierkegaard posited the individual and the subjective. This achievement resounds throughout the twentieth century and provides a touchstone for interiority, phenomenology, and those seeking to comprehend the constituent nature of consciousness and historicity.

From this basis, Buber, Marcel, and Levinas emerge amidst Nietzsche, Heidegger, Foucault, and Derrida. Their dialogue and development owes foundational homage to Kierkegaard's anti-Hegelian affirmation of subjectivity. Articulating the basic structures and dynamics of inner experience, Kierkegaard provided a new vocabulary to confront modernity and what Marcel later called mass man. The quest for individuality amidst a growing modern conformity cast Kierkegaard into a search for religious existence that he knew was not cut from the cloth of bureaucracy and the universal hypocrisy of state religion. In Christ, he saw a dynamic of spirit free from the law and the universals. And this goes to the heart of Levinas's evaluation of Kierkegaard. Levinas realizes and appreciates the contributions of Kierkegaard, but he pushes farther and affirms the ethical as congruent with faith. For Levinas, the post-Kierkegaardian Abraham reaffirms the ethical in relationship with the other. And that happens when Abraham listens to the second voice of the angel, drops his knife, and unbinds Isaac.

In "A Propos of 'Kierkegaard vivant,'" Levinas tells us that the two things that bother him about Kierkegaard are his "completely naked subjectivity that, in its desire to avoid losing itself in the universal, rejects all form," and his shocking violence.[5] Levinas describes Kierkegaard's achievement as positing a self that is tensed upon itself and unable to accept any form because it defies objectivity and universality. Levinas sees this inability as a progenitor for reactionary movements of structuralism, Marxism, and idealism and other systems that reduce subjectivity to a concept or a correlative of thought. This insight echoes the onslaught of movements that stress radical freedom and result in isolation and alienation. In the anxiety of human existence one gets lost in the angst and trauma of everydayness. In Kierkegaard, the inward alienated self creates truth through its own suffering and despair which further isolates it. The Kierkegaardian Abraham is forced to rise above this isolation by rejecting all form, rejecting the ethical, choosing a religious state that relies only upon self-alienation and choice. Ironically, it distorts relationships.

Levinas alludes to the violence of Kierkegaard's subjectivity and notes "that harshness of Kierkegaard emerges at the exact moment when he 'transcends ethics.'"[6] Kierkegaard achieves his radical transformation by philosophizing disruptively. He referred to himself as the 'fork' poking at and overturning comfortable ways of thinking and being. The violence supposes subjectivity "tensed on itself, existence as the care that a being takes for its own existence, and a kind of torment over oneself."[7] Affirming, denying, or modifying this

---

5. Levinas , "A Propos of 'Kierkegaard vivant,'" in *Proper Names*, 76.

6. Ibid.

encapsulated self is the source of much of the philosophical debate in the twentieth century.

Another question raised by the story of Abraham is "How does God speak to us?" Levinas explains for this to have meaning, we must look to God's communication as being a "disruption." In *Of God Who Comes to Mind*,[8] Levinas extends a line of argument and analyses that stretches from the Talmud, to the early Christian fathers, Augustine, and Anselm; and builds on a neglected notion from Descartes. "It did not interest Descartes, for whom the mathematical clarity and distinctness of ideas were enough, but whose teaching on the priority of the idea of the Infinite relative to the finite is a precious indication for any phenomenology of consciousness."[9] A key notion to Levinas is the infinite expressed in us. God speaks to us in our innermost selves and access to this voice of God within us demands attention to our inner interiority. It is primarily a relationship, and it orders other relationships. But it almost always disrupts our everyday notions of reality and being. Thus enters Abraham, the knight of faith, as Kierkegaard calls him. Truly and in everyday ways, he was disrupted. The disequilibrium that this caused impels him to do things he never would dream of executing: keeping information from his wife, bringing his most beloved son to the sacrificial altar, binding him who is innocent and who is loved. The juncture here is critical for Levinas's interpretation of Abraham as disrupted—will he listen to the voice that impels him to obey a command that is clearly paradoxical in nature as Kierkegaard suggests, or will he respond in a way that truly represents the divine? In "God and Philosophy" Levinas says, "our question is whether, beyond being, a meaning might not show itself whose priority, translated into ontological language, will be called prior to being."[10] The key for Levinas relies not on the self but on something prior. "Biological human fraternity . . . is not a sufficient reason that I be responsible for a separated being."[11]

Levinas tells an interesting story attributed to Picard in the essay, "Max Picard and the Face," in *Proper Names*, about a person who disarmed the violence of a murderer through sheer inner conviction, noninvolvement, and peace.[12] Levinas states clearly that he did not agree with Picard, but he respected

---

7. Ibid.

8. Levinas, *Of God Who Comes to Mind*, trans. Bettina Bergo (Stanford: Stanford University Press, 1998).

9. Ibid., xiv.

10. Levinas, "God and Philosophy," in *Of God Who Comes to Mind*, 57.

11. Ibid., 71.

12. Levinas, "Max Picard and the Face," in *Proper Names*, 97.

his inner and poetic approach. To Levinas, more is required. Picard's notion of a deep connection to silence and inward meaning portends to be an antidote to the violence that surrounds us. Ironically, though Levinas did not articulate it, this seems apropos of the story of Isaac. As disarming, and naïve, Picard's story highlights Levinas's understanding of the implications concerning the encapsulated version of the Akedah. And it illustrates why Levinas's interpretation went beyond the encapsulation of Kierkegaard's self, while yet continuing Kierkegaard's legacy in important ways.

Kierkegaard's encapsulated subject, tensed upon itself and requiring a leap and a suspension of all ethical bonds, has two consequences: Kierkegaard responded to a truncated notion of the ethical and his defense of the subject was also truncated because it overcame alienation through a leap that assumed a chasm between faith, ethics, and God. His accusatory analysis against Christianity and for the leap of faith was a reaction against critical and Hegelian thought that exposed and overrode the subject. But, the resultant subject had few resources. The self, exposed and isolated, was encouraged to resist and be disruptive. A more empowered self needed relational resources that were more than confrontational. It is not that conflict was to be eliminated, but that relationships are more than confrontations. And this is what Kierkegaard sacrificed in both personal and theoretical terms.

Levinas develops his analysis and assessment of the truncated subject in his essay, "The Other in Proust:" "The theme of solitude" is to his mind, "the basic incommunicability of the person." Levinas calls this the "despair of impossible communication."[13] To Levinas, even collectivism shares this same "despair." In light of this one can gain an insight into Levinas's understanding of the Kierkegaardian limitation, and why Levinas sees Kierkegaardian violence as a form of unsuccessful overcoming. The genius of Levinas is to recognize the achievements of Kierkegaard and yet seek another way to resolve the challenge to relationships, community, and God.

Beyond Kierkegaard—Levinas and Jewish Philosophy

For Levinas, Franz Rosenzweig's thought, rooted in a return to Judaism, presents itself as a revolt against Hegel.[14] In the Hegelian system the individual becomes but a moment. To this Rosenzweig posits the "'individual in spite of it all' and the inexhaustible newness of life's instants."[15] Two movements of

---

13. Levinas, "The Other In Proust," in *Proper Names*, 103.

14. Levinas, "Franz Rosenzweig: A Modern Jewish Thinker," in *Outside the Subject*, trans. Michael B. Smith, (Stanford: Stanford University Press, 1994), 53.

thought go beyond the totality of being so emphasized from Thales to Hegel, and with Kierkegaard, Rosenzweig attempts to break free from this Hegelian totality to realize an "irreducible singularity; he is (like the Kierkegaardian man passing from the ethical to the religious stage) meta-ethical."[16] But what is essential for us in this essay is to underscore Levinas's treatment of Rosenzweig. "But as soon as man discovers that he is meta-ethical and leaves the totality, God also withdraws from the totality and returns to his meta-physical essence"[17]. Once separated from the totality of being, we are isolated. This isolation is not "the reality of our lived experience."[18] Important for Levinas is the observation that for Rosenzweig, the second movement of his thought breaks this isolation. Levinas explains that since isolation is not the reality of our lived experience, intelligence cannot without violence break through that isolation, whereas in humanity's concrete and living experience, God, man, and world are in relation. "The entering into relation is accomplished, not by the effect of the philosopher's synoptic gaze, but by the life of the elements overflowing their essence, forming time."[19]

In this isolation rests solitude, which for Levinas is the realm, not of existential angst, but of a way to nonviolently overcome the isolation and separation from the totality. In an insightful analysis in "Time and the Other" he builds upon the foundation laid by Rosenzweig to explain that overcoming solitude goes beyond the encapsulation of Kierkegaard's knight of faith, Abraham.[20] The insights from Jewish thought set a non-Greco-Roman platform for him to both assess and add to the analysis that has captured the attention of postmodern thought. He states, "in thus going back to the ontological root of solitude I hope to glimpse wherein this solitude can be exceeded. Let me say at once what this exceeding will not be. It will not be a knowledge, because through knowledge, whether one wants it or not, the object is absorbed by the subject and duality disappears. It will not be an ecstasis, because in ecstasis the subject is absorbed in the object and recovers itself in its unity. All these relationships result in the disappearance of the other."[21]

---

15. Ibid., 54.

16. Ibid., 55.

17. Ibid., 56.

18. Ibid.

19. Ibid.

20. Levinas, "Time and The Other," in *Time and the Other and Additional Essays,* trans. Richard A. Cohen (Pittsburgh: Duquesne University Press, 1987), 41.

21. Ibid.

At this point it is appropriate to place this analysis in the context of Abraham, who was groping with the messages that God sent to him but did not see his son as the other. His regard of Isaac was to treat him as an object of God's command and wishes. For Levinas, apropos of Rosenzweig and Buber, this was not an adequate interpretation of the story, because Kierkegaard had him in a solitude that only a violent leap of faith could overcome. Levinas's understanding of Jewish relational thought gave him insights that pushed the analysis further. The unbinding of Isaac became the issue because in the relationships that overcome totality, God can command love. Traditional Jewish thought held the independence of the Jewish people against history because the people of God had the Torah's command to love, regardless of history and power.

This asymmetrical relationship of God commanding love is only realized as the solitary subject avoids making ideas into itself or losing oneself in the object. The relationship comes to be in the other, in making the choice to accept and care for this extrinsic being that in other modes can either kill or entrap. Levinas tell us, "to conceive a situation wherein solitude is overcome is to test the very principle of the tie between the existent and its existing. It is to move toward an ontological event wherein the existent contracts existence. The event by which the existent contracts its existing I call hypostasis [standing under]."[22] Levinas tells us that in relation to the other, "I hope to show that the relationship with the Other is entirely different from what the existentialists propose as it is from what the Marxists propose."[23] This leads us to understand how Abraham went beyond the subject and dropped his knife, so to speak. His repetition of "Here I am," enigmatic as it may seem, is prescient of what came to be—the instantiation of Isaac as the father of Israel and the progenitor of a people. "Relationship with the future, the presence of the future in the present, seems all the same accomplished in the face-to-face with the Other. The situation of the face-to-face would be the very accomplishment of time; the encroachment of the present on the future is not the feat of the subject alone, but of intersubjective relationship."[24] Here we have Levinas's key contribution to the long standing commentary on the Akedah: the focus and explanation of the centrality of intersubjective relationships. Relational movement beyond the subject was the missing key that the Kierkegaardian Abraham did not possess as he attempted to fulfill his understanding of the commands. Levinas unpacks the riddle with which the Kierkegaardian Abraham struggled and

22. Ibid., 43.
23. Ibid., 79.
24. Ibid.

provides a hermeneutical cue that opens the door to developing a more nuanced understanding of the continued significance of the Abrahamic story and the Akedah. The future in the present that eluded the early Abraham, and certainly Kierkegaard, was what the God of the Jews wanted—a covenant for all time that saw in the present a fecundity of the future. Levinas's understanding of the intersubjective basis of our story has much to offer the philosophical analyses of relationships, nonviolence, and the ethical life.

BEYOND BUBER: LEVINAS'S TRIADIC OTHER

In the *Eclipse of God*, in the chapter "Religion and Ethics," Buber lays the foundations of his critique that in large measure owes debt to his Jewish origins. He tells us that as Christianity "flowing over the world from the source of Israel and strengthened by mighty influxes, especially the Iranian and the Greek, arose at a time in Hellenistic civilization, and especially in its religious life, when the element of the people was being displaced by that of the individual."[25]

The emphasis away from a people to an individual is an essential insight that comes through the intellectual and spiritual heritage and experience of the Jews as a chosen people. This hermeneutical lens allows Buber to critically see developments in Christianity and philosophy. He notes that Christians "did not stand, like Israel, in a fundamental relationship to Him as the people of the covenant."[26] One can see that this insight is foundational to Levinas as well. The shift to relationships and foundations becomes the interpretive wedge that illumes the critique Levinas levels at Western ontology and, more specifically, at Kierkegaard's excessive individualism. Once again, Buber makes this explicit: "In connection with this Christian individualism, moreover, the relationship between the ethical and the religious was impaired."[27] With this interpretive foundation, one can make sense of the Buberian reaction to Kierkegaard's interpretation and application of the Akedah. Buber tells us, "Christianity is 'Hellenistic' insofar as it surrenders the concept of a 'holy people' and recognizes only a personal holiness. Individual religiousness thus attains a hitherto unheard-of intensity and inwardness."[28]

Buber tells us this foundational inwardness and separation of the religious and the ethical is evident in *Fear and Trembling*. Through the story of Abraham,

---

25. Buber, *Eclipse of God: Studies in the Relation between Religion and Philosophy*, (New York: Harper and Row, 1957), 105.

26. Ibid., 106.

27. Ibid.

28. Ibid., 105.

Kierkegaard's knight of faith, "the ethical, the universal and the universally valid, is relativized."[29] Ironically, the relation of God to "the Single One" forms the basis for action, "that is, in direct personal relation with the individual."[30] Moreover, "'that which the Single One is to understand by Isaac,' says Kierkegaard, 'can be dreaded only by and for himself.' That means, clearly and precisely, that he does not learn it, at least not mistakenly, from God. . . . His interpretation will always be determined by his life-circumstances in this hour."[31] This isolated individual, "'This knight of faith,' says Kierkegaard, 'is left to his own resources, single and alone, and therein lies the dreadful.'"[32]

One can now understand how both Buber and Levinas work to overcome the excessive encapsulation of the subject. In "Martin Buber's Thought and Contemporary Judaism," Levinas tells us that, "Jewishness does not present itself in terms of principles, nor should it be judged on that basis."[33] Buber showed the world "that Judaism exists as a contemporary form of life and thought."[34] In Buber, "the human I is the reuniting of the sacred and the profane. It is not a substance but a relationship."[35] Seeing the human I as a relationship proffers an escape from the isolation of the knight of faith. "To exist is to gather up the dispersion of the sacred in the profane."[36] As Levinas states, this is much different than finding us "thrown and abandoned in the absurd."[37] Levinas holds that for Buber the instant of meeting God does not become a personal isolated experience; it is "meeting, dialogue, opening to others but at the same time presence to self. The instant is not transcended in the impersonal, but in the interpersonal."[38]

Levinas agrees that Buber's greatest contribution to Western thought is the Meeting, Buber's term for the I-Thou; this going beyond the subject-object, or I-It, is foundational to the Buberian worldview.[39] Buber's contribution to Western thought and philosophy highlights the key elements of analysis and dialogue. "He privileges the special case of the relation and the meeting that takes place between beings who do not know each other."[40] Though Levinas

29. Ibid., 115.

30. Ibid., 116.

31. Ibid., 117.

32. Ibid.

33. Levinas, "Martin Buber's Thought and Contemporary Judaism," in *Outside the Subject*, 4.

34. Ibid., 5.

35. Ibid., 7.

36. Ibid.

37. Ibid.

38. Ibid., 10.

39. Ibid., 7.

affirms Buber's achievement, he states that the formalism of the Meeting is "foreign to the Jewish genres."[41] For its philosophical import, Levinas claims the Meeting is a particular case of presence that is not representation but an "irreducible proximity" that can disturb the order of life. This is "the theme of an inquiry that does not posit God as a very great being, . . . an inquiry that wishes, before speaking to God, to express proximity, to describe whence the voice comes and how the trace is left."[42] With this, Levinas affirms the achievement of Buber, makes it his own, and provides a step that advances his own analysis and work.

In "Martin Buber, Gabriel Marcel and Philosophy," Levinas stakes his claim to expound how these works renewed philosophy and how the traditional privilege of ontology is affected by this new approach, in which the source and the model for the meaningful are sought in inter-human relations.[43] This foundational thesis is what separates Levinas, Marcel, and Buber from Nietzsche, Heidegger, Foucault, and Derrida, who he sees as heirs to Kierkegaard's excessive, isolated, and violent self-encapsulation. The Levinasian-identified commonality rests in "the fact of the proximity of persons, neither lost in mass nor abandoned to their solitude."[44] Levinas builds upon Buber's work in everyday terms: "In relation to others, that interiority is immediately broken open and language—the saying that says, if only implicitly, thou—is not just the (always optional) account of a Meeting. It is the account of that Meeting itself, the very bursting forth of thought dialogically coming out of itself."[45]

This original achievement of Buber becomes a foundational insight for Levinas because non-social proximity and interaction is no longer a derivative or degradation of the rational or conceptual. "It is a fully meaningful order of the ethical relation, a relation with the inassimilable, and thus, properly speaking in-com-prehensible (alien to grasp, to possess in) alterity of others."[46]

Though Levinas builds upon the achievements of Buber, he does diverge on a very important point that has direct relevance to the Akedah. If we have recognized the essential over-isolation of Abraham, Buber's solution is to see in the I-Thou, God as the Eternal Thou. Levinas goes in another direction.

<hr>

40. Ibid., 17.

41. Ibid., 18.

42. Ibid., 19.

43. Levinas, "Martin Buber, Gabriel Marcel and Philosophy," in *Outside the Subject*, 20.

44. Ibid., 21.

45. Ibid., 41.

46. Ibid.

Levinas does not feel the "divine person resides in the Thou of dialogue. . .
Levinas . . . has "recourse to the third person, to what I have called illeity. . . God
is personal insofar as He brings abut interpersonal relations between myself and
my neighbors."[47] This claim of Levinas is another interpretive key to Levinas's
understanding of the story of Akedah.

In *Proper Names*, Levinas unfolds his view openly, affirming the philosophy
of dialogue that emerged with Buber and Marcel and extending Kierkegaard's
turn toward the subject. Marcel challenged "the classical idea, the eminent
value of *autarkia*, or personal self-sufficiency."[48] This shatters the reading of
Kierkegaard's Akedah. The interpretation of Abraham as the singular one is
valued as the turn to a subjectivity that counters the objectification of the ideal,
but left unchecked it leads to relativity and isolation because it did not continue.
As Marcel states, "what counts here is the spiritual exchange between beings."
Levinas comments, "This is an important text. . . . Here being is not conscious
of self; it is relation to the other than self . . . and the other than self—is that not
the Other [*Autrui*]?"[49]

Welcoming the "other as thou" is key for Levinas and undergirds his
notion that "opens up a passage from the same to the other, where there is as
yet nothing in common."[50] It is essential to realize that this dialogic relation is
also a rupture that leads to "awakening of the Self to the Other, of me by the
stranger, of me by the stateless person, that is, by the neighbor who is only
nearby."[51] And, especially relevant for philosophy, he states, it is "an awakening
that is neither reflection upon oneself nor universalization."[52] In this rupture
and awakening, "a transcendence beyond ontology unfolds."[53] This awakening
entails a responsibility for the other; it comes to a person who by it does not
avoid it, but "instead of being alienated, it is intensified by my irreplaceability."[54]
In this we have the kernel of Levinas's turn away from the objectification
of Being, and his following of Buber and Marcel in breaking the solitude of
Kierkegaard's encapsulated Abraham. In overcoming the violence inherent in
Kierkegaard's leap he also adds to the work of the dialogue Buber and Marcel
started, by positing the relation to the other as an awakening to, not the Divine,

47. Ibid., 47.
48. Levinas, *Proper Names*, 5.
49. Ibid.
50. Ibid., 6.
51. Ibid.
52. Ibid.
53. Ibid.
54. Ibid.

but an ordinary thou, the other who to needs to be fed, who eats, who lives like me, but is not me. This asymmetrical relationship becomes an essential hallmark of Levinas's contribution to the philosophy of dialogue that proceeds *otherwise than being.*

As Levinas turns to the ordinary other, he achieves the overcoming of Kierkegaard's subject that is tensed on and in itself. Turning toward the other does not destroy the I, nor does it lose it in totality, it discovers an interiority that brings it to total altruism.[55] Rather than yielding, in the Akedah, a Kierkegaardian subjectivity rising to the religious God above the ethical order, he gives the story a different twist. "Perhaps Abraham's ear for hearing the voice that brought him back to the ethical order was the highest moment in this drama."[56] As Levinas tells us, "life receives meaning from an infinite responsibility, a fundamental *diacony* that constitutes the subjectivity of the subject—without that responsibility, completely tendered toward the Other, leaving any leisure for a return to self."[57] Levinas sums up his assessment of the Akedah: "That he [Abraham] obeyed the first voice is astonishing: that he had sufficient distance with respect to that obedience to hear the second voice—that is the essential."[58] Levinas interprets the story in a decisive way: "Abraham's attentiveness to the voice that led him back to the ethical order, in forbidding him to perform a human sacrifice, is the highest point of the drama."[59]

Beyond Levinas: Toward Synchronistic Relationships

Our study leads us to the following conclusions that stem from our analysis of Levinas's interpretation of the Akedah. First, the essential facet of the story is that Levinas's Abraham returned to the ethical when he listened to the second voice not to commit human sacrifice. This is the highlight of the story, in a sense, "the unbinding of Isaac." Second is the development through and beyond Kierkegaard that becomes the backbone of Levinas's philosophy and which forms his basic critique of idealism, materialism, Heideggerian Being, and postmodern subjectivism and violence. This foundational analysis places Levinas in a position to offer a critique of philosophic thought that both emerges from and follows Kierkegaard's encapsulated and violent self. Levinas presents a distinctive base for developing new patterns of analysis that balance

55. Levinas, "Kierkegaard: Existence and Ethics," in *Proper Names*, 73.

56. Ibid., 74.

57. Ibid.

58. Ibid., 77.

59. Ibid.

interiority, relationships, dialog, responsibility, justice, the state, and nonviolence in a postmodern world. Levinas, following Buber's analysis, effectively criticizes Kierkegaard's interpretation and provides a potent reinterpretation of Kierkegaard's existentialism with its inherent limits. Levinas identifies the essential encapsulation of Kierkegaard's Abraham, the violence inherent Abrahams' leap, and reaffirms the ethical.

Third, close reading of the Levinasian texts related to the Akedah reveal that Abraham listened to the second voice, eschewed the infanticide he was perpetrating, and came back to the ethical. Nowhere does Levinas invoke his concept of the Face to imply that Abraham suddenly changes his course of action when he saw Isaac's face. This unexpected consequence of the analysis counters articulate commentators such as Katz and Reiss who see the key to the Akedah when Abraham looked into Isaac's face and hence dropped the knife.[60] Unfortunately, as enticing as this thesis appears, it is not substantiated in the texts of Levinas. And, if true, would open up Levinas to serious counterfactuals that belie the pre-rational facticity of the primordial sight of the face. In her interpretative works, Claire Katz correctly states what Levinas said, but in this essay, I have tried to elicit the reasons why he said it. However the course of analysis refutes her claim that it was the sight of Isaac's face that was the turning point, the occasion for Abraham to drop his knife.

In this story of power and violence, the most powerful entity, according to Abraham, has ordered him to do violence to one of the persons he loves the most. The idea that Abraham could do all this and never encounter Isaac's face belies the narrative, and, in my estimation, trivializes both the theory and the relationship. Levinas never comments about the face in the Akedah, so let us not mistakenly apply it where he did not. For Levinas, it is about hearing and finally returning to the ethical by listening to the second voice. Levinas's hermeneutic acknowledges his debts to Kierkegaard, Rosenzweig, and Buber, and forms a way he can both align to and distinguish himself from them. He identifies a split in the philosophical road, which, after separating left and right Hegelians, understands Kierkegaard's truncated and encapsulated self and those that followed his path—Nietzsche, Heidegger, and Derrida. In contrast, Levinas charts out a path that is relational, intersubjective, non-encapsulated and less violent. For these reasons, I take a more strictly exegetical approach. Katz's eisegesis render Levinas subject to Derrida's criticism. In that case,

---

60. Claire Katz, "The Voice of God and the Face of the Other: Levinas, Kierkegaard, and Abraham," *Journal of Textual Reasoning* 10 (2001), http://jtr.lib.virginia.edu/archive/volume10/Katz.html; Moshe Reiss, "Abraham's Moment of Decision: According to Levinas and Rembrandt," *Jewish Bible Quarterly* 35, no.1 (2007): 56–59.

Levinas' contribution would be limited in any philosophical account of peace and nonviolence.

Fourth, future research is necessary to sort out how Levinas's notion of the tripartite "other" is the genesis of this return from infanticide to nonviolence. For philosophers concerned with the possibility of peace and nonviolence, Levinas offers a determined effort to overcome the violence of contemporary thought since Hegel. Derrida presents a critique of Levinas that undermines the possibility of nonviolence and peace. In the struggle to articulate an archaeology of peace, the dynamics of violence and nonviolence are exposed through the tensions elicited through the tension between Derrida[61] and Levinas.[62]

Fifth, Levinas's accomplishments provide a benchmark to developing an archaeology of peace. It is important to realize that peace involves both violence and nonviolence. The deconstruction of Levinas's position by Derrida proves less than successful, and also forms a basis of an approach to peace. The task of developing this archaeology of peace supersedes and goes beyond both thinkers, beyond even the reverence for Abraham and his people. The Akedah is a story of power, violence, and disquietude. Abraham is at a loss as he prepares and carries out an act of extreme violence commanded, he thinks, by a Supreme Being. The ultimate resolution is for any reader to affirm or deny. But if we follow Levinas's path we must go beyond Derrida's criticisms.

I agree with Martin Hagglund's claim that we must disassociate Derrida from Levinas.[63] A conflated view leads to a standstill intellectually. What is important for our essay is to understand that they function from two different foundational tropes: for Levinas it is relationships and intersubjectivity, and for Derrida it is a deconstructive method that overturns and subverts each statement. In Derrida nothing is finalized, all things are subject to deconstruction. In this sense Buber, Marcel, and Levinas are more optimistic because they attempt to articulate a phenomenology of interior human experience, one of the most elusive tasks of the last and present centuries. Derrida, according to Hagglund, undermines its possibility. Hagglund's argument that Levinas did not get alterity right is key to maintaining that Levinas contributes to a philosophy of nonviolence and peace. Derrida seeks to prove that it was not inherently possible because the other is a phenomenon

61. Jacques Derrida, "Violence and Metaphysics: An essay on the Thought of Emmanuel Levinas," in *Writing and Difference*, trans. Alan Bass (Chicago: University of Chicago Press, 1978): 79–153.

62. Levinas, "Jacques Derrida: Wholly Otherwise," in *Proper Names*, 55–62.

63. Martin Hagglund, "The Necessity of Discrimination: Disjoining Derrida and Levinas," *diacritics* 34, no. 1 (2004): 40–71.

that keeps changing and is indeterminably violent. As Derrida proclaims, the most nonviolent is the most violent. Unlocking this aporia is essential if one is to affirm that Levinas provides a way for Abraham to move from infanticide to unbinding, and most importantly, that Derrida's arguments hold if relationships and the other are discursive phenomena. In contraposition, Levinas's position holds if we understand others as non-discursive and pre-logical. A form of synchronicity, which Jung identified as an a-causal connection of two or more psycho-physic phenomena, is an essential basis for creating an adequate sense of relationships. The resolution of the Levinas/Derrida conflict suggests, and contemporary global thinkers seek, an enhanced theoretical trope that will allow for a reinterpretation of the story of the Akedah. This essay acknowledges Levinas's contributions and posits the need for an archaeology of peace that goes beyond Levinas's triadic other and Derrida's deconstruction. The root tropes change during this analysis from encapsulated subject, to dyadic dialogue between "I and Thou," to the triadic other of Levinas, past Derrida's undermining of Levinas through deconstructive skepticism. For a post-Levinasian archaeology of peace, relationships are regarded as synchronistic, following laws beyond dialectics, beyond discursive didactic thought.

Our study encourages further research into a peculiar sort of contemporary intellectual problem that has become acute in this age of instantaneous communication and global networking, a problem engendered by the prevailing situation in this late modern/postmodern milieu. This problem has been taken to extremes unimagined by many: the simultaneous experience of multiple interpretations coming from different sources, credible and non-credible, and from each vantage point, sufficient and insufficient. Existential and relational incommensurability seemingly undermines the axioms of interpretation because it makes discursive dialectics insufficient. On the positive side, the interpretive limits of dialectics open the exploration and study of synchronicity and simultaneous relations, which I call *hyperlectics*. The traditional subject/object viewpoint expands into a coming to know as a synchronistic relational situation. Our search for a prioritized vantage point yields to a synchronistic notion of engagement and causality. The need to envision simultaneous behavior and structure demands an intellectual process redefined to its purpose. Hyperlectics reveal multiple vantage points simultaneously and demands foundational and structural ways of envisioning moving viewpoints.

These insights arise from what can be aptly characterized as postmodern vertigo—a condition brought upon as one attempts to listen to and react to the myriad cultures and societies that are vying for survival in our contemporary world. As one listens to and attempts to form a coherent theory of meaning, the many proponents of the intellectual heritage of the modern West fail us and require a re-visioned response. As Levinas reminds us, "the encroachment of the present in the future is not the feat of the subject alone, but of intersubjective relationship."[64]

In summary, Levinas traces Kierkegaard's retrieval of subjectivity from the dialectics of Hegel, to the relation of Buber's "I-Thou" (Meeting), and establishes the triadic notion of the other both ordinary and divine. Derrida correctly identifies the further complexity of relationships but his method of deconstruction relies on past dialectics that critique peace and nonviolence because of the inherent variability of human experience and engagement. When going beyond Levinas into the hyperlectic and synchronistic structure of relationships, one realizes that Levinas, though groundbreaking, did not articulate the full complexity of relationships. It was not naïveté that kept Levinas from falling into the skepticism and lack of possibilities that Derrida affirms; his method brought him quite far.

Our post-Levinasian situation now demands retelling and interpretation of the Akedah that travels through the synchronistic tensions that pervade the story. Abraham and Isaac were pulled in many directions simultaneously. Abraham has lied to Sarah, loves his son, obeys a Supreme Being, leads a clan, is an elder who has charge of many—all at the same time. This is the hydra-like dynamic of the story that shatters "encapsulation," goes beyond the dyadic meeting and the triadic sense of other. Levinas was wise not to appeal to Isaac's face, because the value of this notion is primordial; by contrast, Isaac was familiar, was loved, and was a companion. Abraham is immersed in his relation to Isaac and listens to his questions. The notion of Abraham torn in various directions simultaneously does not undermine, as Derrida supposes, peace or nonviolence. Abraham had to break the Gordian knot of his relationships because great violence to loved ones and obedience to a Supreme Being were antithetical and tension producing. The nature of relationships create limits that Abraham had to live through; his choice was nonviolence.

In Levinas, the naturalism of Aristotle is found in the ethical priority for the flourishing of the other. It was Aristotle's mistake to think that few attain this ethical dimension, whereas in Levinas we find the relational self confronted with an asymmetrical synchronistic obligation to choose. And, it is otherwise than by being that one yields to ethics . . . it was otherwise than being that led Abraham to choose his son. Levinas's achievement beckons to us to build on

64. Levinas, "Time and The Other," 79.

his thought and to articulate the full complexity of synchronistic intersubjective relationships that have the potency to be nonviolent, ethical, and religious.

9

DERRIDA

Derrida and the Test of Secrecy

Chris Danta

Jacques Derrida[1] ends his 1993 essay "Passions: 'An Oblique Offering'" by confessing his taste in books. "Literature I could, fundamentally do without, in fact, rather easily," writes Derrida there. "If I had to retire to an island, it would be particularly history books, memoirs, that I would doubtless take with me, and that I would read in my own way, perhaps to make literature out of them."[2] What fascinates Derrida is not literature itself but rather the potential of the nonliterary text to become literary. Derrida explains this idea of the becoming-literary of the nonliterary text in one of his mediations on Genesis 22, the 1999 essay *Literature in Secret: An Impossible Filiation.* "Every text that is consigned to public space," he writes, "that is relatively legible or intelligible, but whose content, sense, referent, signatory, and addressee are not fully determinable *realities*—realities that are at the same time *non-fictive* or *immune from all fiction,* realities that are delivered as such, by some intuition, to a determinate judgment—can become a *literary* object."[3] Literature arises for Derrida wherever a text becomes decontextualized in some way as a result of its content, sense, referent, signatory or addressee being rendered indeterminate.

Literary writing is thus for Derrida writing that resists contextualization or writing that remains open to decontextualization. If we are wont to think

---

1. Some of the contextualizing material in the chapter appears in my book *Literature Suspends Death: Sacrifice and Storytelling in Kierkegaard, Kafka and Blanchot* (London: Continuum, 2011).

2. *On the Name,* ed. Thomas Dutoit (Stanford: Stanford University Press, 1995), 27–28.

3. *The Gift of Death and Literature in Secret,* trans. David Wills (Chicago: University of Chicago Press, 2008), 131. Original emphasis.

187

of deconstruction as a mode of literary criticism or a mode of thought whose essential object is literary writing, this is because Derrida associates the power of the literary with the power of decontextualization. One of Derrida's characteristic reading practices—we might even say, one of his interpretative ticks—is to isolate a decontextualizing phrase or sentence and then apply that decontextualizing phrase or sentence to a nonliterary text in order to facilitate its becoming-literary. This is precisely what he does in *Literature in Secret* when he goes to read the story of Abraham's near-sacrifice of Isaac in Genesis 22. Derrida begins this essay by formulating and then analyzing the following cryptic and idiomatic French sentence: *Pardon de ne pas vouloir dire.* There are a couple of ways of translating this sentence. The most literal translation would be "Pardon for not wanting to say." But one could also translate it "Pardon for not meaning," since *vouloir dire* means "to mean" in French. After first leaving it untranslated in *Literature in Secret*, David Wills then tries to capture the pun in Derrida's sentence by rendering it thus: "Pardon for not meaning (to say)" (119). What fascinates Derrida about this phrase *Pardon de ne pas vouloir dire* is that it seems to decontextualize itself and so becomes literary. "Is this, such an utterance, a sentence?" he asks.

> A phrase from a prayer? A request about which it is still too early, or already too late, to know whether it has simply been interrupted, whether it requires or excludes suspension points at the end? "Pardon for not meaning (to say) [. . .]" . . .
>
> An archaeologist might well wonder if the phrase is complete: "Pardon for not meaning (to say) . . . ," but what in fact? And to whom? Who to whom?
>
> There there is secrecy [*il y a là du secret*], and we sense that literature is taking over these words, without, for all that, appropriating them in order to fashion them to its purpose. (119, original square brackets)

"Pardon for not meaning (to say)" is a communication that paradoxically attempts to put an end to any further communication—that actively separates itself from its preceding context without at the same time establishing an alternative context of meaning that would enable further discourse. The sentence asks its reader's or its listener's forgiveness for the way it inexplicably suspends communication. It implies a desire for secrecy on the part of the author. But it gives the reader or listener no chance to interrogate this desire. The plea for forgiveness is in this sense a wholly defensive maneuver. While a secret is implied, the secret is effectively impenetrable because of the prohibition on further communication. To quote Derrida from the earlier essay "Passions," we might thus say that the sentence "Pardon for not meaning (to say)" keeps "a secret that is without content, without a content separable from its performative experience, from its performative tracing" (24).

In the way it performs the suspension of communication, "Pardon for not meaning (to say)" recalls the famous refrain of Herman Melville's unforgettable character Bartleby the scrivener: "I would prefer not to." In Melville's novella, the first-person narrator, an elderly Wall Street lawyer, tells of Bartleby's extraordinary career as a law-copyist in his New York practice. Initially, Bartleby throws himself into his new job and does an enormous amount of writing for the lawyer: "As if long famishing for something to copy," the narrator reports, "he seemed to gorge himself on my documents."[4] But feast turns to famish on the third day of Bartleby's employment when he responds to his new boss's request that the two of them read over a small paper together by saying, "'I would prefer not to'" (29). This whimsical response stuns the narrator: "'Prefer not to,' echoed I, rising in high excitement, and crossing the room with a stride. 'What do you mean? Are you moon-struck? I want you to help me compare this sheet here—take it'" (30). Like Derrida's "Pardon for not meaning (to say)," Bartleby's "I would prefer not to" disables further communication. It actively separates itself from the semantic context of professional duty without at the same time establishing another context of meaning in its place. Or, rather, it does establish an alternative context of meaning, but this alternative context is a purely private one, one that is entirely Bartleby-shaped. As Gilles Deleuze writes in his essay "Bartleby; or, The Formula":

> The formula I WOULD PREFER NOT TO excludes all alternatives, and devours what it claims to conserve no less than it distances itself from everything else. . . . If Bartleby had refused, he could still be seen as a rebel or insurrectionary, and as such would still have a social role. But the formula stymies all speech acts, and at the same time, it makes Bartleby a pure outsider [*exclu*] to whom no social position can be attributed. This is what the attorney glimpses with dread: all his hopes of bringing Bartleby back to reason are dashed because they rest on a logic of presuppositions according to which an employer "expects" to be obeyed, or a kind friend listened to, whereas Bartleby has invented a new logic, a logic of preference,

4. "Bartleby the Scrivener," in *The Piazza Tales* (New York: Russell & Russell Inc., 1963), 28.

which is enough to undermine the presuppositions of language as a whole. As Mathieu Lindon shows, the formula "disconnects" words and things, words and actions, but also speech acts and words—it severs language from all reference.[5]

This is why the lawyer-narrator accuses Bartleby of being "moon-struck": he realizes that the two men are no longer communicating with each other as if they are on the same planet. Deleuze explains this disconnect by suggesting that Bartleby invents a new logic, a logic of preference that undermines a logic of presuppositions. The lawyer expects Bartleby to help him look over the document because Bartleby's social role is to be a copyist. But by responding to the lawyer's demand to work with "I would prefer not to," Bartleby renounces this social role without at the same time actively adopting any other. Rather than a rebel or an insurrectionary, he turns himself into a "pure outsider"—someone with no social role whatsoever.

Deleuze's analysis of Bartleby's formula helps us to sharpen our understanding of Derrida's strange formulation "Pardon for not meaning (to say)." Like "I would prefer not to," "Pardon for not meaning (to say)" supplants a logic of presupposition with a logic of preference. Derrida says of his formula that it resembles a prayer because, like a prayer, it willfully retreats from the social realm into the private realm. It removes its writer or speaker from the social network and so makes him or her into a pure outsider: a Bartleby. While it asks for forgiveness (again, in the mode of a prayer), it only asks to be forgiven for suspending further communication or for retreating into silence and non-meaning. It diverges from a prayer in being addressed to all others, including God, and in withdrawing its speaker from the society of all others, including God. We might thus call it a secular, existential, or even literary prayer.

If we feel literature to be taking over utterances such as "Pardon for not meaning (to say)" and "I would prefer not to," I think this is because literary writing allows a logic of preference to overtake a logic of presupposition. Literature is utopian in this precise sense: in order to challenge or contradict our preconceptions about the world, the literary writer prefers the world to be otherwise than it is. As Jacques Rancière puts it in his essay "Deleuze, Bartleby, and the Literary Formula," "the unique power of literature finds its source in that zone of indeterminacy where former individuations are undone, where the eternal dance of atoms composes new figures and intensities every moment."[6] The effect of Bartleby and of his formula upon the narrator of Melville's story is

5. "Bartleby; or, The Formula," in *Essays Critical and Clinical*, trans. Daniel W. Smith and Michael A. Greco (New York: Verso, 1998), 73–74.

in this sense a literary effect: "With any other man I should have flown outright into a dreadful passion," the narrator tells us, "scorned all further words, and thrust him ignominiously from my presence. But there was something about Bartleby that not only strangely disarmed me, but, in a wonderful manner, touched and disconcerted me" (31). This strangely disarming aspect of Bartleby that simultaneously touches and disconcerts narrator and reader alike is his literariness: the sense in which he confounds our preconceptions about how people should be in the world.

At a number of points in his work, Derrida argues that literature is consubstantial with democracy—that literature's power to decontextualize something aligns with the twin democratic rights of the modern citizen to free speech and privacy. "Literature is a modern invention," writes Derrida in "Passions":

> Inscribed in conventions and institutions which, to hold on to just this trait, secure in principle *its right to say everything*. Literature thus ties its destiny to a certain noncensure, to the space of democratic freedom (freedom of press, freedom of speech, etc.). No democracy without literature; no literature without democracy. . . . The possibility of literature, the legitimacy that a society gives to it, the allaying of suspicion or terror with regard to it, all that goes together—politically—with the unlimited right to ask any question, to suspect all dogmatism, to analyze every presupposition, even those of the ethics or the politics of responsibility. . . . This authorization to say everything (which goes together with democracy, as the apparent hyper-responsibility of a "subject"), acknowledges a right to absolute nonresponse, just where there can be no question of responding, of being able to or having to respond. (28–29, original emphasis)

In the terms Derrida here develops, "Pardon for not meaning (to say)" constitutes the negative limit of the literary. It is a form of nonresponse that is "more original and more secret than the modalities of power and duty because it is fundamentally heterogeneous to them" (Derrida, "Passions," 29). Like Bartleby's "I would prefer not to," it momentarily suspends power relations between self and other by undoing previous individuations. As Bartleby's formula does the lawyer-narrator in Melville's story, Derrida's formula equally

6. "Deleuze, Bartleby, and the Literary Formula," in *The Flesh of Words: The Politics of Writing*, trans. Charlotte Mandell (Stanford: Stanford University Press, 2004), 149.

touches and disconcerts its listeners or readers by returning them to a state of pre-individuation. (It is interesting to note in this regard that the narrator in Melville's novella remains anonymous and so, in some sense, pre-individuated.)

Derrida's phrase "Pardon for not meaning (to say)" performs the right to nonresponse or secrecy that he associates with the modern institution of literature. But, as I've already mentioned, Derrida formulates and analyzes this secret of a literary type in order to tie it to a biblical rather than a literary character: to Abraham rather than Bartleby. His remarkable claim in *Literature in Secret* is that Abraham is the literary prototype of Bartleby. "Among all those, infinite in number throughout history, who have kept an absolute secret, a terrible secret, an infinite secret," he writes:

> I think of Abraham, starting point for all the Abrahamic religions, but also the origin of this fund without which what we call literature would probably never have managed to emerge as such and under that name. . . . I think of Abraham who kept the secret—speaking of it neither to Sarah nor even to Isaac—concerning the order given him [to sacrifice Isaac], in a tête-à-tête, by God. (121)

Rather than anachronistically applying a literary formula to a biblical text in order to make literature out of it, Derrida is in fact claiming to derive the literary formula from the biblical text itself. "Pardon for not meaning (to say)" is, for him, a fictive testament to the Abrahamic origin of literature.

Derrida's reading of Genesis 22 has the heretical effect of transforming Abraham from the father of faith into the father of secrecy: "Unilaterally assigned by God," Derrida writes, "the test imposed on Mount Moriah would consist in proving whether Abraham was capable of keeping a secret: in short, 'of not meaning to say . . .'" (*The Gift of Death,* 122, original emphasis). Indeed, Derrida urges us to go even further than this: insofar as the right to nonresponse or secrecy is constitutional to the modern institution of literature, he thinks we should understand Abraham's experience of secrecy in Genesis 22 not simply as an archetypal religious experience but also as an archetypal literary experience.

Derrida's interpretation of Genesis 22 in *Literature in Secret* is both paradoxical and overdetermined. Derrida here decontextualizes Genesis 22 by making it into a story about literature rather than faith; he applies a literary formula to the story of religious faith in order to facilitate its becoming-literary. But then (as if to shore up his interpretation) he claims, perhaps even more strangely, that the story itself calls for this act of decontextualization, or that the deconstruction of the religious by the literary is somehow already underway in Genesis 22 irrespective of his intervention. So what is it about the story that leads him to think this? Very simply, it is Abraham's acceptance of God's incredible command for him to sacrifice his beloved son Isaac and thus destroy the condition of possibility for his covenant with God. In Gen. 17:19, just after the covenant of circumcision, God says to Abraham, "your wife Sarah will bear you a son, and you will call him Isaac. I will establish my covenant with him as an everlasting covenant for his descendants after him." In Gen. 21:2, "Sarah became pregnant and bore a son to Abraham in his old age, at the very time God had promised him." Yet, God's extraordinary demand in Genesis 22 signals the imminent cancellation of all his former promises to Abraham. According to E. A. Speiser:

> Isaac was to Abraham more than a child of his old age, so fervently hoped for yet so long denied. Isaac was also, and more particularly, the only link with the far-off goal to which Isaac's life was dedicated (see xxi 12). To sacrifice Isaac, as God demanded, was to forego at the same time the long-range objective itself. The nightmare physical trial entrains thus a boundless spiritual trial.[7]

How can God ask Abraham to sacrifice Isaac when he is the very embodiment—and future—of God's covenant with Abraham? As the Danish philosopher Søren Kierkegaard, whose 1843 "dialectical lyric" *Fear and Trembling* exerts an enormous and direct influence on Derrida, ruminates in his journals: "The terrifying thing in the collision is this—that it is not a collision between God's command and man's command but between God's command and God's command."[8]

God's initial demand in Genesis 22 for Abraham to sacrifice Isaac makes no sense. In the terms I've been developing, it replaces a logic of presupposition, according to which Abraham supposes that God will establish his covenant with Isaac, with a logic of preference. What God is in effect saying to Abraham at the beginning of Genesis 22 is, "I would now prefer that you sacrifice Isaac." As Derrida notes in *Literature in Secret*, from the moment that Abraham accepts God's demand for him to sacrifice Isaac as absolutely binding, "there is nothing more sacred for Abraham, for he is ready to sacrifice everything. This test would thus be a sort of absolute *desacralization* of the world" (154, original emphasis).

<hr>

7. *Genesis*, Anchor Bible 1 (Garden City, NY: Doubleday, 1964), 164.

8. *Fear and Trembling*, trans. Howard V. Hong and Edna H. Hong (Princeton: Princeton University Press, 1983), 248.

In going to sacrifice Isaac, Abraham shows his willingness to give up on the meaning of the world as it comes to him from the divine.

We can now see why Derrida chooses to begin *Literature in Secret* with this phrase "Pardon for not meaning (to say)." What Abraham is asked to put an end to in Genesis 22 is not just the life of his beloved son but also the sense of his relation with God. The opening scene of Genesis 22 is thus a paradoxical moment in the Bible in which holy history seems to be at odds with itself. For Derrida, crucially, the temporary desacralization of the world that Abraham brings about as a result of following God's command to sacrifice Isaac is what allows for the later emergence of literature. Literature, Derrida writes in *Literature Suspends Death*,

> surely inherits from a holy history within which the Abrahamic moment remains the essential secret (and who would deny that literature remains a religious remainder, a link to and relay for what is sacrosanct in a society without God?), while at the same time denying that history, appurtenance, and heritage. It denies that filiation. It betrays it in a double sense of the word: it is unfaithful to it, breaking with it at the very moment when it reveals its "truth" and uncovers its secret. Namely that of its own filiation: impossible possibility. This "truth" exists on the condition of a denial whose possibility was already implied by the binding of Isaac. (157)

Derrida's point here is that the institution we have since the eighteenth century called literature is in some sense perpetually breaking with the religious, always denying its affiliation with holy history without being able to break decisively from this history. And what allows literature to enter into the religious text in order to break with it in this way, he thinks, is the moment of Genesis 22 in which Abraham goes at God's request to sacrifice the condition of possibility of the covenant.

So we might call Derrida's sentence "Pardon for not meaning (to say)" literary in one more sense: it expresses an impossible filiation with the Bible. In being a secular or an existential prayer, it denies its filiation with the religious. But, in keeping "a secret that is without content, without a content separable from its performative experience, from its performative tracing," it furtively and fugitively refers to Abraham's test of secrecy in Genesis 22.

"Above all, no journalists!"

In *Literature in Secret*, Derrida reduces literature and Genesis 22 alike to a primal scene of (non)communication. His reading of Genesis 22 and the literature that stems from this story depends entirely on the sense he gives to the initial exchange between God and Abraham over the sacrificial demand in verses 2 and 3 of the narrative:

> Then God said, "Take your son, your only son Isaac, whom you love, and go to the region of Moriah. Sacrifice him there as a burnt offering on one of the mountains I will tell you about."
>
> Early the next morning Abraham got up and saddled his donkey. He took with him two of his servants and his son Isaac. When he had cut enough wood for the burnt offering, he set out for the place God had told him about.

These two verses bear out Erich Auerbach's famous observation in *Mimesis: The Representation of Reality in Western Literature* that there is in the text of Genesis 22

> the externalisation of only so much as is necessary for the purpose of the narrative, all else left in obscurity; the decisive points in the narrative alone are emphasized, what lies beyond is nonexistent; time and place are undefined and call for interpretation; thoughts and feelings remain unexpressed, are only suggested by the silence and fragmentary speeches.[9]

Indeed, the Akedah, or the binding of Isaac, is so clipped or elisional in its mode of presentation that at times it is difficult to ascertain exactly what happens in it. The text says nothing about Abraham's emotional or psychological reaction to the divine command to sacrifice his beloved son. It only tells us what Abraham does the morning after receiving this command: gather together the sacrificial party and equipment and head out to the region of Moriah. The elliptical nature of the narrative at this point immediately begs the question: Does Abraham tell anyone about what God has asked him to do? Does he communicate the gruesome purpose of the journey to Moriah to his wife Sarah, his son Isaac, or even the two servants he takes on the journey to Mount Moriah?

---

9. *Mimesis: The Representation of Reality in Western Literature*, trans. Willard R. Trask (Princeton: Princeton University Press, 1953), 9.

For a number of prominent readers of the Genesis story there can be no doubt about the matter: Abraham kept God's sacrificial command to him a secret from any of the ethical authorities around him (his wife Sarah, son Isaac, and two servants). The interpretative gambit of Kierkegaard's *Fear and Trembling* is that Abraham somehow concealed his sacrificial intention from the other members of his household. "Was it ethically defensible of Abraham to conceal his undertaking from Sarah, from Eleazar, from Isaac?" (82), asks Kierkegaard's pseudonym Johannes de silentio in the third and concluding *problema* of *Fear and Trembling*. But Kierkegaard is certainly not the first to impute a form of silence or secrecy to the patriarch. Three important earlier readings of the story arrive at just this conclusion. Philo of Alexandria writes in his work *De Abrahamo*:

> Mastered by his love for God, [Abraham] mightily overcame all the fascination expressed in the fond terms of family affection, and told the divine call to none in his household, but taking out of his numerous following two only, the oldest and most loyal, he went forth with his son, four in all, as though to perform one of the ordinary rites.[10]

First century Jewish historian Flavius Josephus, draws the same inference as Philo in his *Antiquities of the Jews* (93 CE): "[Abraham] concealed this command of God, and his own intentions about the slaughter of his son, from his wife, as also from every one of his servants, otherwise he should have been hindered from his obedience to God."[11] Martin Luther is another commentator who attributes silence to the patriarch:

> I have said . . . that we cannot comprehend this trial; but we can observe and imagine it from afar, so to speak. . . . The text says nothing about Sarah, whether she was aware of this command or not. Perhaps . . . Abraham concealed this matter from her. . . . What do you suppose the sentiments of Abraham's heart were in this situation? He was a human being, and, as I have stated repeatedly, he was not without natural affection. Besides, the fact that he did not dare divulge to anyone what was happening made his grief greater. Otherwise all would have advised against it, and the large number of those who advised against it would perhaps have influenced him.

---

10. *De Abrahamo*, trans. F. H. Colson (Cambridge, MA: Harvard University Press, 1959), 87.

11. *The Works of Flavius Josephus*, trans. William Whiston (Edinburgh: William P. Nimmo, 1869), 36.

Therefore he sets out on the journey alone with young slaves and his son.[12]

In *Fear and Trembling*, Kierkegaard radicalises the silence Philo, Josephus and Luther readily impute to Abraham. For Kierkegaard, significantly, at no point in his trial did Abraham convey his sacrificial intention to another. "The relief provided by speech," de silentio claims, "is that it translates me into the universal" (113). By speaking, I make my actions intelligible to those around me. As Hegel puts it in the *Phenomenology of Spirit*: "Language is self consciousness existing *for others* . . . and as *this* self-consciousness is universal. . . . It perceives itself just as it is perceived by others."[13] Whereas in Genesis 21 Abraham is openly distressed when Sarah says to him, "Get rid of that slave woman [Hagar] and her son [Ishmael], for that slave woman's son will never share in the inheritance with my son Isaac" (Gen. 21:10), in Genesis 22 he seems to conceal his reaction to the divine command from others, thereby removing it from the realm of universal or ethical communication. According to de silentio, not only does Abraham refuse to disclose his sacrificial plans to anyone, he also continues to conceal the true purpose of the sacrifice even when Isaac asks him on the way to Mount Moriah, "The fire and the wood are here . . . but where is the lamb for the burnt offering?" (Gen. 22:7). Abraham's speculative response to this question—"God himself will provide the lamb for the burnt offering, my son" (Gen. 22:8)—must be ironic, de silentio thinks, "for it is always irony when I say something and still do not say anything" (118). If we are to understand "Abraham's total presence in that word" (118), then he did not speak. In a dramatic irony of the highest order, he bore God's demand entirely within himself. Abraham thus stands silent—and, as such, absolutely isolated—before the prospective reproach of others about the senselessness of his act: "When Abraham's heart is moved, when his words would provide blessed comfort to the whole world, he dares not offer comfort, for would not Sarah, would not Eliezer, would not Isaac say to him, 'Why do you want to do it, then? After all, you can abstain'" (114).

Like Kierkegaard, Derrida hears nothing more—or other—in the gap between verses 2 and 3 of the Genesis narrative than Abraham's silence. Derrida follows Kierkegaard in assuming that Abraham conceals his sacrificial mission in Genesis 22. But he goes one step further than Kierkegaard by labeling this assumption indisputable—"an absolute axiom" (*Literature in Secret*, 128). "No

12. *Luther's Commentary on Genesis*, trans. T. Theodore Mueller, vol. 2 (Grand Rapids, MI: Zondervan, 1958), 96, 98.

13. *Phenomenology of Spirit*, trans. A. V. Miller (New York: Oxford University Press, 1977), § 652.

one would dare dispute that the very brief account of what is called the sacrifice of Isaac or Isaac bound," writes Derrida in *Literature in Secret*:

> leaves no doubt as to this *fact*: Abraham keeps silent, at least concerning the truth of what he is getting ready to do, as far as what he knows about it but also as far as what he doesn't know and finally will never know. Concerning God's precise, singular call and command, *Abraham says nothing and to no one.* Neither to Sarah, nor to his own, nor to humankind in general. He does not reveal his secret or divulge it in any familial or public, ethical or political space. (128, original emphasis)

Here is a clear example of Derrida over-reading the Genesis narrative in order to shore up his interpretation against possible alternatives. But surely one anxiously overdetermines the matter of the story by calling Abraham's silence a fact? God never asks Abraham to keep his sacrificial command a secret in Genesis 22. It is not like that odd moment in Genesis 18, when the three mysterious visitors ask Abraham, "Where is your wife Sarah?" (18:9), as if to make sure that the patriarch is alone before he receives the good but unbelievable news from God that his wife will soon bear him a son. God never swears Abraham to secrecy—as Prince Hamlet swears Horatio and Marcellus to secrecy about the appearance of the ghost in Shakespeare's play. Nor do we read anywhere in the Bible that Abraham actively concealed his sacrificial purpose from those around him. This is rather something that the commentator deduces from the gaps in the text in the manner of a midrash—for example, as Luther does, from the fact that the "text says nothing about Sarah, whether she was aware of this command or not." A midrash is a response to the Bible that aims to fill a gap in the original text through fantasy and legend, explication and interpretation. Imagining Abraham to have kept the sacrificial command a secret satisfies the commentator's desire to account for Sarah's peculiar absence from the scene. Spelling out Abraham's motivations toward the rest of his household also imbues the event with a degree of psychological realism.

But if it seems psychologically plausible to imagine Abraham concealing his sacrificial mission as he leaves his home in Beersheba to set out for Moriah, it certainly strains the bounds of psychological probability to think that Isaac fails to intuit what is going on as the two approach the summit of Mount Moriah. When does Isaac realize that he is the one meant for the sacrifice? By the time he asks Abraham about the lamb for the sacrifice on the way to Moriah? When he is being bound to the altar? When Abraham takes the knife to slay him?

Rather than addressing this significant problem of Isaac's reaction to the sacrifice, Derrida and Kierkegaard simply ignore it by making the crucial point of the narrative what happens between God and Abraham. Each reads God's initial demand in Genesis 22 as a demand for absolute secrecy or silence on Abraham's part. Given that God is asking Abraham to murder his son, Kierkegaard thinks to himself, how can the patriarch be expected to speak of it to anyone else? Wouldn't they all respond to him by urging him to abstain from killing his beloved son? For the German Enlightenment philosopher Immanuel Kant, it is not just the content of God's command that is incredible but also the fact that a man believes he is speaking with God. Kant dismisses the Akedah most memorably in his 1798 text *The Conflict of the Faculties*:

> For if God were really to speak to man, the latter could after all never know that it is God who is speaking to him. It is utterly impossible for man to apprehend the Infinite through his senses, to distinguish him from sensible objects and thereby know him. He can, though, no doubt convince himself in some cases that it cannot be God whose voice he believes he hears; for if what it commands him to do is contrary to the moral law, he must regard the manifestation as an illusion, however majestic and transcending the whole of Nature it may seem to him to be.
>
> For example, consider the story of the sacrifice which Abraham was willing to make at the divine command by slaughtering and burning his only son—what is more, the child unwittingly carried the wood for the sacrifice. Even though the voice rang out from the (visible) heavens, Abraham ought to have replied thus to this supposedly divine voice, "It is quite certain that I ought not to kill my innocent son, but I am not certain and I cannot ever become certain that you, the 'you' who is appearing to me, are God."[14]

Here, Kant's focus on the rational has the comic effect of divesting the Akedah of all its dramatic tension. "Act in such a way that you always treat humanity, whether in your own person or in the person of others, never simply as a means, but always at the same time as an end," avers Kant famously in the *Groundwork of the Metaphysic of Morals*.[15] Abraham's sin in Genesis 22, as far as

---

14. Quoted in Robert L. Perkins, *Kierkegaard's Fear and Trembling: Critical Appraisals* (Birmingham, AL: University of Alabama Press, 1981), 32.

15. *Groundwork of the Metaphysic of Morals*, trans. H. J. Paton (New York: Harper, 1964), 96.

he is concerned, is to treat his son as a means to an end rather than an end in himself.

The problem with Kant's position on the Akedah is that "the hypothetical case of an acceptable yet religious sacrifice never arises."[16] What Kant is dismissing, then, is the very notion of sacrifice, which depends on the sacrificial victim—whether we consider this to be human or animal—becoming a means to an end. For Kierkegaard, if what Abraham does in Genesis 22 is rationally inexplicable, this is because "faith begins precisely where thought stops" (*Fear and Trembling*, 53). Faith is an end that justifies the terrible means of human (or animal) sacrifice. Contra Kant, Kierkegaard thus seeks to preserve the meaningfulness both of God's call "from the (visible) heavens" and of Abraham's response to this call. "If occasionally there is any response at all these days to the paradox," he notes in *Fear and Trembling*, "it is likely to be: One judges it by the result" (62). For Kierkegaard, in approaching Genesis 22 with an attitude of "that's to be judged by the outcome," thought skips too quickly to the happy end and so avoids thinking the terrible time of the trial: those three days Abraham spent approaching Moriah. Kierkegaard thinks Abraham is justified in keeping quiet about the sacrificial command because this silence preserves the prospective meaningfulness of this (and, indeed, of any other kind of) sacrifice. In this sense, Abraham is not just the father of faith, but also the father of sacrifice. This, no doubt, is why Kierkegaard came to think of the patriarch when he broke his engagement with Regine Olsen in November 1841, two years prior to publishing *Fear and Trembling* in October 1843.

Like Kierkegaard, Derrida also wants to preserve the meaningfulness of sacrifice against the kind of rationalist attack that Kant offers in *The Conflict of the Faculties*. For Derrida, however, the secret Abraham keeps has less to do with the content of the command than with the absolutely singular relationship that the command establishes between Abraham and God. The axiom that Abraham kept quiet about the sacrifice "obliges us to pose or to suppose a demand for secrecy," he writes, "a secret asked by God, by him who proposes or promises the covenant" (*Literature in Secret*, 154). Like Kierkegaard, Derrida obsesses about the implications of God's sacrificial demand. As he muses—quite amusingly—in his 2001 essay "Above All, No Journalists!":

What *must* God have said to Abraham? What did He tell him, necessarily, at the moment when he gave him the order to climb

16. Emil Fackenheim, *Encounters between Judaism and Modern Philosophy* (London: Jason Aronson, 1994), 62

Mount Moriah, accompanied by Isaac and his donkey, in view of the worst possible sacrifice?[17] What *could* and *should* He have told him? . . . What He must have told him can be summarized thus: "Above all, no journalists!"

To translate: What happens here, my summons and your response, your responsibility ("Here I am")—all of this must remain absolutely secret: just between us. It must remain *unconditionally* private, our internal affair and inaccessible: "Don't tell anyone about it." Reread the story: it underlines (and Kierkegaard amplified this point) the near-total silence of Abraham.[18]

A little later in "Above All, No Journalists!" Derrida renders the implications of God's command even more comically:

> God: "So, no mediator between us (not even Christ, who will have been the first journalist or news-man [*nouvelliste*], like the Evangelists who bring the Good News), no media between us. No third. The ordeal that binds us must not be newsworthy. This event must not be news: neither good nor bad." (57)

For Derrida, what God asks Abraham to prove in Genesis 22 is that he is "capable of keeping a secret" (*Literature in Secret*, 121). The *OED* defines *secret* as "some fact, affair, design, action, etc., the knowledge of which is kept to oneself or shared only with those whom it concerns or to whom it has been confided; something that cannot be divulged without violation of a command or breach of confidence."[19] But, for Derrida, Abraham's is not a secret in this ordinary or everyday sense of the word. As he notes in *Literature in Secret*, Abraham's "secret does not have the sense of something to hide as Kierkegaard suggests. . . . It is a secret without content, without any sense to be hidden, any secret other than the request for secrecy, that is to say the absolute exclusivity of the relation between the one who calls and the one who responds 'Here I am'" (154). On Derrida's account, it is almost as if God demands Isaac's sacrifice because he is ontologically jealous.

---

17. Derrida is wrong here about the donkey accompanying Abraham and Isaac up Mount Moriah. In Gen. 22:5, Abraham tells his servants when he sees Mount Moriah in the distance: "'Stay here with the donkey while I and the boy go over there. We will worship and then we will come back to you.'"

18. Derrida, "Above All, No Journalists!" in *Religion and Media*, ed. Hent de Vries and Samuel Weber (Stanford: Stanford University Press, 2001), 56, original emphasis.

19. *Oxford English Dictionary*, s.v. "secret," def. 3a.

Derrida's analysis of the Akedah in *Literature in Secret*, as well as in the earlier essay *The Gift of Death*, hinges on the fact that Abraham keeps two distinct but related kinds of secret in the event:

> First secret: he must not reveal that God has called him and asked the greatest sacrifice of him in the tête-à-tête of an absolute covenant. This is the secret he knows and shares. Second secret, super-secret: the reason for or the sense of the sacrificial demand. In this regard, Abraham is held to secrecy quite simply because the secret remains a secret for him. He is therefore held to secrecy not because he shares God's secret but because he doesn't share it. Although he is, in fact, as if passively held to the secret he doesn't know, any more than we do, he also takes passive *and* active responsibility, such as leads to a decision, for not asking God any questions, for not complaining as Job did, of the worst that seems to threaten him at God's request. (129, original emphasis)

According to the logic of the super-secret that Derrida develops in this passage from *Literature in Secret*, however actively or fastidiously Abraham pursues God's sacrificial request, he still remains in the dark as to its ultimate meaning. Since Abraham relates to the divine demand not just actively but also passively, he approaches Mount Moriah with as much uncertainty about what will happen there as his son.

The fact Abraham doesn't know what is going to happen on the summit of Moriah—the super-secret, as Derrida calls it—affects the way we read his response to Isaac. As Derrida points out in *The Gift of Death*, Abraham says something to Isaac "that is not nothing and that is not false. He says something that is not a non-truth, something moreover that, although *he doesn't know it yet*, will turn out to be true" (60, original emphasis). Although from an ethical point of view evasive, Abraham's reply to Isaac that the Lord will provide the lamb for the burnt offering is also a dim prophesy of the end of the story where the ram substitutes for the son. At this point in his reading, Derrida links Abraham to Bartleby. "If Abraham has already consented *to make a gift of death*," he writes in *The Gift of Death*, having just mentioned Bartleby,

> and to give to God the death that he is going to put his son to, if he knows that he will do it unless God stops him, can we not say that his disposition is such that he would, precisely, *prefer not to*, without being able to say to the face of the world what is involved? Because

he loves his son, he would prefer that God didn't let him do it, that he would hold back his hand, that he would provide a lamb for the holocaust, that the instant of this mad decision—once the sacrifice had been accepted—would lean on the side of nonsacrifice. He will not decide *not to*, he has decided *to*, but he would prefer *not to*. He can say nothing more and will do nothing more if the Other continues to lead him toward death, to the death that is offered as a gift. (75–76)

Abraham's response to Isaac substitutes a logic of preference for a logic of presupposition. Given the absence of the lamb at the point of Isaac's question, it is fair to assume that Isaac himself will be the sacrificial victim. But in his response to his beloved son, Abraham shows that he would prefer it to be otherwise. Abraham's reply is not simply ironic (as Kierkegaard says) but also properly literary—or utopian—in that it actively prefers the world to be otherwise than it is.

What is strange or unexpected about Derrida's Kierkegaardian account of the Akedah is that it fails to take note of a deconstructive consequence that follows from its positing of the super-secret. According to the logic of the super-secret, the sacrifice requires both activity and passivity on the part of the sacrificial subject, since it orients this subject toward an unknown—indeed, an unknowable—future. But if this is the case, if Abraham relates both actively and passively to God's demand in Genesis 22, then why can't he tell others about what he has been asked to do? Why must Abraham take sole and terrible responsibility for the sacrifice? Why must he interiorise his despair as Isaac's father and remain silent about the death sentence that God has passed down? Of course, it is always possible to locate this activity and this passivity within the one subject, as both Kierkegaard and Derrida do by having their Abrahams take sole responsibility for the sacrificial event. But it is certainly not necessary that we do so. We might just as well locate the paradoxical interplay of activity and passivity in the intersubjective space that sacrifice necessarily opens up between human beings and between species. Indeed, given that the sacrificial event in Genesis 22 involves both Isaac and the ram, this would seem to be a much more natural line of interpretation to adopt than the one taken by Derrida and Kierkegaard.

My point here is that the Akedah does not just concern what happens between Abraham qua single individual and God. In thinking about the sacrifice we must take into account not just the patriarch's tacit decision to follow God's command but also Isaac's tacit decision to follow Abraham's command. The sacrifice in Genesis 22 depends for its meaning not simply upon the one who decides in secret to sacrifice (Abraham) but also upon the one who decides in secret to be sacrificed (Isaac). It depends, moreover, upon the sacrificial communion that father and son willingly enter into as they approach Moriah together with a quiet heart.

Derrrida's reading of the Akedah as a test of secrecy has the surprising—and one might say, literary—effect of emptying the Genesis story of its content. The more weight Derrida gives to the implications of God's initial command for Abraham to sacrifice Isaac the less what follows this scene seems to matter. "In order for this request to have the sense of a trial," Derrida writes in *Literature in Secret*,

> the veritable object of the divine injunction had to be something other than putting Isaac to death. Moreover, what interest could God have in the death of this child, even if it were offered as a sacrifice? That is something he will never have said or meant to say. The putting to death of Isaac therefore becomes secondary, which is an even more monstrous eventuality. In any case it is not the thing to be hidden, the content of a secret that is to be safeguarded. It has no sense. And everything will hang on this suspension of sense. God's injunction, his command, his request, his imperious prayer, are designed only to test Abraham's endurance, to put it to the test of an absolutely singular appeal. It is only a matter of his determination, his passive-and-active commitment not-to-be-able-to-mean-to-say, to keep a secret even under the worst conditions, hence unconditionally. To enter into an unconditionally singular covenant with God. Simply in order to *respond*, in a responsible way, to answer to the coresponsibility that is committed to by means of the appeal. That is the test of unconditionality in love, namely the oath sworn between two singularities. (155, original emphasis)

Derrida's focus on the secret ultimately falls prey to the same problem as Kierkegaard's focus on silence: it gives Abraham all the power in the situation by allowing him to interiorize the sacrificial decree, which is to say, to take both active and passive responsibility for it.

In making the crux of Genesis 22 what happens between God and Abraham, Derrida and Kierkegaard fail to offer an account of the victim of the sacrifice. Or else they consider this victim to be Abraham. In *Fear and Trembling*, silence figures a form of betrayal—specifically, the betrayal of one being by another. Silence is the demon's trap: by concealing the purpose of his sacrificial mission, Kierkegaard's Abraham betrays ethics since ethics demands disclosure and punishes secrecy. The only acceptable silence, as far as Kierkegaard is concerned, is that which the father of faith keeps with the divine, Abraham with God. This silence marks the exclusiveness of Abraham's covenant with God. It would be, Derrida remarks in *Literature in Secret*,

> as if God were to have said to Abraham, "Don't speak of it to anyone. Not so that nobody *knows* (and in fact, it is not a question of *knowledge*), but so that there is no third party between us, nothing of what Kierkegaard will call the generality of the ethical, political, or juridical. Let there be no third party between us, no generality, no calculable knowledge, no conditional deliberation, no hypothesis, no hypothetical imperative, so that the covenant remains absolute and absolutely singular in its act of election. You will undertake not to open yourself up to anyone else". . . . In short, the secret to be kept would have, at bottom, to be without an object, without any object other than the unconditionally singular covenant, the mad love between God, Abraham, and what descends from him. His son and name. (154–56, original emphasis)

Derrida once again goes too far here in arguing that the secret Abraham keeps with God in Genesis 22 is without an object and involves no third party. For, in so doing, he strangely occludes the problem of the victim of the sacrifice—whether we consider this victim to be Isaac or the ram that eventually substitutes for Isaac.

Dominick LaCapra picks up on this occlusion in his book *History and Its Limits*:

> The fact that the question of the victim does not become a key problem for Derrida [in *The Gift of Death*] may seem surprising since in sacrifice the typical gift is the victim. The actual sacrifice of the ram as a substitute for Isaac is a seeming nonissue, as it tends to be in other accounts of the Abraham story. The ram (caught in a thicket by its horns—as if already trapped and bound) seems at best to be an "extra" that remains offstage. And Isaac as potential sacrificial victim plays at most a cameo part. At least in *The Gift of Death* [but we can also say in its follow-up, *Literature in Secret*], the dialogue is almost exclusively one that involves Abraham, God, and Derrida. Neither

the human nor the other-than-human animal as sacrificial victim is given a "voice" or significant role in the excessive focus on the excessive gift.[20]

Rather than in terms of "voice," we might just as well put the problem in terms of "silence": there is not just Abraham's silence to consider in Genesis 22, but also Isaac's silence, the ram's silence, the silence of the two servants who accompany Abraham and Isaac to Moriah, not to mention the silence of the one who doesn't: Abraham's wife Sarah.

We might now say that silence is not simply the demon's trap but also the commentator's trap. This is because silence overspills the limits—and the control—of the single individual by putting that individual in relation to others, whether these be human or nonhuman. As soon as one imagines Abraham to have remained silent in Genesis 22 then all kinds of other silences come into play—silences that act in relation to Abraham's and that show him to be still acting in relation to others. Both Derrida and Kierkegaard try to make the crucial point of the narrative what happens—in secret—between God and Abraham. But this attempt to sequester the individual's relation to the divine ultimately comes unstuck because it crucially alters our sense of the sacrifice's eventuality. By making the Akedah solely a matter between God and Abraham, by occluding the problem of the sacrificial victim, Derrida and Kierkegaard stop us from imagining the sacrifice eventuating as it did—happily for its human participants, with the ram's substitution for Isaac. Or rather, both lead us into a kind of hermeneutic temptation by allowing us to imagine the sacrifice as eventuating in a way that it didn't. Kierkegaard writes in *Fear*

---

20. *History and Its Limit: Human, Animal, Violence* (London: Cornell University Press, 2009), 182. Derrida does briefly give the ram in Genesis 22 a voice in his essay "Rams": "One imagines the anger of Abraham's and Aaron's ram, the infinite revolt of the ram of all holocausts. But also, figuratively, the violent rebellion of all scapegoats, all substitutes. Why me?" *Sovereignties in Question: The Poetics of Paul Celan*, ed. Thomas Dutoit and Outi Pasanen (New York: Fordham University Press, 2005), 157. He also considers the ram's perspective parenthetically in *The Animal That Therefore I Am*: "(ask Abraham's ass or ram or the living beast that Abel offered to God: they know what is about to happen to them when men say "Here I am" to God, then consent to sacrifice themselves, to sacrifice their sacrifice, or to forgive themselves)" *The Animal That Therefore I Am*, ed. Marie-Louise Mallet, trans. David Wills (New York: Fordham University Press, 2008), 30. But LaCapra is right to point out that Derrida largely ignores the problem of the victim of the sacrifice in *The Gift of Death*. Derrida raises the question of the animal victim of sacrifice in this text in relation to his pet cat (perhaps the same one who sees him step naked from his shower and inspires his essay *The Animal That Therefore I Am*): "How would you ever justify the fact that you sacrifice all the cats in the world to the cat that you feed at home every morning for years, whereas other cats die of hunger at every instant?" (71).

and Trembling: "We glorify Abraham, but how? We recite the whole story in clichés: 'The great thing was that he loved God in such a way that he was willing to offer him the best.' . . . So we talk and in the process of talking interchange the two terms *Isaac* and *the best*, and everything goes fine" (28, original emphasis). For Kierkegaard, we only become sleepless when we stop speaking so metaphorically about the story and imagine ourselves actually taking Abraham's place in the journey to Moriah. But this existential thought experiment also requires us to forget that Abraham never has to sacrifice Isaac in Genesis 22. LaCapra notes that a similar confusion vitiates Derrida's analysis in *The Gift of Death*: "Derrida recognises that God (or his angelic messenger) stops the human sacrifice and that Abraham displaces it onto the animal. But Derrida understands the Akeda 'as if Abraham had already killed Isaac' in the instance of Abraham's decision" (182).

"Who would I show it to"

Rather than allowing us to take account of the surprising end of the Genesis story in which the angel of the Lord stops Abraham's hand and draws attention to the hapless ram caught in a thicket that is to be substituted for Isaac, what I've tried to show here is that Derrida's reading of the Akedah constantly throws us back to the mad moment at the beginning of the story when Abraham decides, perhaps in secret, to accept God's sacrificial request. For Derrida, Genesis 22 shows us that there is something like the trauma of the address in which the Other's demand for the self to sacrifice the very sense of the world traumatically casts that self into a state of irremediable secrecy. But what the end of the Akedah shows us is that the living self can never be completely isolated from the rest of the world. The ram's substitution for Isaac illustrates that absolute secrecy—the isolation of one being by another—is impossible or that, to reverse Derrida's formulation in *Literature in Secret*, there is always a third party between us. If Genesis 22 is a kind of animal fable, then its lesson is that the human being is drawn out of itself into the realm of generality at the point at which the animal sacrificially takes its place.

According to Derrida in *Literature in Secret*, "there is no literature that does not, from its very first word, ask for forgiveness. In the beginning was forgiveness. For nothing. For meaning (to say) nothing" (157). But if literature asks for forgiveness from its very first word, this is because it betrays the singularity or the privacy of the relation between self and other. Literary writing cannot help but expose the particular to the general. Bartleby's literary refrain "I would prefer not to" empties the speaking subject of its qualities or particularities by invoking an empty, withdrawn and abstract sense of interiority. As Deleuze writes:

> Bartleby is the man without references, without possessions, without properties, without qualities, without particularities: he is too smooth for anyone to be able to hang any particularity on him. Without past or future, he is instantaneous. I WOULD PREFER NOT TO is Bartleby's chemical or alchemical formula, but one can read inversely I AM NOT PARTICULAR as its indispensable complement. ("Bartleby; or, The Formula," 74)

We might say the same thing of Isaac at the moment the ram takes his place in the sacrifice: namely, that he is not particular but is instead being defined by something outside him that takes his place. If literature (as Derrida suggests) is a form of secrecy without content, this is because it communicates by sacrificing the self's absolute particularity.

By way of conclusion, let me very briefly analyze a short poem that makes this point and that recalls both Derrida's discussion of Abraham in *Literature in Secret* and Melville's character Bartleby. The American poet W. S. Merwin's poem "Elegy"—surely one of the shortest in the English language—consists of a single, unpunctuated line: "Who would I show it to."[21] In this poem, we hear both Bartleby's "I would prefer not to" and Derrida's "Pardon for not meaning (to say)." The poet, overcome with grief, would prefer not to write the poem that laments the other he has lost. To prevent his relationship with his subject from being exposed to the media, from becoming news so to speak, he empties the poem of any content so that the only name it bears is that of its genre: elegy. But there is a price to be paid for sacrificing the absolutely particular to the general in this way: the poet must ask forgiveness both from his subject and his reader. "Pardon for not meaning (to say)," he might thus say. Pardon for not being more specific. Like Bartleby's and Derrida's literary formulas, Merwin's poem keeps a literary secret, "a secret that is without content, without a content separable from its performative experience, from its performative tracing."[22] In so doing, it alludes to Abraham's test of secrecy in Genesis 22—not just to the mad moment at the beginning of the story when Abraham decides in secret to sacrifice his "only son," whom he loves, Isaac, but also to the equally mad

21. W. S. Merwin, *The Second Four Books of Poems: The Moving Target / The Lice / The Carrier of Ladders / Writings to an Unfinished Accompaniment* (Port Townsend, WA: Copper Canyon Press, 1993), 226.

22. Derrida, *On the Name*, 24

moment at the end of the story when this secret loses its specificity as Abraham decides to sacrifice the ram instead of Isaac.

PART IV

Today

Our Journeys to Moriah

Bradley Beach

In this world there is nothing more difficult to comprehend than the murder of a child by a parent. Who can fathom the motives of a person who would intentionally take the life of his or her own child? For most of us such actions can only be explained in terms of either madness or profound duress—and even duress often seems a questionable motive. It is because of the incomprehensibility of such actions that the biblical account of Abraham taking his son Isaac to the mountains of Moriah is so odious. How can one morally comprehend the actions of Abraham, the patriarch of Israel and the father of Judaism, Islam, and Christianity? Such an occurrence seems foreign to the justice and benevolence of God and it also seems repugnant for Abraham to acquiesce to such a request from God. It would be better for us if this story never existed or were expunged forever from the sacred traditions of religion. Unfortunately, we do not have this luxury. We are forced to confront the narrative and to make sense of it in light of our understanding of God, faith, and moral duty. How is it that Abraham can be called the father of faith and be held up as an example for his obedience and faithfulness to God in Heb. 11:17-19? What would ordinarily be called an act of either homicide or madness is instead praised in the religious traditions as the epitome of faithfulness to a holy, righteous, and just God. For the believer, the persistent question is how can Abraham's actions at Moriah be reconciled with our understanding of God?

For some there remains a simple, clear, and unreflective response to this question. To the person of pure, innocent, and unwavering belief, the story is a call to exercise complete faith in God—regardless of costs or consequences. It is predicated on the assumptions that God is ultimate moral authority and that God will make all things right in the end. Under this view, the belief that God requires Abraham to sacrifice his only son is, ultimately, all that matters. The covenant made between God and Abraham, the promises by God to produce through Isaac a great nation and to bless all peoples through his descendants, even the moral justice of a righteous and holy God are put into abeyance for this simple believer in light of God's command that Abraham sacrifice his son. In this case, all focus is on the demand and upon Abraham's response. Does Abraham love God enough and trust God enough to do *whatever* God requires of him? Does our faith run deep enough that we can believe that God will do literally *anything* to bring God's plans to fruition—even resurrecting a dead child? In this reading of the account, all that matters is faith and nothing else. Reason does not matter, logical consistency does not matter, even God's goodness and unchanging character does not matter. From this perspective, God is putting our faith to the test and it becomes an either/or. Either we will fail to put God first and let our own volitions supplant God's will, or we will trust exclusively in God and allow God's desires to reign over our own. In the end, the question for such a person is simply do we have enough faith in God to trust God *no matter what*?

In truth there is something attractive about this interpretation. Can we simply believe in God and not be swayed by any other influences? Is God truly first in the life of the believer, or has the believer held in reserve some part that is off limits to everyone . . . including God? This is, no doubt, a powerful archetype that confronts the person who claims to be faithful to God. A very simple and concise alternative that must be resolved for the believer, it is an either/or.

But the problem confronting Abraham in Genesis 22 is much more subtle, layered, and nuanced than the simple either/or and it demands much more of us than simply a decision for or against God. It raises the matter of attunement with the divine and the specter of whether we are truly listening to the voice of God. Are we listening to God or have we allowed other voices (ourselves, our culture, madness, etc.) to usurp the divine will? In addition, it raises concerns about the nature of God. Is a person who would require the sacrifice of our child worthy of admiration and devotion? How can a truly good God demand a human sacrifice? Is such a request consonant with a morally good God, a God who loves us and wants what is good for us? Does God not have to keep promises because of who God is? Can reason be abrogated because it is God who gives the command? And if the answers to all of these questions are affirmative, then on what grounds can the believer come to put her trust in such a God? Why choose to love and follow one who is not what we understand to be good, right, holy, and rational? If something is right simply because the words: "God says" are attached to it, then is there any sense to the claim that one ought to worship and love God? All of these points are salient to this confrontation between God and Abraham. So much more is at stake than simply whether or not one will be found faithful. Belief itself rests on whether it is possible to reconcile Abraham's decision to take Isaac to Moriah with our understanding of who God is. Simple faith sounds very enticing, but it may very well become a trap in which to become ensnared. For the theist who claims that God is on our side and that we are right to believe in God, it must be both reason and faith that are at work. Reason requires that it be logically coherent to believe and that there is a deontic sense in which we are obligated to submit to God. It is not simply *doxa* but duty that the theist insists is behind decisions to obey God, including Abraham's judgment to sacrifice his son, his only son—Isaac.

These points should not be too quickly agreed to and passed over. There are, unquestionably, unique logical considerations in the Akedah story that make it troublesome for the faithful. Obviously there are an ample number of cases in history where parents were compelled to sacrifice their own children for some higher end. For example, there is the instance of Brutus who sentences his own sons to death for the good of the Republic. Jephthah, who promises a sacrifice to God for success in battle, never conceives that his own daughter will be the first to meet him upon his return and so must be his promised sacrifice. Agamemnon calls upon the gods for a favorable wind to Troy and is instructed to offer his daughter Iphigenia as a sacrifice; she willingly agrees to be killed for the good of the nation. In each of these instances, there is the belief that the sacrifice was necessary in order to bring about a greater good. There is a sense in which we can understand how such decisions could be made. Søren Kierkegaard identifies these individuals as tragic heroes.[1] We can morally understand such tragic heroes and can sympathize with their decisions. But as Kierkegaard notes in his work *Fear and Trembling*, Abraham is far from a tragic hero. There is nothing tragic or heroic in Abraham's decision. In choosing to sacrifice his son, he has decided for something lesser. This is not done for the good of the nation, nor for some higher end, not even for the good of someone else. Tragic heroes we can understand because they put their own wishes aside for some greater good. But this is not the situation with Abraham, since his behavior is not the behavior of a hero but rather that of an antihero. If this act

---

1. In Fear and Trembling Kierkegaard identifies the tragic hero in problema 2: Is there an absolute duty to God? He points out that the tragic hero is ethically understandable as well as sympathetic. The tragic hero makes personal sacrifices for something greater than personal ends. This we can understand and we sympathize with the hero.

is not heroic and not madness, how does it become an archetype of faithfulness and emblematic of how we should live before God?

A more complete and satisfying answer to these concerns is developed in a variety of different religious perspectives as well as philosophical writings within the Judeo-Christian-Islamic tradition. One of the most compelling voices to attempt an answer has been the previously mentioned Danish philosopher Søren Kierkegaard, in his work *Fear and Trembling*. In many ways, Kierkegaard's interpretation of the Akedah story has become the focal point for clarity about Abraham and his sacrifice of Isaac. Many of the modern interpretations of the Akedah story have been influenced by Kierkegaard, as the essays in this book clearly reflect. Franz Kafka is haunted by Kierkegaard's *Fear and Trembling*, using Kierkegaard's interpretation as a means of revealing the utter transcendence of God as well as God's hiddenness. Our own sense of alienation and of being alone in the world is what is at the heart of Abraham's confrontation with God at Moriah, as Kafka reads Kierkegaard. The absurdity that Kierkegaard identifies as inherent in and essential to the movement of faith brings to high relief our aloneness and our alienation, according to Kafka. Such notions, which are intended to complete the understanding of Genesis 22, are uncovered for Kafka in Kierkegaard's *Fear and Trembling*.

Emmanuel Levinas presents his views of the Akedah story in reaction to the Kierkegaardian understanding of the Abrahamic encounter with the Divine. Levinas rejects Kierkegaard's belief in the event as a teleological suspension of ethical duty; instead Levinas views the encounter as a restoration of the ethical in Abraham. It is not merely a subjective and particularized tête-à-tête between God and Abraham, but rather a tripartite relational encounter that makes clear to Abraham his moral obligations to God and to Isaac. Similarly, Jacques Derrida's interpretations of Abraham's action and its significance also stems from his reading of Kierkegaard. God's command to Abraham is understood by Derrida as a direct challenge to God's own commands. In agreeing to sacrifice his son, Abraham is giving up the meaning of the world as it comes from the Divine. It is the desacralization of holy history to offer such a sacrifice and as such must be met with silence from Abraham. As Derrida himself points out, Kierkegaard recognizes the silence of Abraham before the moral authorities—his wife Sarah, his servant Eleazar, and even his son Isaac. In *Fear and Trembling* Kierkegaard begins *problema 3* by asking the question: "Was it ethically defensible of Abraham to conceal his purpose from Sarah, from Eleazar, from Isaac?"[2] Derrida, following Kierkegaard's lead, interprets this silence as instrumental to and indicative of Abraham's "faith of secrecy." Abraham's silence is required because of the secrets that he shares with God.

First, there is the secret that it is God who has called him to sacrifice his son—a secret they share. More importantly, there is the super-secret that Abraham cannot share with anyone else, namely, the *reason* for this sacrifice. Derrida believes this cannot be shared because Abraham himself does not share this secret with God and so cannot communicate this information to others. Abraham does not know the purpose of God's command to sacrifice Isaac and so remains in the dark. Yet he chooses to actively participate in the divine plan while elliptically expressing his preference not to do so by answering Isaac's query about the sacrifice with the response: "God will provide a sacrifice." The Akedah story becomes a test of secrecy for Abraham, according to Derrida, an interpretation first revealed in Kierkegaard.

Not only are those who succeed Kierkegaard influenced by him in their interpretations of the Akedah story and in their attempts at reconciliation, but those who precede Kierkegaard also seem to be best approached in terms of his account. When we turn to Immanuel Kant, we encounter a thinker who insists that God is accessible to us only by means of the ethical via the voice of the moral conscience. In light of this epistemic gateway to the supersensible, is it possible that God could command Abraham to violate the universal and necessary moral dictates by sacrificing his only son? For Kant the answer must be a resounding NO! If you "hear" a voice commanding you to violate the moral law, Kant states you can be sure that it cannot be the voice of God. But of even more significance for Kant is the question of the role that history and historical events may play in religious belief formation and salvation. The question is framed for us and examined by Kierkegaard in his work *Philosophical Fragments*. In the *Fragments*, Kierkegaard begins the work by asking, "can a historical point of departure be given for an eternal consciousness; how can such a point of departure be of more than historical interest; can an eternal happiness be built on historical knowledge?"[3] Is it possible for someone who occupies history to come to know what is eternal and is it possible to base salvation upon such historically grounded information? Kant must insist that such knowledge cannot be acquired historically and that the Akedah story cannot be a point of departure on the pathway to personal salvation. Kierkegaard will unequivocally disagree with Kant on this matter, and he will say as much in both the *Fragments* and the *Concluding Unscientific Postscript*. It is Kierkegaard who becomes the foil

2. Søren Kierkegaard, Fear and Trembling, trans. Alistair Hannay (London: Penguin Books, 2003), 109.

3. Søren Kierkegaard, Philosophical Fragments, trans. David Swenson (Princeton: Princeton University Press, 1962), 1 (title page).

for Kant and it is Kierkegaard, unlike Kant, who finds the story of Abraham to be meaningful to the believer.

Hegel, too, is best contrasted with Kierkegaard in explaining his interpretation of the Akedah story; this is most easily explained by the fact that Kierkegaard himself is responsible for setting up the dichotomy. Hegel interprets the religious in terms of the social and the political. As such, for Hegel it is impossible for the particular to rise above the universal and for the individual to transcend societal expectations and demands. The state must be the earthly manifestation of God and it functions as God's presence on earth, according to Hegel. Kierkegaard proposes, in *Fear and Trembling*, that Abraham, as the knight of faith, can enter into an absolute relationship with the absolute through a teleological suspension of the ethical. Such a relationship is not to be availed in Hegel's conception of God and faith. Under Hegel's understanding of the ethical, Abraham stands condemned for his deed as a murderer. In Hegel's purification process, it is Abraham himself who is ultimately washed away. In *Fear and Trembling*, Kierkegaard essentially intends to provide an antidote to what he takes to be the limitations of the Hegelian views on God and Abraham.

Even the historical interpretations of the Akedah story as formulated within the Judeo–Christian–Islamic religious traditions take on a richer and more robust exegesis when filtered through the prism of Kierkegaard. The Islamic emphasis upon submission to God's will through Abraham's willingness to sacrifice his son is echoed in the pages of *Fear and Trembling*. Kierkegaard does not have Abraham confer with his son about God's demand nor does the son consent to become a sacrifice to God. These aspects of the Islamic version of the Akedah story stand in opposition to Kierkegaard's interpretation; in doing so they change the moral nature of the story. It becomes an account of submission to God by both father and son, their submission presenting an opportunity for disguised blessing from God. By highlighting a different set of aspects in the story, this explanation gives an ethical dimension to Abraham's actions. This is something that stands out in contrast to Kierkegaard's views.

The Christian eisegesis of Genesis 22 connects the sacrifice of Isaac, the son of Abraham, with the sacrifice of Christ, the son of God. It becomes a story that prefigures the atonement and is meant to provide an historical arch to salvation history. This Christian approach to the Akedah story shares with Kierkegaard's rendition an emphasis upon the need for God's grace. In both accounts there is the recognition of our own insufficiency and the need to throw ourselves upon the mercy of God's grace.

Finally, the Judaic interpretation of Abraham once again challenges Kierkegaard and his views. Behind God's seemingly cruel demand there is a higher purpose present, a purpose yet to be revealed. We must look forward to an eschatological verification of Abraham's actions; God's ultimate plans for Israel are yet to be made known. It functions as a type of covenantal relationship between God and the nation of Israel. God will remain always loyal to Israel, saving them from destruction, if Israel will remain faithful to God. For Kierkegaard there is the emphasis upon the subjective character of Abraham and his actions. Abraham acts as a solitary figure, acting alone and individually before God. For Kierkegaard, Abraham's behavior cannot be an example for us but rather is intended to point us toward God. As such, Abraham does not act on behalf of others but acts in isolation.

All attempts to reconcile God and Abraham in fuller, more complete, and intellectually satisfying terms have, either directly or indirectly, made their way through Søren Kierkegaard. He acts as either a catalyst or as a foil. Regardless how one views the Akedah story, it seems clear that all of us must confront certain fundamental human concerns inherent in the narrative. Each of us must follow the path of Abraham and make our way to the mountains of Moriah. In the life of the believer there inevitably arise moral dilemmas that require one to struggle in choosing between conflicting duties. More substantively, the theist must wrestle with the ineffable nature of the divine, the paradoxes of religious belief, and the mysteries of faith in a hidden God. It has been said that to become a wholehearted believer it is necessary to be persuaded not merely with the passions, but with the whole person. The "heart" of the individual is the ruling center of the entire person, so that rational functions are ascribed to the heart and not just emotive functions. To believe with the whole heart is to assert that we are committed at the very roots of our existence. In this sense of wholehearted commitment, one must be convinced equally with the passions and with the reason. The objects of faith must not only have existential import for us but must be rationally convincing for us as well. Such notions of wholehearted commitment hardly seem congruent with the story of Abraham and yet I believe this is precisely the point of convergence. The journey to the mountains of Moriah is made in order to satisfy the heart, to make the person of faith satisfied in her understanding of God and what it is that God requires of us. Kierkegaard insists that only the knight of faith can understand what it is to enter into an absolute relationship with the absolute. For all others this movement of faith is absurd. From the perspective of Abraham, who has completed the sacrifice of his only son, the movement of faith to God makes perfect sense. It is for us, as "objective" observers, that these requirements of God seem paradoxical and absurd. If Abraham returns from the mountains of Moriah with the same dread with which he left, then all is lost. There is merely mystery, confusion, and ultimately silence. For the sojourner to Moriah, the point of the journey is to enter into a new relationship with the absolute. Abraham returns to Beersheba no longer with fear and trembling but persuaded that he has now entered into a new and complete relationship with God.

We would prefer to suspend judgments about God until we have sufficient evidence. However, there is no such safe and neutral ground from which to approach God. The evidence we seek in knowing God is not going to become available to us until we make the journey to Moriah. This journey is essential to our faith, for it is the means by which the believer can become wholeheartedly committed—or turned away forever. It is in the struggle with the divine that the reason can finally be convinced and we can achieve the requisite evidence for whole-hearted commitment. Like Abraham we must each make our own way to the mountains of Moriah, and yet it is possible for Abraham to help illuminate our way. It is in the Akedah story that each of us can find the truths to help us chart our course to Moriah with fear and trembling.

Bibliography

Ackroyd, P. R., and C.F. Evans, eds. *The Cambridge History of the Bible: From the Beginnings to Jerome.* Cambridge: Cambridge University Press, 1970.

Ambrose. *Letters.* Translated by Mary Melchior Beyenka, OP. Fathers of the Church, vol. 26. New York: Catholic University Press, 1954.

Anderson, Gary A. *The Genesis of Perfection: Adam and Eve in Jewish and Christian Imagination.* Louisville: Westminster/John Knox, 2002.

Aquinas, Thomas. *The Collected Works of St. Thomas Aquinas.* Electronic edition. Charlottesville, VA: InteLex Corporation, 1993.

———. *Summa Theologiae.* Blackfriars Edition. New York: McGraw-Hill, 1964.

'Arabi, Ibn. *The Bezels of Wisdom.* Translated and introduction by R. W. J. Austin. New York: Paulist Press, 1980.

Asad, Muhammad. *Message of the Qur'an.* Gibraltar: Dar al-Andalus, 1984.

Ash'ari, Abu'l Hasan Ali Ibn Ismail al-. *Al-Ibana 'an Usul ad-diyanah.* Translated and introduction by Walter C. Klein. New Haven, CT: American Oriental Society, 1940.

Auerbach, Erich A. *Mimesis: The Representation of Reality in Western Literature.* Translated by Willard R. Trask. Princeton: Princeton University Press, 1953.

Augustine. *The Works of Saint Augustine.* 3rd release. Electronic edition. Charlottesville, VA: InteLex Corporation, 2001.

Bailie, Gil. *Violence Unveiled: Humanity at the Crossroads.* New York: Crossroads, 1997.

Barth, Karl. *Church Dogmatics.* Vol. 3, pt 3. Edited by Geoffrey W. Bromiley and Thomas F. Torrance. Edinburgh: T& T Clark, 1936.

———. *Dogmatics in Outline.* Translated by G. T. Thompson. New York: Harper, 1959.

Bialik, Hayim Nahman and Yehoshua Hana Ravnitzky, eds. *Sefer Ha-Aggadah, The Book of Legends from the Talmud and Midrash.* Translated by William Braude. New York: Schocken Books, 1992.

Bijlefeld, W. A. "Controversies around the Qur'anic Ibrahim Narrative and Its 'Orientalist' Interpretations." *The Muslim World* 72 (1982): 81–94.

Blanchot, Maurice. *The Space of Literature.* Translated by Ann Smock. Lincoln: University of Nebraska Press, 1982.

Blumenthal, David. *Facing the Abusive God: A Theology of Protest*. Louisville, KY: Westminster John Knox, 1993.

Brandom, Robert. *Tales of the Mighty Dead: Historical Essays in the Metaphysics of Intentionality*. Cambridge, MA: Harvard University Press, 2002.

Brod, Max. *Franz Kafka: A Biography*. New York: Da Capa Press, 1960.

Buber, Martin. *Eclipse of God: Studies in the Relation between Religion and Philosophy*. New York: Harper and Row, 1957.

———. *I and Thou*. Translated by Ronald Gregor Smith. New York: Scribner, 2000.

Caesarius of Arles. *Sermons*. Translated by Mary Magdeleine Mueller, OSF. Fathers of the Church, vol. 47. Washington, DC: Catholic University Press, 1964.

Calder, Norman. "From Midrash to Scripture: The Sacrifice of Abraham in Early Islamic Tradition" in *Interpretation and Jurisprudence in Medieval Islam*, ed. Jawid Mojaddedi and Andrew Rippin, 375–402. London: Ashgate, 2006.

Calvin, John. *Institutes of the Christian Religion*. Translated by Henry Beveridge. Grand Rapids, MI: Eerdmans, 1953.

Chittick, William C. "Ibn 'Arabi's Own Summary of the *Fusūs*: 'The Imprint of the Bezels of the Wisdom.'" *Journal of the Muhyiddin Ibn 'Arabi Society*, Vol. 1 (1982). http://www.ibnarabisociety.org/articlespdf/naqshalfusus.pdf.

Cohen, Ralph, ed. *New Directions in Literary History*. Baltimore, MD: Johns Hopkins University Press, 1974.

Danielou, Jean, SJ. *From Shadow to Reality: Studies in the Biblical Typology of the Fathers*. Translated by Wulstan Hubbard. CreateSpace, 2011.

Dawson, John David. *Christian Figural Reading and the Fashioning of Identity*. Berkeley: University of California Press, 2002.

Deleuze, Gilles. *Essays Critical and Clinical*. Translated by Daniel W. Smith and Michael A. Greco. New York: Verso, 1998.

Derrida, Jacques. "Above All, No Journalists!" in *Religion and the Media*, edited by Hent de Vries and Samuel Weber, 56–93. Stanford: Stanford University Press, 2001.

———. *The Animal That Therefore I Am*. Edited by Marie-Louise Mallet. Translated by David Wills. New York: Fordham University Press, 2008.

———. *The Gift of Death and Literature in Secret*. Translated by David Wills. Chicago: University of Chicago Press, 2008.

———. *On the Name*. Edited by Thomas Dutoit. Stanford: Stanford University Press, 1995.

————. *Sovereignties in Question: The Poetics of Paul Celan.* Edited by Thomas Dutoit and Outi Pasanen. New York: Fordham University Press, 2005.

————. *Writing and Difference.* Translated by Alan Bass. Chicago: University of Chicago Press, 1978.

Ephrem the Syrian. "Commentary on Genesis" in *Selected Prose Works.* Translated by Edward G. Mathews Jr. and Joseph P. Amar. Fathers of the Church, vol. 91. Washington, DC: Catholic University Press, 1994.

Fackenheim, Emil L. *Encounters between Judaism and Modern Philosophy.* London: Jason Aronson, 1994.

Finlan, Stephen. *Problems with Atonement: The Origins of, and Controversy about, the Atonement Doctrine.* Collegeville, MN: Liturgical, 2005.

Fowl, Stephen E., ed. *Engaging Scripture: A Model for Theological Interpretation.* Eugene, OR: Wipf & Stock, 2008.

————, ed. *The Theological Interpretation of Scripture: Classic and Contemporary Readings.* Oxford: Blackwell, 1997.

Freedman, H., and Maurice Simon, eds. *Midrash Rabbah.* and Maurice Simon. Vol.1, *Genesis.* London: Soncino, 1939.

Geach, Peter. *Reference and Generality: An Examination of Some Medieval and Modern Theories.* 3rd ed. Ithaca: Cornell University Press, 1980.

Grant, Robert M. and Tracy, David. *A Short History of the Interpretation of the Bible.* 2nd ed. Philadelphia: Fortress Press, 1984.

Green, Ronald. *Kant and Kierkegaard on Time and Eternity.* Macon, GA: Mercer University Press, 2011.

————. *Kierkegaard and Kant: The Hidden Debt.* Albany: State University of New York Press, 1992.

————. *Religion and Moral Reason.* New York: Oxford University Press, 1988.

Gunkel, Hermann. *Genesis.* Translated by Mark E. Biddle. Macon, GA: Mercer University Press, 1997.

Gupta, Anil. *The Logic of Common Nouns: An Investigation in Quantified Modal Logic.* New Haven: Yale University Press, 1980.

Haleem, Abdel. *The Qur'an: A New Translation.* Oxford: Oxford University Press, 2005.

Harmless, William, SJ, ed. *Augustine in His Own Words.* Washington, DC: Catholic University of America Press, 2010.

Harris, H. S. *Hegel's Development: Night Thoughts, 1801–1806.* New York: Oxford University Press, 1983.

————. *Hegel's Development: Toward the Sunlight, 1770-1801.* Oxford: Oxford University Press, 1972.

Hazm, Abu Muhammad 'Ali bin Ahmad Ibn. *Al-Fasl fi al-milal wa al-ahwai fi al-nihal,* vol. 5. Edited by M. I. Nasr and A. 'Umayra. Beirut: Dar al-Jil, 1982.

Hegel, G. W. F. *Lectures on the Philosophy of History.* Translated by J. Sibree. New York: Willey Book Co., 1944.

———. *Lectures on the Philosophy of Religion.* Vol. 1, *Introduction and the Concept of Religion.* Translated by R. F. Brown, P. C. Hodgson, J. M. Stewart, J. P. Fitzer, and H. S. Harris. Edited by Peter C. Hodgson. Berkeley: University of California Press, 1984.

———. *Lectures on the Philosophy of Religion.* Vol. 2, *Determinate Religion.* Translated by R. F. Brown, P. C. Hodgson, J. M. Stewart, J. P. Fitzer, and H. S. Harris. Edited by Peter C. Hodgson. Berkeley: University of California Press, 1987.

———. *Lectures on the Philosophy of Religion.* Vol. 3, *The Consummate Religion.* Translated by R. F. Brown, P. C. Hodgson, J. M. Stewart, J. P. Fitzer, and H. S. Harris. Edited by Peter C. Hodgson. Berkeley: University of California Press, 1985.

———. *Phenomenology of Spirit.* Translated by A.V. Miller. New York: Oxford University Press, 1977.

———. *Science of Logic.* Translated by A.V. Miller. New York: Humanity Books, 1969.

Holz, Barry W. *Back to the Sources: Reading the Classic Jewish Texts.* New York: Summit Books, 1984.

Jacobs, Louis. *Principles of the Jewish Faith: An Analytical Study.* New York: Basic Books, 1964.

Jerome. *Saint Jerome's Hebrew Questions on Genesis.* Translated by C. T. R. Howard. Oxford: Clarendon, 1995.

Johnson, Luke Timothy. *The Writings of the New Testament: An Interpretation.* Minneapolis: Fortress Press, 1999.

Josephus, Flavius. *The Works of Flavius Josephus.* Translated by William Whiston. Edinburgh: William P. Nimmo, 1869.

Kafka, Franz. *The Blue Octavo Notebooks.* Edited by Max Brod. Translated by Ernst Kaiser and Eithne Wilkins. Cambridge, MA: Exact Change, 1991.

———. *The Diaries: 1910-1923.* Edited by Max Brod. Translated by Joseph Kresh and Martin Greenberg. New York: Schocken Books, 1976.

———. *Letters to Family, Friends, and Editors.* Translated by Richard and Clara Winston. New York: Schocken Books, 1977.

Kant, Immanuel. *Critique of Practical Reason.* Translated by Lewis White Beck. Indianapolis: Bobbs-Merrill, 1956.

———. *Religion and Rational Theology*. Edited and translated by Allen Wood and George Di Giovanni. Cambridge: Cambridge University Press, 1996.

Keeler, Annabel. *Sufi Hermeneutics: The Qur'an Commentary of Rashid al-Din Maybudi*. Oxford: Oxford University Press, 2006.

Kierkegaard, Søren. *Eighteen Upbuilding Discourses*. Translated by Howard V. Hong and Edna H. Hong. Princeton: Princeton University Press, 1990.

———. *The Essential Kierkegaard*. Edited by Howard V. Hong and Edna H. Hong. Princeton, NJ: Princeton University Press, 2000.

———. *Fear and Trembling*. Translated by Alastair Hannay. New York: Penguin Books, 1985.

———. *Fear and Trembling and The Book on Adler*. Translated by Walter Lowrie. New York: Alfred A. Knopf, Inc., 1994.

———. *Journals and Papers*. Electronic edition. Charlottesville, VA: InteLex Corporation, 1995.

———. *Philosophical Fragments. Johannes Climacus*. Edited and translated by Howard V. Hong and Edna H. Hong. Princeton: Princeton University Press, 1985.

———. *Works of Love*. Edited and translated by Howard V. Hong and Edna H. Hong. Princeton: Princeton University Press, 1998.

Kugel, James L. and Greer, Rowan A. *Early Biblical Interpretation*. Philadelphia: Westminster, 1986.

LaCapra, Dominick. *History and Its Limit: Human, Animal, Violence*. London: Cornell University Press, 2009.

Lampe, G. W. H., ed. *The Cambridge History of the Bible: The West from the Fathers to the Reformation*. Cambridge: Cambridge University Press, 1969.

Lash, Nicholas. *Theology on the Way to Emmaus*. Eugene, OR: Wipf & Stock, 2005.

Lerch, David. *Isaaks Opferung Christlich Gedeutet*. Tübingen: J. C. B. Mohr, 1950.

Levenson, Jon D. *The Death and Resurrection of the Beloved Son: The Transformation of Child Sacrifice in Judaism and Christianity*. New Haven: Yale University Press, 1993.

Levinas, Emmanuel. *Of God Who Comes to Mind*. Translated by Bettina Bergo. Stanford: Stanford University Press, 1998.

———. *Outside the Subject*. Translated by Michael B. Smith. Stanford: Stanford University Press, 1994.

———. *Proper Names*. Translated by Michael B. Smith. London: Athelone, 1996.

———. *Time and the Other, and Additional Essays*. Translated by Richard A. Cohen. Pittsburgh: Duquesne University Press, 1987.

Louth, Andrew. *Discerning the Mystery: An Essay on the Nature of Theology*. Oxford: Clarendon, 1983.

Luther, Martin. *Luther's Commentary on Genesis*, vol. 2. Translated by T. Theodore Mueller. Grand Rapids: Zondervan Publishing House, 1958.

———. *Luther's Works*. Edited by Jaroslav Pelikan and Helmut T. Lehman. Philadelphia: Fortress Press, and St. Louis, Concordia, 1957–86.

———. "Sermons on Gospel Texts for Advent, Christmas, and Epiphany," in *Sermons of Martin Luther*, vol. 1. Electronic edition. Charlottesville, VA: InteLex Corporation, 1995.

———. "Sermons on Gospel Texts for the 1st to the 12th Sundays after Trinity," in *Sermons of Martin Luther*, vol. 4. Electronic edition. Charlottesville, VA: InteLex Corporation, 1995.

Mahallī, Jalal al-din and al-Suyuti, Jalal al-din al-. *Tafsīr al-Jalalayn*, Edited by 'Abd Allah Rabī Mahmud. Lebanon: Maktaba Lubnan, 1998.

Melville, Herman. *The Piazza Tales*. New York: Russell & Russell Inc., 1963.

Merwin, W. S. *The Second Four Books of Poems: The Moving Target / The Lice / The Carrier of Ladders / Writings to an Unfinished Accompaniment*. Port Townsend, WA: Copper Canyon Press, 1993.

Moltmann, Jürgen. *The Crucified God: The Cross of Christ as the Foundation and Criticism of Christian Theology*. Minneapolis: Augsburg Fortress, 1993.

Noort, Ed and Eihert, Tigchelaar, eds. *The Sacrifice of Isaac: The Aqedah (Genesis 22) and its Interpretations*. Leiden: Brill, 2002.

O'Keefe, John T. and Reno, R. R. *Sanctified Vision: An Introduction to Early Christian Interpretation of the Bible*. Baltimore: Johns Hopkins University Press, 2005.

Origen. *Homilies on Genesis and Exodus*. Translated by Ronald E. Heine. Fathers of the Church, vol. 71. Washington, DC: Catholic University Press, 1982.

Penchansky, David. *What Rough Beast? Images of God in the Hebrew Bible*. Louisville, KY: Westminster John Knox, 1999.

Perkins, Robert L., ed. *Kierkegaard's Fear and Trembling: Critical Appraisals*. Birmingham, AL: University of Alabama Press, 1981.

Philo. *De Abrahamo*. Translated by F.H. Colson. Cambridge, MA: Harvard University Press, 1959.

Rad, Gerhard von. *Genesis: A Commentary*. Translated by John H. Marks. London: SCM 1972.

Rancière, Jacques. *The Flesh of Words: The Politics of Writing.* Translated by Charlotte Mandell. Stanford: Stanford University Press, 2004.

Razi, Fakr al-din al-. *Tafsir al-Kabīr,* vol. 26. Egypt: al-Matba'ah al-Bāhiyah al-Misrīya, n.d.

Renard, John. *All the King's Falcons: Rumi on Prophets and Revelation.* New York: SUNY Press, 1998.

Rorty, Richard. *Achieving Our Country: Leftist Thought in Twentieth-Century America.* Cambridge, MA: Harvard University Press, 1998.

Rosenzweig, Franz. *The Star of Redemption.* Translated by Barbara E. Galli. Madison, WI: University of Wisconsin Press, 2005.

Rumi. *The Mathnawi of Jalalu'ddin Rumi.* Translated and commentary by R. A. Nicholson. Cambridge: E.J. Gibb Memorial Trust, 1930.

Schechter, Solomon. *Aspects of Rabbinic Theology: Major Concepts of the Talmud.* New York: Schocken Books, 1961.

Schulweis, Harold M. *Consciences: The Duty to Obey and the Duty to Disobey.* Woodstock: Jewish Lights, 2008.

Schwartz, Regina M. *The Curse of Cain: The Violent Legacy of Monotheism.* Chicago: University of Chicago Press, 1997.

Seitz, Christopher R. *Figured Out: Typology and Providence in Christian Scripture.* Louisville: Westminster John Knox, 2001.

Sheridan, Mark. ed. *Genesis 12-50* Vol. 2 of *Ancient Christian Commentary on Scripture: Old Testament.* IVP Academic, 2002.

Sherwood, Yvonne. "Binding–Unbinding: Divided Responses of Judaism, Christianity, and Islam to the 'Sacrifice' of Abraham's Beloved Son." *Journal of American Academy of Religion* 72, no. 4 (2004): 821–61.

Speiser, E.A. *Genesis.* Anchor Bible 1. Garden City, NY: Doubleday, 1964.

Spiegel, Shalom. *The Last Trial: On the Legends and Lore of the Command to Abraham to Offer Isaac as a Sacrifice: The Akedah.* New York: Pantheon, 1967.

Stern, Chaim, ed. *Gates of Repentance: the New Union Prayerbook for the Days of Awe.* New York: Central Conference of American Rabbis, 1978.

Sternberg, Meier. *The Poetics of Biblical Narrative: Ideological Literature and the Drama of Reading.* Bloomington: Meir Sternberg (Author) Indiana University Press, 1987.

Stewart, Jon. *Kierkegaard's Relations to Hegel Reconsidered.* New York: Cambridge University Press, 2003.

Taftazani, Sad al-Din. *A Commentary on the Creed of Islam: Sad al-Din al-Taftazani on the Creed of Najm al-Din al-Nasafi.* Translated and introduction by E. E. Elder. New York: Columbia University Press, 1950.

Watt, W. Montgomery. "Isḥāḳ." *Encyclopaedia of Islam*. 2nd ed. Edited by P. Bearman, Th. Bianquis, C. E. Bosworth, E. van Donzel, and W. P. Heinrichs. Leiden: Brill, 2011.

Westermann, Claus. *Genesis 12-36: A Commentary*. Translated by John J. Scullion. Minneapolis: Augsburg Publishing House, 1985.

Wilken, Robert L. *The Spirit of Early Christian Thought: Seeking the Face of God*. New Haven, CT: Yale University Press, 2005.

Yazir, Elmalili Hamdi M. *Hak Dini Kur'an Dili*. Edited by I. Karacam, E. Isik, N. Bolelli, and A. Yucel. Yenibosna. Istanbul: Feza Yay, 1992.

Young, Frances M. *Biblical Exegesis and the Formation of Christian Culture*. Cambridge: Cambridge University Press, 1997.

Index of Names

Ali Shariati, 80–81, 83
Ambrose, 50
Anselm, 173
Aquinas, Thomas, 38, 52, 87
Aristotle, 187
Athanasius, 50
Auerbach, Erich, 46, 195
Augustine, 36, 42–43, 50, 52–55, 173

Barnabas, 41
Barth, Karl, 51, 55
Bauer, Felice, 150, 158, 168
Baum, Oskar, 151
Brandom, Robert, 118
Brod, Max, 149, 158, 160–62
Buber, Martin, 169–71, 176–83, 185

Caesarius of Arles, 40, 46–48
Calvin, John, 35, 44
Chrysostom, 50
Clement of Alexandria, 42
Cohen, Norman, 4

Danielou, Jean, 33, 35
Davenport, John, 131–32, 134–37, 142
Davis, Ellen, 37
Deleuze, Gilles, 189–90, 207
de Lubac, Henri, 30
Derrida, Jacques, 171, 179, 182–85,
    187–198, 200, 214–15
Descartes, Renee, 173

Fakhr al-dīn al-Razi, 62, 67
Firestone, Reueven, 64
Foucault, Michel, 171, 179

Hagar, 60, 66, 197
Hagglund, Martin, 183
Hannay, Alastair, 140

Hawthorne, Nathaniel, 101
Hegel, Georg W. F., xiii, 101–30,
    174–75, 183, 185, 197, 216
Heidegger, Martin, 171, 179, 182
Hoffman, Lawrence, 24
Holtz, Barry, 4

Ibn Hazm, 62, 72–73, 82
Imam Abu Hanifa, 65
Iser, Wolfgang, 5
Isaac, xi, xii, 3, 6, 11–25, 27–29, 31–35,
    38–40, 42–50, 52–54, 60–61, 63–66,
    75–76, 78, 83, 87, 90, 131, 133–35,
    139–41, 145, 155–57, 164–65,
    169–72, 174, 176, 178, 181–82, 185,
    188, 192–198, 200–8, 211, 213–16
Ishmael, 12, 35, 60–61, 63–66, 75–78,
    80–83, 197

Jalal ad-Din Rumi, 73–79, 83
Jerome, 40–41
Job, 75, 105, 107, 202
Johannes de silentio, 101–2, 129, 131,
    133–37, 139–40, 142–45, 154,
    196–97
Josephus, Flavius, 196–97
Jung, Carl, 184

Kafka, Franz, 149–53, 158–68, 214
Kant, Immanuel, xiii, 31, 87–100, 123,
    199–201, 215–16
Katz, Claire, 182
Khidr, 76–77
Kierkegaard, Sören, xii, xiii, 90, 99–100,
    101–2, 131–35, 137–42, 145, 149,
    150–58, 160–63, 165, 167, 169–78,
    180–82, 185, 193, 195–201, 203–7,
    213–17

Klopstock, Robert, 160–61, 163

LaCapra, Dominick, 205, 207
Levinas, Emmanuel, 169–85, 214
Lindon, Mathieu, 189
Luther, Martin, 28, 33–34, 38–39, 41, 43–47, 49–50, 52, 55, 196–98

Marcel, Gabriel, 169, 171–72, 179–80, 183
Melville, Herman, 189–91, 207
Merwin, W. S., 208
Moses, 6, 7, 8, 14, 22, 32, 58, 72, 73, 76, 77, 82
Muhyiddin Ibn 'Arabi, 70–73, 83

Nietzsche, Friedrich, 171, 179, 182

Olsen, Regine, 200
Origen, 27, 29 –31, 37, 41–45, 49, 50–52, 53

Perkins, Robert, 142
Peirce, Charles Sanders, 109–13

Philo of Alexandria, 196–97
Picard, Max, 173–74

Rancière, Jacques, 190
Reiss, Moshe, 182
Renard, John, 62
Rosenzweig, Franz, 169–70, 174–76, 182

Schulweis, Harold, 8
Schwartz, Regina, 39
Seitz, Christopher, 40
Sherwood, Yvonne, 82
Speiser, E. A., 193
Spiegel, Shalom, 19, 22–23
Stewart, Jon, 101–2

Tertullian, 50
Thales of Miletus, 175

Wellhausen, Julius, 31
Wills, David, 188
Wohryzek, Julie, 166

Index of Biblical References

Genesis
12:1—17:27......9
12:2-3......53
13:16......35
14:14......45
15:5-6......53
15:6......35
17:4-8......53
17:10......34
17:19......193
17:23-27......48
18:1—22:24......10
18:14......47
21:2......193
21:5......48
21:10......197
22:1-19......3
22:1......10
22:2......34
22:4......16
22:7......197
22:8......197
22:9......15, 16

Exodus
12......29
32......15

Numbers
16......8

Leviticus
16......29

2 Chronicles
3:1......40

Psalms
11:5......11

76......40
119......8

Proverbs
1:7......53

Isaiah
2......40

Daniel
12:2......33

Zechariah
6......40

Matthew
12:38-42......37
22:32......34

Luke
2:41-50......39
11:29-32......37
20:37......34

John
11:26......55

Acts
1:7......52

1 Corinthians
15:55......33

Hebrews
11:1......32
11:17-19......32, 99, 211
11:17......38
11:19......48

James
2:21-22......35

2:21......32

Index of Quranic References

2:124......59
2:127......78
2:127-128......60
2:130......59
2:132-133......62
2:132-136......65
2:133......60
2:135......59
2:136......60
2:140......60
2:228......77
2:243......77
2:244......76
2:246......76
2:258......59
3:19......62
3:84......60
3:85......62
3:95......59
3:96......60
3:97......62
4:54-55......60
4:125......59
4:163......60
4:164......59
6:25......63
6:61......59
6:76......59
6:80-81......59
6:118......60
8:31......63
9:105......63

11:71......64
12:38......60
14:37......60
14:39......60
16:24......63
18:79......77
18:72......77
19:42-46......59
19:54......60
20:39......73
21:51......59
21:71......59
22:26-37......61
22:26-28......79
22:34-35ff.......79
22:36......62, 79
22:78......79
26:70-89......59
27:19......75
28:7......73
29:16-27......59
29:26......59
33:21......62
37:83-98......59, 60
37:99......59
37:101......64
37:104-105......72
37:107......79
37:99-111......61
40:78......59
43:26-28......59
60:4-6......62

CPSIA information can be obtained at www.ICGtesting.com
Printed in the USA
BVOW02s0348150114

341851BV00007B/121/P